POLITICS OF THE
CHACO PEACE CONFERENCE
1935–1939

LESLIE B. ROUT, JR., is not only a historian but also a jazz musician, and he has published several articles on jazz. He became interested in the Chaco War and its subsequent settlement while traveling in Latin America as a member of a United States government-sponsored musical group. Informed that unpublished documents could be made available, Dr. Rout returned to Brazil, Argentina, Uruguay, and Bolivia in 1965 to prepare the present study. Dr. Rout received the Ph.D. degree from the University of Minnesota and is associate professor of history at Michigan State University, where he was a recipient of the 1969 Teacher-Scholar Award for publishing and classroom teaching excellence.

Latin American Monographs, No. 19
Institute of Latin American Studies
The University of Texas at Austin

POLITICS OF THE
Chaco Peace Conference
1935-1939

By LESLIE B. ROUT, JR.

PUBLISHED FOR THE INSTITUTE OF LATIN AMERICAN STUDIES
BY THE UNIVERSITY OF TEXAS PRESS, AUSTIN & LONDON

International Standard Book Number 0-292-70049-0
Library of Congress Catalog Card Number 70-130589
Copyright © 1970 by Leslie B. Rout, Jr.

TO KARIN, KAREN, AND MOMA

each of whom played a role
they will never understand.

PREFACE

The word *chaco* appears to be derived from the Quechua word *chacu*, meaning "hunting" or "hunting ground,"[1] but authorities disagree on its exact meaning. The so-called Gran Chaco includes portions of Argentina, Bolivia, and Paraguay, but the area that served simultaneously as *cause célèbre*, battlefield, and mass burial ground in the conflict between Paraguay and Bolivia was the Chaco Boreal, or that portion of the Chaco lying beyond the Pilcomayo River. The approximate coordinates of the Chaco Boreal are 57°21′41″ to 63°26′54″ of west longitude, and 17°55′43″ to 25°21′41″ of south latitude.[2] While its generally accepted eastern and south-southwestern boundaries are the Paraguay and Pilcomayo rivers, its exact northern and western frontiers are uncertain.[3] About 297,000 square kilometers is generally given as the region's total area.[4]

---

[1] United States, National Archives, Washington, D.C., Department of State, RG 59, Decimal File 724.3415/28, no. 104, p. 3, Oscar L. Milmore (Geographic Section) to Sec'y State, February 23, 1916. Enrique de Gandía (*Historia del Gran Chaco*, p. 17) finds that the word can refer not only to "hunting ground" but also to the local Indians who obtained their livelihood by hunting.

[2] League of Nations, *Dispute between Bolivia and Paraguay: Report of the Chaco Commission*, Political, C.154.M.64. VII (1934), p. 12. The same figures are found in Margaret La Foy, *The Chaco Dispute and the League of Nations*, p. 1.

[3] League of Nations (*Report of the Chaco Commission*, C. 154. M. 64. VII [1934], p. 12) holds that the north-northeastern limits are the "Choci Mts." and the "Rio Negro." The north-northwestern limits have also been placed along the Parapetí River and the "Sierra Chiriguana." Emerson B. Christie in *Chaco Boreal Memorandum* (U.S., Archives, RG 59, Decimal File 724.3415/652½, July 31, 1929) agrees with Manuel Domínguez (*El Chaco Boreal fué, es y sera del Paraguay*, p. 31) that the northeast boundary of the Chaco is the Otuquis River rather than the "Rio Negro." Christie takes issue with Domínguez where the latter recognizes a "cordillera Chiriguana" to the northwest; Christie mentions that the American Geographical Society denied the existence of a "cordillera" in the north-northwest Chaco (see Christie, *Chaco Boreal Memorandum*, in U.S., Archives, RG 59, Decimal File 724.3415/652½, p. 2).

[4] La Foy, *Chaco Dispute*, p. 1; Christie, *Chaco Boreal Memorandum*, in U.S.,

The Chaco is hardly a tourist attraction. Vast swamps or *bañados* are found in the northeast, northwest, and southwestern sectors. The extreme west is arid and sloping, whereas the central and southern regions may be described as a tangle of forests occasionally broken by tracts of flat savannah. From May to November the sun, an incandescent globe, scorches the savannahs, while clouds of dust and swarms of insects battle each other for supremacy of the skies. The earth dries, bakes, and finally becomes almost as cracked as the Texas-Oklahoma plain. November's showers are succeeded by December's tropical storms, which flood the rivers, inundate the plains, and make all but aerial transportation hazardous for three or four months.

The Chaco War is unique in that it remains the only full-scale conflict fought between American states in the twentieth century. The Chaco Peace Conference deserves critical attention because it terminated that war and because it remains one of the few contemporary conferences that has provided a lasting settlement to an international crisis; since 1939 Paraguay and Bolivia have been peaceful neighbors, and the old *fortines*[5] that once dotted the Chaco have almost disappeared. Because formerly restricted material has recently become accessible, two major questions can be considered in this study: Why were the other American states unable or unwilling to bring the three-year conflict between Paraguay and Bolivia to a halt more quickly? Since the peace conference ultimately proved successful, what lessons may be derived from it and possibly applied to other inter-American disputes?

In the late summer of 1965 I visited the inscrutable Chaco. After returning to Asunción, I concluded that the brutal 1932–1935 combat again demonstrates that politically and/or economically unstable states do not act in a rational manner when perceived national interests are jeopardized. For Bolivia and Paraguay the cost of defending these

Archives, RG 59, Decimal File 724.3415/652½, p. 2; and League of Nations, *Report of the Chaco Commission*, C.154.M.64.VII(1934), p. 12. Oscar Milmore gives the total area as 106,922 square miles (U.S., Archives, RG 59, Decimal File 724.3415/28, no. 104, p. 5, Milmore to Sec'y State, Feb. 23, 1916). The Chaco area is also given as "close to 150,000 sq. miles" (United States, Department of State, *The Chaco Peace Conference*, Publication 1466, no. 46, p. 3).

5 *Fortines* were small military posts, usually of crude wood and mud construction.

interests proved prohibitive. War again may erupt in the Americas, but it is hoped that next time the nonbelligerent states will take the steps necessary to bring about rapid termination of hostilities—or at least that they will try to reduce the number of casualties.

ACKNOWLEDGMENTS

Directly across from me sat a diplomatic official, whose name, I was later informed, it would be "unwise to disclose." I had requested the use of certain documents, and the diplomat had just given me a stringent lecture, complete with gestures, explaining why these documents would remain classified. Since it seemed obvious that the necessary cooperation would not be forthcoming, I asked the official if any documents relating to the Chaco Conference of Peace could be made available to me. He expressed his pessimism and sought to impress upon me the sensitivity of the question, both in his nation and in several neighboring republics; I could only express my sympathy with his viewpoint and hope for the best.

After about thirty seconds of silence, the official suddenly broke into English. "What city are you from?" he asked. "Chicago," was my response. "Ahh! I remember Chicago," he said. Wistfully, he recalled pleasant memories of a "black-and-tan" club on the South Side that had been very fashionable in the nineteen-thirties and forties. I had played with an orchestra in this club during the fifties, and from the diplomat's recapitulation of happy times at the once-famous nightspot, it became apparent that he and I had a mutual acquaintance—a bartender. As the bartender was my friend, the diplomat was now certain that I was "simpatico." He took me down a hall to a closed room and opened a safe. The office personnel were then informed that the documents in the safe were to be placed at my disposal. All I could think was: who would ever believe this story?

I never did see the bartender again, but in the creation of this work there are numerous institutions and people whom I would like to thank. Of unparalleled help were the foreign offices and foreign office archival staffs of the Republics of Argentina, Bolivia, Paraguay, and Uruguay, and the Diplomatic, Legal, and Fiscal Branch of the National Archives of the United States. Both the Pan American Union Library and the

John Hay Whitney Foundation provided invaluable assistance. Also indispensable was the aid of former United States Ambassador Spruille Braden; of such illustrious Paraguayans as Dr. Efraím Cardozo, Dr. Carlos Pastore (now in Uruguay), Dr. Juan Isidro Ramírez; and of Mr. John Barton, United States cultural attaché in La Paz, Bolivia, in 1966–1967. I would also like to extend recognition for their help to Captain Enrique Bozzano, Paraguayan navy retired; Victor Mérida, former Bolivian army officer; Monroe Davids of the University of Maryland for his work on the maps; and Sra. Rosalia Ramón of Buenos Aires, Argentina, for certain pictures. Lastly, it is necessary to single out my former mentor, Dr. W. D. Beatty of the University of Minnesota, whose idea set in motion the entire project; Dr. Edward Gargan of the University of Wisconsin, whose previous training laid the basis for the research; and my colleague, Dr. Charles Cumberland, who read the manuscript and made the kind of suggestions only "old pros" can.

CONTENTS

ILLUSTRATIONS

(*Following page 94*)

MAPS

PART ONE
Preliminary Diplomatic Maneuvers

1. ROOT OF THE CONFLICT

> *The tongue of land between the Pilcomayo and the Paraguay [rivers,] up to the Brazilian border, Paraguay regards as vital to her existence.*
>
> United States Minister to Paraguay John Stevens to Secretary of State Hamilton Fish, June 5, 1872

> *The Republic of Bolivia ... has maintained and is maintaining the integrity of its territorial rights, in the zone situated between the west bank of the Paraguay River from the northern boundary of the Brazilian possessions, ... up to the left bank of the Pilcomayo River.*
>
> Ricardo Mujía, *Bolivia-Paraguay*

𝍸𝍸

ARTICLE 4 OF THE 1853 Argentine-Paraguayan Recognition Treaty stated that the Paraguay River "shall belong from bank to bank in full sovereignty to the Republic of Paraguay down to its confluence with the [Río] Paraná."[1] Promulgation of the treaty elicited a sharply worded protest from Juan de la Cruz Benavente, Bolivian consul in Buenos Aires. Benavente proclaimed that Bolivia, as a riparian republic, was entitled to an area along the Paraguay River, specifically to that area between parallels 20, 21, and 22. The Argentine

---

[1] Great Britain, *British and Foreign State Papers*, 1853–1854, XLVII, 1257.

government replied that in the treaty it had not conferred any judicial titles and tactfully suggested that Bolivia take up the matter with Paraguay. Officials in the Andean capital did not follow the Argentine suggestion, and when no comment emanated from Asunción, the question simply lapsed as a diplomatic controversy.

During the eighteen-fifties, Paraguay became increasingly involved both in Platine politics and in territorial disputes with Brazil and Argentina. A crisis was reached in 1864 when Paraguay intervened to support the Blanco Party of Uruguay in a civil war in which Buenos Aires and Rio de Janeiro had made the Colorado Party their protégé. The Blanco Party was crushed and President Francisco Solano López of Paraguay subsequently found himself leading his landlocked nation in a dauntless but imprudent sally against Brazil, Uruguay, and Argentina. On May 1, 1865, the enemies of Paraguay formed a secret Triple Alliance. They acknowledged that a state of war existed between them and Asunción and pledged, among other things, never to make separate peace treaties with Paraguay.

Of utmost importance were the treaty articles that allowed Brazil and Argentina to settle their long-festering territorial disputes with Paraguay entirely at the latter's expense. Article 16 of the treaty declared: "The Brazilian Empire will be divided from the Republic of Paraguay by the line of the Apa River, the mountain range of Amambay and Maracayú, to the Siete Caídas Falls and the Paraná River."[2] In effect, Brazil was establishing its claim to all Paraguayan territories east of the Apa and Paraguay rivers, occupied or disputed. Argentina also hastened to assert its intentions of territorial acquisition. Article 16 further read: "The Argentine Republic will be divided from the Republic of Paraguay by the Paraná and Paraguay Rivers up to the boundaries of the Brazilian Empire which are, in the Chaco, Bahía Negra."[3] The Buenos Aires government planned to annex the province of Misiones, all land between the Bermejo and Pilcomayo rivers, as well as the relatively unexplored Chaco Boreal.

With the fall of Asunción in January 1869 and the flight of Presi-

---

[2] Eduardo Amarilla Fretes, *La liquidación de la guerra de la triple alianza contra el Paraguay*, p. 24.
[3] *Ibid.*

dent López into the interior of the Chaco, the factors responsible for Argentine-Brazilian cohesion disappeared. These nations were traditional rivals, and each suspected the other of harboring plans for the total acquisition of a prostrate Paraguay. It was their mutual antipathy that allowed Paraguay to act as both pawn and participant in the duel that followed.

Buenos Aires struck first. The Argentines found it difficult to exert pressure since Brazilian troops occupied most of Paraguay. On November 21, 1869, however, Argentine troops crossed the Pilcomayo River and occupied Villa Occidental, the largest settlement in the Chaco Boreal. This move did not go unnoticed in Rio de Janeiro. In December 1869 the State Council of Empire, the agency responsible for shaping Brazilian foreign policy, submitted a confidential memorandum to the emperor. The document contended that the "Triple Alliance is not definite and perpetual in regard to boundaries."[4] The document further argued that a separate peace with Paraguay was desirable and that under no circumstances was Argentina to acquire territory east of the Pilcomayo River.

A Paraguayan provisional government was set up in August 1869. On June 20, 1870, the allied powers and the Paraguayans agreed that while the conditions of the Triple Alliance must be accepted, Paraguay might propose and reserve for final adjustment modification of the boundaries defined in the alliance. In November 1870 a duly elected Paraguayan republican government took office. Under pressure from both Argentina and Brazil to grant the territorial demands mentioned in article 16 of the Triple Alliance treaty, the Paraguayans chose to resist Argentine demands. The Paraguayans were faced with the dual problem of ridding the nation of Brazilian occupation while saving as much of the national patrimony as possible. Cooperation with Brazil seemed more advantageous partly because of the number of Brazilian troops in Paraguay and partly because Brazil might help Paraguay to hold the Chaco Boreal against Argentina. Thus, from January 9 to January 18, 1872, Brazil and Paraguay signed four treaties governing boundaries, trade, and navigation and reestablishing amity between the two na-

[4] Delgado de Carvalho, *História diplomática do Brasil*, p. 94.

tions.[5] This brazen violation of the Triple Alliance was a direct affront to Argentine *amour propre*. Argentine Foreign Minister Carlos Tejedor threatened reprisals, but eventually soldier-president Bartolomé Mitré was sent as special ambassador to Rio de Janeiro to establish friendly relations. The most he could obtain, however, was an ambiguous Brazilian promise of adherence to the Triple Alliance.[6] Just how much this promise meant Mitré discovered in 1873 when he was sent to Asunción only to find the Paraguayans as adamant as ever regarding cession of the Chaco Boreal.

Argentina was, however, soon presented with an excellent opportunity to intervene in Paraguayan affairs. A slowly reviving Paraguayan nation had begun to stir uneasily under continued Brazilian interference. Since Brazilian occupation could end only after the celebration of definitive treaties with all the former Triple Alliance partners, concessions to Argentina were deemed necessary by some Paraguayan politicians.[7] In August 1874 President Salvador Jovellanos dispatched Jaime Sosa as special envoy to Brazil. In that nation's capital Sosa reopened negotiations with Carlos Tejedor, now Argentine ambassador to Brazil. In May 1875 a treaty was agreed upon whereby Paraguay ceded the Villa Occidental Zone to Argentina in exchange for cancellation of the war debt.

Although Sosa appears to have exceeded his instructions in signing such a treaty, his action hardly warranted the retribution taken against

---

[5] Cecilio Báez, *Historia diplomática del Paraguay*, II, 217. The Brazilian plenipotentiary was Baron de Cotegipe. Carlos Loizaga was the Paraguayan signatory. Following signature of the treaties Cotegipe secretly promised Juan Bautista Gill, president of the Senate, that if the treaties were ratified Brazil would support Paraguay in resisting Argentine demands in the Chaco (*ibid.*, p. 218).

[6] *Ibid.*, p. 218. The protocol (no. 5 in a series signed between General Bartolomé Mitré and the Marquis de São Vicente, Brazilian plenipotentiary) provided Argentine recognition of the Loizaga-Cotegipe treaties in exchange for Brazilian recognition that the terms of the Triple Alliance of May 1865 were still in effect.

[7] The Paraguayan authors cited above are unusually vague on this question. Harris Gaylord Warren (*Paraguay*, p. 262) states that early in 1874 several leading members of the Jovellanos government entered into a plot to cede the Chaco Boreal to Argentina, for Brazilian occupation of Paraguay would end only after a treaty had been signed with Argentina. According to Warren, the Baron of Araguaya, Brazil's minister in Asunción, heard of the plot and thwarted it.

him.[8] The announcement of the Tejedor-Sosa agreement created understandable anger among Brazilians, who were quick to reassert their influence in Paraguay. In May 1875 Juan Bautista Gill, who had replaced Salvador Jovellanos as Paraguayan president in November 1874, received a virtual ultimatum demanding Paraguay's disavowal of the treaty.[9] Gill immediately complied, and in June 1875 Jaime Sosa was denounced as a traitor. Once more Brazil's demands had been accepted whereas Argentina had failed to acquire the desired territorial rights. Clearly, Paraguayans could continue to ignore Argentine ire only because they had Brazilian support. If Argentina wanted the Chaco Boreal, it would have to fight Brazil. A bloody war for the acquisition of a territory populated by primitive Indians, jaguars, and anteaters was hardly conceivable.

Shifts in circumstances finally provided diplomats with the necessary room to maneuver. The cost of occupation placed an increasingly intolerable burden on the Brazilian treasury. Furthermore, a new ministry that was more inclined to end the territorial impasse came to power in Rio de Janeiro late in 1875. Negotiations between Argentina and Paraguay recommenced and progressed rapidly as President Juan Bautista Gill managed to shake off some of the strictures of Brazilian authority. On February 3, 1876, Facundo Machaín, Paraguayan foreign minister, and Bernardo de Irigoyen, his Argentine counterpart, signed a new territorial agreement. By its terms, Paraguay ceded outright only that

---

[8] John Basset Moore, ed., *History and Digest of the International Arbitrations of Which the United States Has Been a Party*, II, 1935. By the terms of the Tejedor-Sosa pact, Paraguay was to cede the town of Villa Occidental "with a territory two leagues to the south, four to the north, and four to the west" (*ibid.*). Báez (*Historia diplomática del Paraguay*, II, 223) and Amarilla Fretes (*La liquidación de la guerra*, p. 112) both insist that Sosa exceeded his diplomatic instructions in signing the agreement. According to Philip Raine (*Paraguay*, p. 206), President Jovellanos had confidentially instructed Sosa to agree to Argentine terms "even if it meant giving up all the Chaco."

[9] Amarilla Fretes (*La liquidación de la guerra*, pp. 110–111) admits that Paraguay had no choice but to accede to Brazilian demands. Both Báez (*Historia diplomática del Paraguay*, II, 223) and Warren (*Paraguay*, p. 262) note that President Juan Bautista Gill was virtually a Brazilian puppet. Delgado del Carvalho (*História diplomática do Brasil*, p. 99) states that the Tejedor-Sosa pact caused extreme vexation in Rio de Janeiro, and the Brazilian minister in Asunción was instructed to demand Paraguayan rejection.

area of the Chaco between the Bermejo and Pilcomayo rivers. The treaty divided the Chaco Boreal territory lying between the main channel of the Pilcomayo River and what later became the port of Bahía Negra into two sections. Argentina renounced all claim to the territory lying between Bahía Negra and the Verde River.

The second section, which included the territory lying between the Verde River and the main branch of the Pilcomayo River, was to be the subject of an arbitration conducted by Rutherford B. Hayes, president of the United States. Hayes's November 12, 1878, decision in favor of Paraguay produced rejoicing in Asunción, and Villa Occidental was later renamed in his honor.

Blunting Argentine territorial expansion provided only temporary relief for the embattled Paraguayans, who were quickly challenged by Bolivia. The Andean state had long assumed that the Chaco Boreal was part of its national domain. About 1836 Bolivia established its first colony in the northern Chaco region. In 1852 and 1853 La Paz declared the Paraguay River open to international traffic and even offered rewards to the first ocean-going vessels to dock at Bahía Negra or Fuerte Olimpo. The Bolivians had also watched nervously while Argentina maneuvered to snatch the entire Chaco. Even before the Hayes Award had been announced Altiplano diplomats informed Washington that they considered the award *res inter alios acta*. In a special memorandum dated April 18, 1878, Bolivian claims to the Chaco Boreal were elaborately presented to Washington, and recognition of Bolivian rights in the Chaco was demanded. Replying on September 6, 1878, United States Secretary of State William Evarts denied the petition on the grounds that Bolivia had not been a signatory of the Machaín–de Irigoyen Treaty of February 3, 1876.[10] Paradoxically then, the Hayes Award, an act of international good will, helped to precipitate new conflict because Bolivian anxiety over its claims increased at the same time that a newly vindicated Paraguay was least inclined to recognize them. Sixty years would elapse before the issue of Chaco proprietorship would fade into obscurity.

---

[10] United States, Commission of Inquiry and Conciliation, *Proceedings of the Commission of Inquiry and Conciliation, Bolivia and Paraguay, March 13, 1929– September 13, 1929*, pp. 1138–1140.

Negotiations between Paraguay and Bolivia to establish Chaco proprietorship started amicably enough. On October 15, 1879, the Quijarro-Decoud Treaty was signed in Asunción.[11] This agreement provided for a frontier to run from the confluence of the Apa and Paraguay rivers, southeasterly to a point on the Pilcomayo River. Pleased with this settlement, the Bolivian National Convention approved it (August 30, 1881) but added the provision that favorable territorial adjustment must be made on the Pilcomayo River so that a port could be established on ground above flood level. José Segundo Decoud, Paraguayan foreign minister, refused to accept such a modification, and on November 12, 1886, the Bolivian National Convention passed the treaty without condition. Unfortunately, their endeavor was to no avail; the Paraguayan Congress had indirectly vetoed the measure by refusing to consider it until after the seven-year limit for ratification had expired.

Both nations now began taking steps to occupy the Chaco. In July 1885 Miguel Suárez Arana began building Puerto Pacheco on the Paraguay River at the site of Bahía Negra, thus establishing for Bolivia a prospective outlet to the Atlantic Ocean. With more port facilities planned and road construction envisioned, Bolivia instructed Isaac Tamayo, its representative in Asunción, to initiate new talks with Paraguayan Foreign Minister Benjamin Aceval. The Tamayo-Aceval Treaty, signed February 16, 1887, divided the Chaco into three sections: one for each party, and a third to be subject to arbitration by King Leopold II of Belgium, or any other mutually acceptable arbiter. Unfortunately, events almost immediately made ratification of this treaty problematic. First, Paraguay gained Bolivian displeasure by granting concessions in the Chaco to foreign entrepreneurs. Secondly, a Paraguayan force seized Puerto Pacheco in December 1887 and drove the Bolivians out. Then on January 13, 1888, the Paraguayan government decreed that the west bank of the Paraguay River up to Bahía

---

[11] Consejo de Ministros Paraguayos, *Acuerdo en consejo de ministros del día 22 de octubre de 1879*, p. 4 (government document in the possession of Señor Carlos Pastore, Montevideo, Uruguay, reviewed August 12–16, 1965). On October 22, 1879, the Paraguayan Council of Ministers and the president of the Republic approved the Quijarro-Decoud Treaty and two others. The Quijarro-Decoud Treaty was then submitted to the Congress for ratification. For a representation of the proposed territorial delineation, see Map 1.

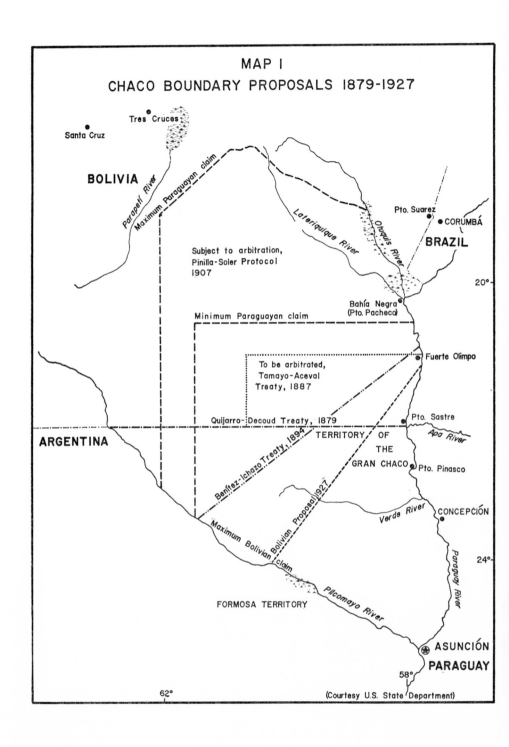

MAP I

CHACO BOUNDARY PROPOSALS 1879-1927

Tres Cruces

Santa Cruz

BOLIVIA

Parapetí River

Maximum Paraguayan claim

Lateriquique River

Otuquis River

Pto. Suarez

• CORUMBÁ

BRAZIL

Subject to arbitration,
Pinilla-Soler Protocol
1907

20°

Bahía Negra
(Pto. Pacheco)

Minimum Paraguayan claim

To be arbitrated,
Tamayo-Aceval
Treaty, 1887

Fuerte Olímpo

Quijarro-Decoud Treaty, 1879

Pto. Sastre

Apa River

ARGENTINA

Benítez-Ichazo Treaty, 1894

TERRITORY OF

THE

GRAN CHACO

Pto. Pinasco

Bolivian Proposal, 1927

Verde River

CONCEPCIÓN

Maximum Bolivian claim

24°

Paraguay River

FORMOSA TERRITORY

Pilcomayo River

ASUNCIÓN

58°

PARAGUAY

62°

(Courtesy U.S. State Department)

Negra was sovereign territory. Bolivia had temporarily broken diplomatic relations with Paraguay over the incident at Bahía Negra (Puerto Pacheco), and the National Convention did not ratify the Tamayo-Aceval Treaty until November 1888, again after the stated period for ratification had lapsed. Actually, the Altiplano politicians need not have bothered with ratification; in September 1889 the Paraguayan Congress declared the document null and void.[12]

Significant diplomatic action was not again forthcoming until 1894. As before, Bolivia initiated the venture by empowering Telmo Ichazo, its minister in Asunción, to negotiate with Foreign Minister Gregorio Benítez. After long months of cautious maneuver, the Benítez-Ichazo Treaty was signed, creating a boundary from Fuerte Olimpo running southeast to the Pilcomayo River at 61°28′ west longitude. Both diplomats may have been satisfied with their endeavors, but the representative bodies that were responsible for ratification were not. The Ichazo-Benítez Treaty was dubiously honored in that neither national assembly ever ratified it.

In 1906 Bolivia began bolstering its territorial claim by constructing a series of military posts in the Chaco. La Paz also dispatched Emeriterio Cano to Asunción to seek a solution to the deadlocked boundary question. Concerned about Bolivian movements in the western Chaco, Paraguayan Foreign Minister Manuel Domínguez was prepared for the serious discussion of a new treaty. The Cano-Domínguez negotiations proved unsuccessful, but they laid the groundwork for eventual success. On January 12, 1907, through the ubiquitous assistance of Argentine Foreign Minister Estanislao Zeballos the Pinilla-Soler Protocol was signed. This proposed solution divided the Chaco into two zones, one of which was ceded to Paraguay, and the other of which was to be submitted to an arbitration conducted by the president of Argentina. Pend-

---

[12] David H. Zook, Jr. (*The Conduct of the Chaco War*, p. 28) suggests that Paraguayan inaction was due to the introduction of several proposed changes by the Bolivian Congress. On the other hand, there is proof that the Paraguayan Council of Ministers approved the treaty and considered it a solution to the Chaco question (Paraguay, Congreso Paraguayo, *Acta de consejo de ministros de 17 de febrero de 1887*, p. 10 [government document in the possession of Señor Carlos Pastore, Montevideo, Uruguay, reviewed August 12–16, 1965]). For a pictorial presentation of the boundary, see Map 1.

ing execution of the agreement, both parties "undertook to refrain from making any change and from pushing forward existing possessions."[13] Maintenance of this status quo was subject to guarantee by the Argentine government once the treaty had been ratified.

Obviously pleased with the new pact, the Paraguayan Congress speedily ratified it. The politicians in La Paz procrastinated, however; they demanded modification of the treaty, but efforts to revise the provisions were soon deadlocked. Unrelated developments in 1909 reduced the Pinilla-Soler Protocol to the status of historical curio. When asked to arbitrate a boundary controversy between Bolivia and Peru, the Argentine president supported the Peruvian claim. Subsequent nationalist fervor triggered anti-Argentine demonstrations in Bolivia, and diplomatic relations were broken on July 20. The following day Argentina informed Paraguay that the diplomatic rupture made it unlikely that Bolivia would allow an Argentine president to play the role stipulated in the Pinilla-Soler Protocol. In 1910 Bolivia unilaterally rejected the proposed solution to the territorial problem.

Paraguay and Bolivia still were disposed to resolve their differences peacefully; on April 5, 1913, they signed the Ayala-Mujía Protocol. This new pact officially canceled the Pinilla-Soler Protocol but charged both nations with maintenance of the status quo in the Chaco. The terms of the protocol gave both governments two years in which to work out a territorial treaty. Failing this, "the high parties shall submit their boundary dispute to arbitration."[14] On July 19, 1915, Fulgencio Ricardo Moreno of Paraguay and Ricardo Mujía of Bolivia affixed their signatures to a new protocol that postponed the time for the commencement of negotiation another twelve months. In 1916, 1917, and 1918 Moreno and Mujía again signed protocols extending the period for direct negotiations over a Chaco boundary. Unfortunately, these extensions of a negotiation that never began produced a debilitating effect.

[13] League of Nations, *Dispute between Bolivia and Paraguay. Records of the Special Session of the Assembly*, Special Supplement 132, p. 2. See also Map 1. The arbitral zone lay "between parallel 20°30′ and the line claimed on the north by Paraguay within the territory between Greenwich meridians 61° and 62°."

[14] United States, Commission of Inquiry and Conciliation, *Proceedings*, p. 857.

Hence, efforts to resurrect the Moreno-Mujía protocols and thereby continue some kind of diplomatic dialogue failed in 1919 and 1921.

Following the obvious failure of diplomatic settlement, the two nations quickly moved toward a crisis in their relations. In 1924 at the request of Carlos Casado, Argentine magnate, the Paraguayan government decreed the settlement of Russian Mennonites in the Chaco.[15] Bolivia proclaimed its ownership of the Chaco and protested the proposed colonization so vigorously that Paraguay temporarily withdrew her ambassador. Both sides now began to increase their networks of *fortines* and purchases of armaments.

The continued construction of advanced military positions coupled with recurring encounters between armed patrols culminated in a series of shooting incidents, the most serious of which occurred near Fortín Sorpresa in February and March 1927. A Paraguayan reconnaissance unit of five men wandered "accidentally" onto the fort. All five were captured, but Second Lieutenant Rojas Silva, commander of the unit, subsequently was killed "trying to escape."[16] Prodded by a concerned Argentina, representatives of the contending republics met in the Bolivian legation in Buenos Aires and signed the Gutiérrez–Díaz León Protocol on April 22, 1927. This agreement provided for the acceptance of Argentine good offices and called for the appointment of plenipotentiaries to meet in Buenos Aires "90 days after the Protocol had been approved by the respective governments."[17]

Neither Bolivia nor Paraguay wasted any time ratifying the agreements, but the joint meetings held in Buenos Aires from September 1927 through July 1928 proved a miserable fiasco. Paraguayan delegates held that the boundaries established in the Pinilla-Soler Protocol were still satisfactory; any zone submitted for juridicial arbitration would have to be similar in its limits to that established in the aforesaid proto-

---

[15] United States, National Archives, Washington, D.C., Department of State, RG 59, Decimal File, 724.3415/65, no. 1436, Southworth (Asunción) to Sec'y State, Oct. 2, 1924, pp. 3–4. The Casado brothers drew up the contract and made the necessary arrangements. William B. Southworth noted that the Paraguayan government was only indirectly involved in the whole business.

[16] Zook, *Conduct of the Chaco War*, pp. 43–44.

[17] United States, Commission of Inquiry and Conciliation, *Proceedings*, p. 279.

col. They also argued that in effect a status quo zone existed in the Chaco into which the forces of neither country were to penetrate. Because Bolivia had built military positions to the east of the zone, she had penetrated into territory indisputably subject to Paraguayan jurisdiction.

Bolivian representatives argued that the status quo line of the 1907 agreement was not the same as the lines that would have been submitted to arbitration. They noted that Bolivia never had ratified the 1907 pact and that the Ayala-Mujía agreement of 1913 canceled whatever arbitral sectors the Pinilla-Soler Protocol might have established. In addition the Bolivians charged that by constructing railways, granting numerous concessions, and establishing military posts, Paraguay had displayed little respect for the status quo it claimed had been established. In an effort to break the stalemate and salvage something from the increasingly bitter sessions, Argentina introduced three proposals calling for demilitarization and evacuation of all Chaco *fortines* and the establishment of a committee of neutral states to guarantee nonaggression, juridical arbitration of the Chaco territorial question, and mutual declarations that *de facto* holdings in the Chaco would not be used in the arbitration as a basis for claims.[18] Both Paraguay and Bolivia speedily rejected this plan, and Argentina withdrew its good offices. However, neither Bolivian nor Paraguayan negotiators seemed prepared to end their verbal dueling. Three more contentious and acrimonious sessions were needed before the representatives of La Paz and Asunción could agree on a joint declaration formally terminating discussions.

The return of the negotiators to their respective capitals was the signal for redoubled military construction and intensified patrol activity on both sides. After a number of skirmishes, a Paraguayan force attacked and partially destroyed the Bolivian Fortín Vanguardia on December 5, 1928, leaving five defenders dead. Three days later Bolivia broke diplomatic relations and in reprisal attacked and captured the Paraguayan Fortín Boquerón on December 14. Each side accused the other of aggression and ordered mobilization.[19] The crisis was com-

18 Consult *ibid.*, pp. 333–336; and Argentina, Ministerio de Relaciones Exteriores y Culto, *La política argentina en la guerra del Chaco*, I, 6.
19 Carlos José Fernández, *La guerra del Chaco*, I, 35–37. Fernández notes that on

pounded by the ineffectiveness of existing inter-American peace machinery. Immediately following the Vanguardia attack, Paraguay requested mediation by the peace committee installed in Montevideo under the terms of the Gondra Convention of 1923.[20] This effort proved abortive because even though the committee was prepared to act the pact had never been ratified by the Bolivian Congress.

Fortunately for the potential belligerents, the International Conference of American States on Conciliation and Arbitration had begun its meetings in Washington to adopt "obligatory arbitration as a means which they [American states] will employ for the pacific solution of international differences of a judicial character."[21] This organization had no *de jure* right to mediate the Chaco affair, but no other nation or organization except Argentina seemed willing to act swiftly enough to prevent expansion of the conflict.[22] Time was the decisive consideration, and on December 17 the Washington conference offered its good offices to Asunción and La Paz. Paraguay accepted almost immediately

---

the Paraguayan side the call for mobilization resulted in hopeless chaos. Both Zook (*The Chaco War*, p. 51) and Fernández (*La guerra del Chaco*, I, 36–37) suggest that mutual military incapacity was the major reason war did not result from the Vanguardia and Boquerón skirmishes.

[20] Russel Cooper and Mary Mattison, "The Chaco Dispute," *Geneva Special Studies*, 5, no. 2 (1934), 17. The Gondra Convention signed at the fifth Pan-American Conference at Santiago, Chile, in 1923, provided for two permanent commissions composed of the longest accredited American diplomatic representatives at Washington, D.C., and Montevideo, Uruguay. In case of any dispute not amenable to direct diplomatic settlement or arbitration, the two parties were to refrain from mobilization and hostile acts and to accept an impartial investigation by a body set up through the agency of one of the permanent commissions.

[21] *Ibid.*, p. 4. The conference had been called in accordance with a resolution of the Sixth Pan-American Conference at Habana in 1928 (*ibid.*). Meetings opened on December 10, 1928.

[22] An official publication of the government (Argentina, Min. de Rel. Ext. y Culto, *La política argentina*, I, 161–162) admits that Argentina made competitive diplomatic overtures to Paraguay and Bolivia in an effort to have the feuding states accept Argentine rather than Washington mediation. These efforts ceased only on January 7, 1929, when Bolivia informed President Yrigoyen that it had definitely decided in favor of Washington. The United States Department of State was fully informed of these Argentine diplomatic maneuvers (see U.S., Archives, RG 59, Decimal File 724.3415/263, no. 60, Dec. 13, 1928, Kaufman [La Paz] to Dept. State [a confidential report]; and Decimal File 724.2415/264, no. 31, Dec. 15, 1928, Kreeck [Asunción] to Dept. State).

but Bolivian acceptance was delayed until December 25, 1928. On January 3, 1929, representatives of the two disputants signed a protocol establishing a cease-fire and initiating investigations to determine the aggressor in the clashes at Vanguardia and Boquerón.

The crisis had been alleviated temporarily and mobilization halted; the contestants again were talking rather than shooting. However, there had been no decrease in chauvinistic agitation, and despite the cries of "peace, peace," the preeminent issue remained how much of the Chaco one contender could secure at the expense of the other.

Since the end of the War of the Triple Alliance in 1870, the Liberal Party and the Colorado Party had traditionally monopolized Paraguayan politics. The Colorados held power at the time of the negotiations of the 1879, 1887, and 1894 treaties. The Colorado-controlled National Council approved the 1879 and 1887 treaties, although neither of these was ever ratified by the Paraguayan Congress. Each of these treaties ceded to Bolivia a littoral on the Paraguay River. Formally organized in 1887 the Liberal Party, which generally fought all opposition-sponsored proposals, was able to attack Colorado efforts to ratify the suggested treaties as measures designed to surrender the national patrimony.[23] Under these circumstances, Colorado deputies and senators were not eager to force an issue that might prove to be a political boomerang.

The situation was reversed in 1907. With the seizure of power by the Liberal Party in 1904, the Colorados assumed the cloak of superpatriotism.[24] The Pinilla-Soler Protocol could be ratified since it did not spe-

---

[23] Efraím Cardozo, Paraguayan historian and former diplomat, interview, Asunción, Paraguay, October 5, 1965. See also Efraím Cardozo, *Breve historia del Paraguay*, pp. 112–114. While many individuals prior to 1887 had been called "liberals" in regard to their views on Paraguayan politics, the party was officially organized by Antonia Taboada. Cardozo, (*Breve historia*, p. 114) notes that one of the major aims of those who founded the Liberal Party was the prevention of the adoption of the 1887 territorial treaty.

[24] Cardozo, *Breve historia*, pp. 119–120. Evidence that the Colorados had even earlier begun to adopt a different attitude toward the problem of Chaco possession can be seen in a letter written by Juan Cancio Flecha (ministro de relaciones exteriores) to Antonio Quijarro (agente confidencial), in *Acta de una reunión realizada por el presidente de la república, Emilio Aceval, con los diputados y senadores y el*

cifically give Bolivia an opening on the Paraguay River. However, the treaty was received with hostility by the Bolivian Congress and the Liberals in Paraguay hardly could have accepted the revisions that would have been demanded. In effect, the Liberals discovered that as rulers they were vulnerable to the same chauvinistic arguments they had used against the Colorados. Adoption of a more conciliatory position gave the opposition a weapon that could be converted into electoral victory or successful coup.

As a psychological issue, the Chaco came to exercise a tremendous influence on Paraguayan opinion. Possibly the first major work attacking Bolivian claims and attributing to Paraguay exclusive Chaco ownership was written by Alejandro Audibert in 1892.[25] Other publicists and academicians, often called "doctores en Chaco,"[26] soon followed with a host of works asserting Paraguayan rights in the Chaco and denying those of Bolivia in terms of their own legalistic precedents. Works by Manuel Gondra asserted the *intangibilidad del litoral* formula;[27] adopted by the Liberal Party, the "Intangibility of the Littoral" doctrine claimed that under no conditions would a port on the Paraguay River be ceded to Bolivia. Manuel Domínquez' *El Chaco-Boreal fué, es y será del Paraguay* (*The Chaco Boreal Was, Is, and Will be Paraguayan*) was adopted by the Paraguayan National Council of Education as an official textbook. Lacking or spurning juridical evidence, Paraguayan writers stressed proximity and territorial occupation.[28] Thus

---

Señor vice-presidente de república y los ministros, secretarios de relaciones exteriores, interior, de hacienda, de justicia, culto, de instrucción pública, y de guerra y marina, 5 de julio, 1901, pp. 14–15 (collection of Carlos Pastore, Montevideo, Uruguay). In the letter read in session at the home of the president, Foreign Minister Flecha stated that Paraguay had never admitted that any part of the right bank of the Paraguay River was subject to litigation. Flecha maintained that Paraguayan possession of the right bank of the Paraguay was "a public, historic and established fact."

[25] Alejandro Audibert, *Los límites de la antigua provincia del Paraguay*, p. 150 and *passim*.

[26] "Doctores en Chaco" was a common term used by Paraguayans to describe those who dealt in juridical problems concerning Chaco ownership. The term was both respectful and derisive. All Paraguayans wanted the Chaco, but the term suggested the "doctores" knew about nothing else.

[27] Cardozo, interview, October 15, 1965.

[28] In 1904 a Paraguayan deputy admitted that Paraguay would have a difficult time proving its Chaco claims, for in the War of the Triple Alliance the nation's

interpreted, the Chaco question was referred to in Paraguayan circles as a *cuestión de límites*—a "question of limits." General José Félix Estigarribia provides an illustrative explanation of the official view: "The administrative centers of Upper Peru [Bolivia] were separated from the Chaco by gigantic mountains and vast deserts stretching over hundreds of miles. Therefore, they [Upper Peru officials] even from a physical point of view were unable . . . to exercise any influence in the Chaco, and actually never did. . . . There remained the precise definition of the boundaries in the hinterlands of the Chaco, which was little explored and little known. . . . The problem was thus reduced to a delimitation of the line of separation between the two republics."[29] The *cuestión de límites* thesis carried the implicit understanding that the entire Chaco was Paraguayan. In fact, Paraguay physically occupied a relatively small part of the area. For theory and reality to agree, Paraguayan policy fixed the Chaco boundaries as far north and west as possible (see Map 2).[30]

Largely through the influence of chauvinistically inclined Paraguayan authors, such geographical barriers as the Paraguay River and publicized political entities like the "Hayes Zone" became sacred symbols. Partly by accident and partly by design Paraguayan academicians and publicists helped to create a psychological climate in which concession to Bolivia became tantamount to treason.

Although the economic importance of the Chaco was overlooked by the legalists, it was never forgotten by many others. The immense

---

national archives had been almost completely destroyed (Paraguay, Congreso Paraguaya, *Acta del Congreso—20 de mayo de 1904—Sesión secreta*, p. 3 [collection of Carlos Pastore, Montevideo, Uruguay]). César Gondra (*La diplomacia de los tratados: Paraguay y Bolivia*, pp. 229–230) declared that while Paraguay held no certain map proving her ownership of the Chaco, he was certain Bolivia had none either. Some years later, Efraím Cardozo (*El Chaco en el régimen de las intendencias*, p. 126) denied that a prolonged study of legal origin or colonial titles was of any great importance in determining Chaco proprietorship.

[29] Pablo Max Ynsfran, *The Epic of the Chaco: Marshal Estigarribia's Memoirs of the Chaco War 1932–1935*, pp. 3–4.

[30] Compare Map 2 with Map 3. In March 1929, when the original from which Map 2 was made was given to United States State Department officials, Paraguay still insisted on its maximum claim, and Bolivia continued to demand all area up to the Pilcomayo and Paraguay rivers.

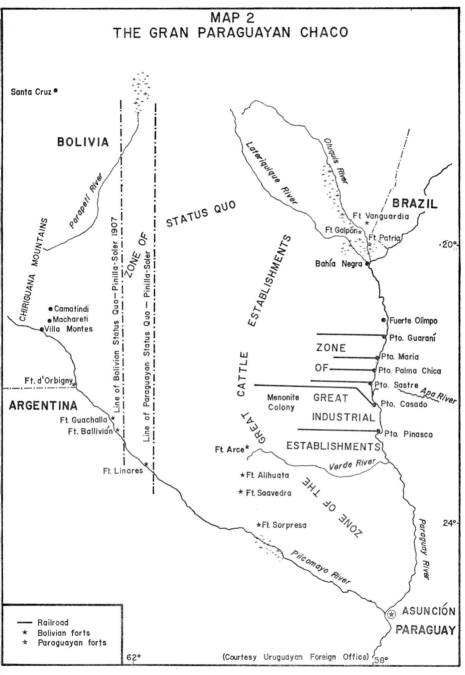

MAP 2
THE GRAN PARAGUAYAN CHACO

Santa Cruz •

BOLIVIA

Parapeti River

CHIRIGUANA MOUNTAINS

STATUS QUO

ZONE OF

Line of Bolivian Status Quo—Pinilla-Soler 1907

Line of Paraguayan Status Quo—Pinilla-Soler

Lateriquique River

Otuquis River

BRAZIL

Ft. Vanguardia

Ft. Galpón

Ft. Patria

·20°·

Bahía Negra •

• Camatindi
• Machareti
• Villa Montes

ESTABLISHMENTS

CATTLE

•Fuerte Olimpo

Pto. Guaraní

ZONE

OF

Pto. Maria

Pto. Palma Chica

Ft. d'Orbigny

Pto. Sastre

Apa River

ARGENTINA

Ft. Guachalla ★
Ft. Ballivián ★

Menonite
Colony

GREAT

INDUSTRIAL

Pto. Casado

Pto. Pinasco

Ft. Arce ★

GREAT

ESTABLISHMENTS

Verde River

Ft. Linares ★

★ Ft. Alihuata

★ Ft. Saavedra

ZONE OF THE

★ Ft. Sorpresa

Pilcomayo River

Paraguay River

24°·

ASUNCIÓN

— Railroad
★ Bolivian forts
★ Paraguayan forts

PARAGUAY

62°

(Courtesy Uruguayan Foreign Office) 58°

This highly stylized map presenting Paraguayan claims to the Chaco Boreal was handed to the United States assistant secretary of state by the chief of the Paraguayan delegation to the Conference of Peace on March 9, 1929.

forests of quebracho trees appeared to defy exhaustion, while the flat, grassy ranges were ideal for cattle raising. With Asunción's blessings, foreign concessionaires moved into the Chaco and developed profitable industries. By 1918 the International Products Company (U.S.A.), based at Puerto Pinasco, had become the leading producer of tannin extract. The holdings of the Paraguayan Land and Cattle Company (U.S.A. and Great Britain) were valued at $1,100,000. Two large interests, the Argentine Quebracho Company and the Farquhar Syndicate, bought large areas of the Chaco with the intention of raising cattle and producing tannin extract for export. The "Baron of the Chaco," however, was Carlos Casado, who owned the largest railroad in the area, a tannin extract company, a port bearing the family name, and four million hectares of Chaco real estate.[31]

By 1928 the capital investment of various companies in Chaco cattle, quebracho, and pettigrain extract had reached $10,000,000. The income from duties and taxes on these activities made possession of the eastern Chaco economically important to Paraguay. Equally significant was the expansion of investment by the companies involved. In this matter, however, an ominous difficulty already had manifested itself. As early as 1913 Bolivian patrols probing south and east had encountered advance agents of several concessionaires pushing westward. The Bolivians had announced their ownership of areas already granted to the companies by Paraguay and were demanding taxes.[32] For Paraguay,

[31] Ronald S. Kain, "Behind the Chaco War," *Current History*, 42, no. 5 (August 1935), 470. Despite the fact that such "giants" as the International Products Company and the Paraguayan Land and Cattle Company represented American or British capital, the majority of the companies and the bulk of capital investment quoted represented Argentine interests (League of Nations, *Report of the Chaco Commission: Dispute between Bolivia and Paraguay*, Political, C.154.M.64.VII[1934], pp. 14–15).

[32] U. S., Archives, RG 59, Decimal File 724.3215/16, no. 126, Lorillard (Paraguay) to Dept. State, Jan. 3, 1913, pp. 2–4. The Farquhar Syndicate and Argentine Quebracho Company ran afoul of Bolivian army patrols in the north central Chaco. The company agents claimed they had paid $2.00 gold per hectare to the Paraguayan government for the territory. The Bolivians refused permission to claim or survey the ground in question. Later, a Bolivian representative informed the companies that as the territory bought did not belong to Paraguay, a charge of $.20 per hectare would be necessary if the companies were to commence operations in the territory.

then, loss of the area would have been a devastating economic blow. Even if the Chaco were not totally lost, Bolivian advances in the area eventually would curtail foreign concessionaire operations and sharply decrease the annual receipts that lined the Paraguayan treasury. Furthermore, Paraguayans realized they had only the Chaco to exploit for future national development. On every count, then, territorial concession to Bolivia seemed exceedingly undesirable.

Informal chronicles may one day tell the history of Bolivia in terms of sea water. This creation of Simón Bolívar and Antonio José de Sucre actually is two nations. One is centered on the high, arid Altiplano, surrounded on the west and north by mountains; the natural outlet for the Altiplano is the Pacific. The other "nation" is the Oriente and the eastern plains of the Beni, with the Atlantic its natural outlet. The split in Bolivia's geographical character has been aggravated by several international misadventures. Following the War of the Pacific (1879–1883), Bolivia lost her Pacific littoral to Chile. In signing the 1904 treaty with the latter state, some Bolivian citizens took solace in the hope that the lost littoral might one day be restored. In reality the country was left without a sovereign outlet. The Bolivian predicament accentuated the Chaco problem, for if Bolivia did not recover its Pacific littoral, an eastern exit would be Bolivia's only opportunity to modify her landlocked status.

The problem of securing a port on the Paraguay River was partially obscured by events. In 1879, 1887, 1894, and 1907, Bolivian diplomats had negotiated settlements that ceded to Paraguay progressively larger areas of the Chaco. Ricardo Mujía, Bolivian diplomat, disrupted the Chaco negotiations of 1915 by introducing into the proceedings an eight-volume study based on the principle of *uti possidetis*.[33] Mujía's action aroused suspicions among the Paraguayans, for it intimated to them that Bolivia intended to claim the entire Chaco.

[33] Bolivia, Ministerio de Relaciones Exteriores y Culto, *Bolivia-Paraguay: Exposición de los títulos que consagran el derecho territorial de Bolivia, sobre la zona comprendida entre los ríos Pilcomayo y Paraguay, presentada por el Doctor Mujía, enviado extraordinario y ministro plenipotenciario de Bolivia en el Paraguay*, prepared by Ricardo Mujía, I, 4–7. In 1915 Mujía submitted an eight-volume work with one folio of maps. The published version consists of only five volumes. *Uti possidetis*, as

After 1915 Bolivia made definite moves to strengthen her claim to the Chaco. The fundamental national objective became the acquisition of a port on the Paraguay River, and a system of forts and communication lines was to be constructed to affirm the legality of this objective.[34] Would such a port, even if obtained, provide a satisfactory outlet for the products of eastern Bolivia? Bolivian politicians and intellectuals could claim little expertise regarding the utility of such a port, but all agreed that as a psychological outlet it provided the means for breaking the confinement they regarded as both real and debilitating.[35]

Unfortunately the bulk of the Bolivian populace, Indian by ancestry, knew practically nothing about either the Chaco or the Pacific littoral. Such questions were of primary interest only to the educated "white"[36] population of the Altiplano. Knowledge of the latter's political orienta-

---

applied in the Americas, states that the territory held by a Spanish colony prior to 1810 (or whatever the date of independence) was to become part of the territory of the new republic. The difficulty with the theory lies in the reality of the situation. Since the Spaniards were not overly concerned with administrative boundaries between colonies, the question to be asked is, exactly what did each colony possess in 1810?

[34] Sumner Welles, ed., *The Intelligent American's Guide to the Peace*, p. 174. Welles maintains that the reacquisition of an outlet to the sea was always Bolivia's major preoccupation despite more menacing declarations by chauvinistic elements. Welles's conclusion is substantiated by reports from other sources (see, for example, U.S., Archives, RG 59, Decimal File 724.3415/600, no. 57, Caffrey [Bogotá] to Dept. State, June 25, 1929, p. 1; and Decimal File 724.3415/59, no. 543, R. Roswell Baker [La Paz] to Dept. State, June 20, 1924, p. 3). Note Map 3, which indicates placement of Bolivian and Paraguayan forts and the thrust of settlement by these two countries.

[35] During the dry season in the Chaco (three or four months annually but occasionally five) the depth of the river falls below 2.20 meters at all Chaco ports (see Paraguay, Ministerio de Hacienda, Dirección General de Estadística y Censos, *Boletín estadístico del Paraguay*, 5, no. 13/15, 10). Despite these navigational difficulties, Bolivian authors such as Eduardo Arze Quiroga (*Documentos para una historia de la guerra del Chaco: Seleccionados del archivo de Daniel Salamanca*, I, 21) and Rogelia Ayala Moreira (*Por qué no ganamos la guerra del Chaco*, p. 96) speak as if they believed a littoral on the Paraguay River would be of great economic value to Bolivia. The construction of a rail and road network would necessarily preclude the effective use of a Chaco port by vessels bearing products for southeastern Bolivia. The Bolivian authors mentioned do not discuss this aspect of the problem.

[36] Bolivians use the term 'white' to refer to an "educated" or "civilized" person (*gente decente*). The definition is social-cultural since the people are physically mestizo.

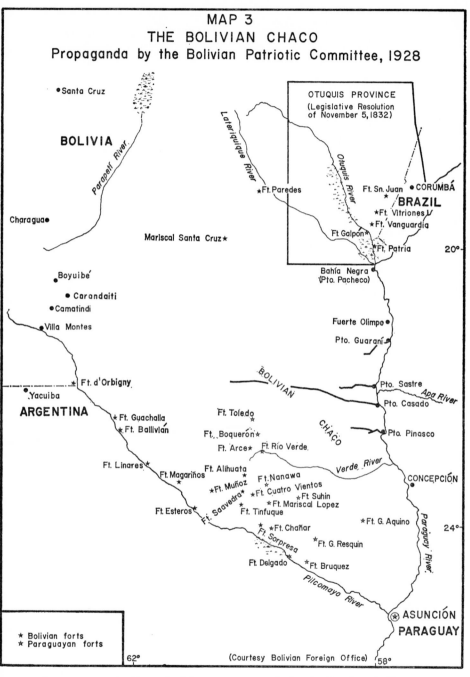

MAP 3
THE BOLIVIAN CHACO
Propaganda by the Bolivian Patriotic Committee, 1928

●Santa Cruz

OTUQUIS PROVINCE
(Legislative Resolution
of November 5,1832)

BOLIVIA

Lateriquique River

Parapeti River

Otuquis River

★Ft. Paredes

Ft. Sn. Juan ●CORUMBÁ
★
BRAZIL
★Ft. Vitriones
★Ft. Vanguardia

Charagua●

Mariscal Santa Cruz★

Ft. Galpon★
★Ft. Patria   20°

.Boyuibe'

Bahía Negra ●
(Pto. Pacheco)

● Carandaiti
●Camatindi

●Villa Montes

Fuerte Olimpo ●

Pto. Guaraní

BOLIVIAN

★ Ft. d'Orbigny

Pto. Sastre
Apa River
Pto. Casado

.Yacuiba
ARGENTINA

★ Ft. Guachalla
★Ft. Ballivián

Ft. Toledo

CHACO

Pto. Pinasco

Ft. Boqueron★
Ft. Arce★ Ft. Rio Verde.

Verde River

Ft. Linares★
Ft. Magariños
★

Ft. Alihuata
★
★Ft. Muñoz
★Ft. Cuatro Vientos
★Ft. Suhin

Ft. Nanawa
★

CONCEPCIÓN
●

Ft. Esteros★
Ft. Saavedra★
★Ft. Tinfuque

★Ft. Mariscal Lopez

★Ft. G. Aquino

Paraguay River

24°

★
★Ft. Chañar
Ft. Sorpresa

★Ft. G. Resquin

Ft. Delgado
★Ft. Bruquez

Pilcomayo River

⊛ASUNCIÓN
PARAGUAY

★ Bolivian forts
★ Paraguayan forts

62°

(Courtesy Bolivian Foreign Office)   58°

As successors to the colonial government of the Audiencia of Charcas,
Bolivia claimed the Province of Otuquis, once controlled by the Audiencia,
and made this claim a partial basis for its Chaco pretensions.

tion required consideration of *reivindicacionismo*, or Bolivian revindi-
cation. This doctrine posited that Bolivia had suffered diplomatic and
military reverses that had made the nation a second-class state. To be
vindicated Bolivia must reemerge as a respected power, and the first
step in this process would be the acquisition of a littoral.[37] The causes
of this phenomenon are rooted in the national history. On the field of
Yungay in 1839, Andrés de Santa Cruz's dream of a united Bolivia and
Peru died aborted. Following the conflict of 1879 Bolivia was thrown
back from the Pacific. In seeking diplomatic advantages, Bolivian representatives had displayed ineptitude. By the terms of a Brazilian treaty
of 1867, Bolivia ceded 100,000 square kilometers in return for "illusory commercial advantages."[38] In 1903 after some desultory fighting, Bolivia ceded to Brazil through the Treaty of Petrópolis the entire
region of Acre in exchange for the promised construction of a railway
and payment of £3,000,000. Brazil failed to make payment and no
further arrangements concerning the projected railroad or the promised
payment were made until 1928.[39] Add to these misfortunes the desire
for a Pacific littoral and fifty years of indecision in the Chaco, and the
damage to the Bolivian national psyche is evident.

Through *reivindicacionismo* the Bolivians intended to terminate an
unrelieved series of military and diplomatic disasters; but they needed
a triumph. Some Altiplano leaders viewed the Paraguayans as ready
foils. President Bautista Saavedra had written, "the offensive action of
Paraguay never would be able to severely injure us."[40] President Daniel
Salamanca believed Paraguay to be the only nation Bolivia could with
certainty defeat in battle.[41] The United States chargé d'affaires, John F.

---

[37] Justo Rodas Equino, *La guerra del Chaco: Interpretación de política internacional americana*, pp. 7–8.

[38] Harold Osborne, *Bolivia*, p. 58.

[39] U.S., Archives, RG 59, Decimal File 724.3415/652 1/2, Special Report by
Emerson B. Christie, July 31, 1929, p. 44.

[40] Paraguay, Ministerio de Relaciones Exteriores, Archivo de Relaciones Exteriores,
Asunción, *La conferencia de paz de Buenos Aires*, File 12, pp. 164–165.

[41] League of Nations, *Dispute between Paraguay and Bolivia. Statement of Paraguayan Case Submitted to the Assembly by the Paraguayan Government*, September
6, 1934, Political, A.19.VII(1934), p. 57. The Paraguayan equivalent of Salamanca's
position was that exhibited by Justo Pastor Benítez, *Estigarribia: El soldado del
Chaco*, p. 45.

Martin, wrote: "There is . . . abundant evidence that Bolivia, generally speaking, would welcome a war with Paraguay. . . . Bolivians everywhere hold a low opinion of the prowess of their Paraguayan neighbors and seem to think that a campaign against them would assume the aspect of a picnic."[42] It would be absurd to conclude that Bolivia deliberately plotted to provoke a conflict with Paraguay. Conversely, however, many felt that if efforts to obtain an outlet from Chile proved ineffectual a similar rebuff from Paraguay might prove well-nigh intolerable.

For La Paz the Chaco was also an economic lure. Practically no profit had been derived from the Oriente area until 1919 and 1920, when petroleum was discovered in the departments of Santa Cruz, Tarija, and Chuquisaca. The presence of "black gold" touched off a scramble among petroleum companies to gain concessions and thus exacerbated the Chaco problem because the discovery of petroleum in territories bordering the Chaco suggested that deposits were to be found there also. Since a trans-Andean pipeline was inconceivable at that time, La Paz concluded that effective exploitation of the petroleum wealth would necessitate a port on the Paraguay River for oil shipment and enough territory across the Chaco for the construction of a pipeline. But under existing circumstances Bolivia held no frontage on the lower Paraguay River. To negotiate with Asunción to obtain such space would be tacit admission that Paraguay held *de jure* rights in the Chaco. Even if Paraguay and Bolivia did choose to negotiate the issue, Paraguay would have to be given a share of the prospective tax revenues in exchange for the right to build a pipeline to the Paraguay River. With the deterioration of Paraguayan-Bolivian relations and the increasing fiscal straits of the Bolivian government,[43] it is understandable that Altiplano leaders were loath to share any prospective windfall.

The recapitulation of events, however, leaves a vague sense of inadequacy. To whom did the Chaco really belong? Which of the con-

---

[42] U.S., Archives, RG 59, Decimal File 724.3415/510, no. 137, John F. Martin (La Paz) to Dept. State, April 10, 1929, p. 2.

[43] Welles, *American's Guide to the Peace*, p. 177. By 1931 the foreign debt had reached $134,000,000.

tending nations had the best claim to it? Rulers in Asunción, both before and after independence, had traditionally exercised control over parts of the Chaco. Bolivian claims rested primarily on the jurisdictional prerogatives of the Audiencia of Charcas. This court, founded in 1559, at one time exercised judicial control over the colonial province of Paraguay, but distance made this mandate impractical, and the Spanish crown never delineated the extent or limits of the court's powers there. The long legal arguments, the masses of maps, the historical documents marshaled by both sides tend to prove little except that a conclusive decision based on legal and historical precedents hardly was possible.

But in 1929 was any kind of solution possible? Consider first the territorial holdings. Bolivia had advanced far into the central Chaco, establishing *fortines* and constructing roads. Paraguayan hinterland holdings perhaps were not as extensive, but Paraguay held the Paraguay River littoral (refer to Maps 2 and 3). Each side was in a difficult position; Paraguay wished to hold the littoral and prevent further Bolivian penetration into the south and central Chaco, whereas Bolivia wished to obtain river frontage on the lower Paraguay while expanding its holdings in the central Chaco. This situation was further complicated because although Asunción never directly opposed arbitration or mediation of the Chaco question, it is unlikely that any proposal that did not regard as inviolate Paraguay's hold on the Paraguay River and the Hayes Zone had any chance of obtaining approval. The coupling of these conditions with Paraguayan determination to halt Bolivia's penetration into the Chaco meant that by 1929 Asunción's diplomats would appear at the bargaining tables with virtually nothing to bargain.

Bolivian predispositions gave little reason for optimism, but events transpiring in 1929 made the situation even more uncertain. On July 28 Chile and Peru signed a treaty ending the Tacna-Arica dispute. Ownership of these provinces along the Pacific littoral had been a central issue arising from the War of the Pacific (1879–1883) and had exacerbated relations between Chile, Peru, and Bolivia since that time. After nearly fifty years of stalemate, Chile had kept Arica, ceded Tacna to Peru, and paid the Peruvian government $6,000,000. Settlement of this problem ended any Bolivian hope of peacefully obtaining a Pacific littoral. But a recourse to arms by Bolivia would certainly result in war with Chile, and probably with Peru; prospects for Bolivian success in such an undertaking were negligible. In an interview with the United States chargé d'affaires, Abon Saavedra, vice-president of Bolivia, declared on August 16, 1929, that the Tacna-Arica settlement had been the "final blow" to Bolivian prestige.[44] Saavedra added that his nation once more had been ignored and humiliated but that such a thing would not be allowed to happen again. Paradoxically, then, the Tacna-Arica détente heightened the prospect of another conflict, because it meant that Bolivia would now seek both the long-desired outlet to the sea and *reivindicacionismo* in the same area: the Chaco.

[44] U.S., Archives, RG 59, Decimal File 724.3415/682, no. 213, Hibbard (La Paz) to Dept. State, August 16, 1929, p. 2.

2. THE ROAD TO WAR

*. . . it would not have been possible to achieve a result so
satisfactory to the two parties and affirming the principles of
peace underlying Panamericanism and continental solidarity,
were it not for the conciliatory spirit of the Delegations of
Bolivia and Paraguay.*

Conclusion of the report of Brigadier General Frank McCoy, chairman of the Commission of Investigation and Conciliation (1929)

*Bolivia has a history of international disasters, the effect of
which must be counter-acted by a victorious war, to prevent the
Bolivian character from becoming daily more and more pessimistic. . . . Paraguay . . . is the only country we are able to
attack with certainties of victory.*

Daniel Salamanca, elected president of Bolivia in 1931

ᘓᘓ

O<small>N</small> JANUARY 3, 1929, Paraguay and Bolivia signed
a protocol providing for the settlement of disputes arising from the
December 1928 conflicts. The story behind the consummation of this
protocol forecast the difficulties that negotiators would encounter in the
future. By December 25, 1928, both Bolivia and Paraguay had agreed
to the creation in Washington, D.C., of an investigatory commission
consisting of two delegates from each of the disputants and one each

from five other American republics. The original commission was to include Argentina, Brazil, Cuba, Uruguay, and the United States. This combination proved to be unacceptable. Argentina, which had not bothered to attend the Washington Conference of Arbitration and Conciliation, and Brazil both declined to take part in Washington-based peace operations. Paraguay then proposed Chilean participation, but vehement Bolivian remonstrances defeated the suggestion. The Commission of Investigation and Conciliation, whose task it was to determine the responsibilities arising from the actions of Vanguardia and Boquerón and to facilitate the restoration of diplomatic relations between Bolivia and Paraguay, finally was composed of representatives from the United States, Cuba, Uruguay, Mexico, and Colombia. The commission failed to include any state that bordered either of the two litigants.

The signature of the January 3, 1929, protocol was little more than an elaborate ceremonial. The commission remained a hypothetical entity for over two months. Following the initial amenities Paraguay and Bolivia swiftly returned to the business of mutual recrimination, and meetings did not begin until March 13, 1929. During the interim, United States State Department officials had successfully transacted the necessary preliminaries for the exchange of prisoners captured during the actions at Vanguardia and Boquéron. Unfortunately, two months of bickering were necessary before a repatriation plan was accepted by the disputants on May 23, 1929.

With the investigatory proceedings finally in progress, State Department officials thought the time propitious to attempt a direct settlement of the Chaco question. On May 31, 1929, Brigadier General Frank McCoy, commission chairman, stated that he considered it "indispensable, in order to prevent further conflicts . . . to procure a settlement of the fundamental question between the two countries."[1] Following guarded agreement by Bolivia and Paraguay, State Department experts began to prepare three exhaustive economic and geographical studies of the Chaco.[2] All three reports recommended a river port for Bolivia,

[1] United States, Department of State, *Papers Relating to the Foreign Relations of the United States, 1929,* I, 864.

[2] The three major studies were by Emerson B. Christie, United States, National

some equitable compensation for Paraguay, and a boundary beginning at the 21° or 22° latitude and running north-northeast from the Pilco-mayo River. On August 16, the commission reached a decision concerning the culpability of Paraguay and Bolivia in the Vanguardia-Bo-querón incidents. On August 26, it began to circulate both its decision and a treaty proposal that would permanently settle the Chaco question. Formally presented to the representatives of La Paz and Asunción on August 31, 1929, the draft treaty called for juridical arbitration, but Article V specifically guaranteed the Hayes Zone to Paraguay and a Paraguay River littoral around Bahía Negra to Bolivia.[3]

Since both nations had long professed their adherence to the principle of arbitration, the presentation of a formal proposal put them in an embarrassing position. As a means of escape, both Paraguayan and Bolivian representatives reaffirmed their commitment to arbitrate but condemned the specifics of the proposed pact. The Bolivians announced, in their reply of September 9, 1929, that since Bahía Negra (Puerto Pacheco) had been illegally seized by Paraguay in 1888, its return constituted an "act of reparation." They severely criticized the award of the Hayes Zone to Paraguay and demanded the exclusion from arbitration of a similar zone, which would be set aside for themselves.[4] The Paraguayans suggested that the neutral commissioners had committed a terrible error in awarding the port of Bahía Negra to Bolivia. They refused to exclude from arbitration any port for Bolivia and argued: "We do not consider substantiated the motives which

---

Archives, Washington, D.C., Department of State, RG 59, Decimal File 724.3415/652 1/2, July 31, 1929; S. W. Boggs, *Notes on the Geographic Aspects of a Practicable Plan for the Settlement of the Bolivia-Paraguay Controversy,* RG 59, Decimal File 724.3415/942, Annex F, pt. 2, Aug. 14, 1929; and Raye Platt, *Suggestions on the Possible Routes for the Bolivia-Paraguay Boundary on the Chaco,* RG 59, Decimal File 724.3415/942, Annex F, pt. 2, Aug. 3, 1929.

[3] U.S., Dept. of State, *Foreign Relations, 1929,* I, 874–880; U.S., Archives, RG 59, Decimal File 724.3415/692, no. 339, Kreeck (Asunción) to Dept. State, Aug. 9, 1929, p. 3, reported that "Bahía Negra as a serviceable port is a fantastic dream . . . or any point thereabouts."

[4] United States, Commission of Inquiry and Conciliation, *Proceedings of the Commission of Inquiry and Conciliation, Bolivia and Paraguay, March 18, 1929–September 13, 1929,* pp. 42–43, 46–47.

require a cession, in advance to Bolivia, of a part of the territory that can be submitted to arbitration."[5]

The commission ignored the refusal of both countries to make meaningful concessions, restated its previous proposal, and on September 12, 1929, called for preliminary arbitration of the Chaco dispute. Caught at a disadvantage, the Bolivians executed a strategic disengagement. The protocol of January 3, 1929, had granted the commission a six-month existence from the time it initiated proceedings;[6] Altiplano representatives waited until twenty-four hours after the commission had legally expired on September 13 before rejecting the proposals of September 12. Further progress concerning territorial negotiation ceased on September 19 when the Bolivian representatives informed United States Secretary of State Henry Stimson that "Bolivian public sentiments"[7] made continuation of talks on the subject impossible.

The Paraguayan response to the commission's September 12 proposals was partially favorable, but other circumstances prevented the Paraguayans from gaining any propaganda advantages at Bolivian expense. The August 16 memorandum of the commission had clearly labeled Paraguay the responsible party in the attacks at Vanguardia and Boquerón. When informed of the commission's decision ten days later, Asunción's representatives hastily advised the commission that they would rebuild Fortín Vanguardia but requested that this condition not be written into the final report. Paraguayan difficulties multiplied after September 9. On that day, Bolivia accepted the conciliation proposals first circulated on August 26. Asunción's representatives then accepted them on September 11, 1929, but with the stipulation that "the supplementary explanation . . . regarding Boquerón and Vanguardia be conditions to be complied with . . . but not . . . part of the signed basis of the conciliation." They also reiterated their request for an informal agreement concerning the problem of rebuilding Fortín Vanguardia.[8] Partly in an effort to forestall the publication of a final

---

[5] *Ibid.*, pp. 46–47.

[6] See the January 3, 1929, protocol, U.S. Dept. of State, *Foreign Relations, 1929,* I, 832. The Commission had begun its meetings on March 13, 1929.

[7] *Ibid.*, p. 900. Minister Eduardo Diez de Medina refused to intimate to Stimson when further negotiation might be initiated.

[8] *Ibid.*, pp. 858–859.

report, the Paraguayans waited until the commission had legally expired and then requested the continuation of its work.

The final protocol approved by the commission on September 12 cannot be said to have been satisfactory to Asunción, since it named Paraguay responsible for the Vanguardia and Boquerón actions and stated that Paraguay must rebuild Fortín Vanguardia.[9] Paraguayan compliance with the protocol seemed doubtful. State Department planners had assumed that difficulties would arise and were more than prepared to meet the issue. Asunción was informed confidentially that unless it accepted the commission's recommendations for conciliation, a special announcement would be made to the effect that the Paraguayans had been the armed aggressors at Fortín Vanguardia. Stimson himself warned the Paraguayan government that "full and complete acceptance of the conciliation plan by Paraguay is necessary immediately."[10] Victim of calculated coercion, Paraguay moodily consented.

Stimson, actual mastermind behind most of the negotiations, realized that hostilities in the Chaco had only been halted temporarily and was determined to settle the conflict permanently. Seizing upon the Paraguayan efforts to extend the life of the commission, Stimson dispatched a memorandum to Asunción on September 13, 1929, which declared that the United States would be glad to continue its good offices in an effort to solve the Chaco problem.[11] By September 18 Stimson was able to persuade the other neutrals to continue their offer of good offices to Bolivia and Paraguay. On October 4 Paraguay formally accepted, and the Commission of Investigation and Conciliation was succeeded by the ill-fated Washington Committee of Neutrals.

Meanwhile, the secretary of state had been busy avoiding trouble with Argentina. Smarting from its earlier failure to prevent a meeting between Bolivia and Paraguay in Washington, Argentina had resumed its enticement. In early August 1929 President Hipólito Yrigoyen had branded Washington-based conciliation efforts as "outside interfer-

9 *Ibid.*, pp. 860–861.

10 U.S., Archives, RG 59, Decimal File 724.3415/69, Stimson to Kreeck (Asunción), Sept. 13, 1929, pp. 1–2.

11 U.S., Dept. of State, *Foreign Relations, 1929*, IV, 10, 859–896, 916.

ence."[12] When the old commission was dissolved in September and the Argentines reopened their diplomatic offensive, Stimson launched a counterattack. On the last day of the month he informed the Argentine government that the United States did not wish to see the Chaco affair become a question of prestige between Washington and Buenos Aires. Stimson added that it made no difference to the United States which city became the seat of negotiations. Buenos Aires now realized it had been outmaneuvered. On October 2 the Argentine foreign minister informed the United States ambassador to Argentina that President Yrigoyen did not feel disposed to make any proposals and had made no new overtures in the Chaco dispute since the autumn of 1928![13] These reassurances convinced no one in Washington.

Stimson's well-executed diplomatic machinations unfortunately were not enough to cope with Altiplano exigencies. It takes two parties to make peace, but neither Stimson's threats nor his cajoleries could lure the Bolivians back to Washington. Since Paraguay indirectly had been named the aggressor, there was little reason for La Paz to continue negotiations once the desired results had been achieved. The year ended with the Commission of Neutrals theoretically alive but neatly short-circuited.

Although hammering out the protocol of September 12, 1929, was difficult, executing its terms proved almost impossible. The task of supervising the repair and exchange of Boquerón and Vanguardia was given to the Uruguayan government, which presented a plan for the exchange to both parties on December 12, 1929. The Uruguayans offered a four-part formula: (1) the Paraguayans would repair Vanguardia; (2) after repairs, the Paraguayans would return Vanguardia to the Bolivians; (3) the Bolivians would return Boquerón to the Paraguayans; and (4) both nations would move to reestablish diplomatic relations by April 10, 1930. La Paz accepted, but Asunción demurred, complaining that the sequence of events proposed by the formula

[12] U.S., Archives, RG 59, Decimal File 724.3415/670, no. 91, Bliss (Buenos Aires) to Dept. State, Aug. 23, 1929, p. 1.
[13] *Ibid.*, Decimal File 724.3415/780, no. 53, Cotton to Kreeck (Asunción), Oct. 12, 1929, p. 1.

tended to brand them as the aggressors in the incident. Calling the
Uruguayan terms "a penal resolution,"[14] the Paraguayans demanded
the simultaneous exchange of Boquerón and Vanguardia.

Paraguayan determination to modify the terms of the September
protocol forced new negotiations. Eventually, on March 14, 1930, a
formula that guaranteed freedom of action for Uruguayan supervisory
personnel and balm for Paraguayan ego was sanctioned by Asunción.
The presentation of the new proposal in La Paz caused Bolivia to adopt
the delaying tactics formerly used by Paraguay. Replying on March 18,
1930, Bolivian diplomats changed the wording of the proposal to fit
their prejudices but unaccountably pushed the date for resumption of
diplomatic relations from April 10 to May 1. Paraguay now demanded
new modifications, and the exasperated Uruguayans played their last
card. They announced that unless the proposal were accepted without
further modification some other nation would have to execute the terms
of the September 12 protocol. For the second time in six months,
Paraguayan diplomats found themselves outdistanced by their peers in
La Paz. Formal agreement for the return of *fortines* occurred on April
4, 1930.

The impasse over Chaco territorial negotiations continued unbroken
throughout 1930 and half of 1931. The period was characterized by
several military skirmishes, ceaseless agitation, and provocative charges
by both litigants in the press of the Americas. Dramatic developments
in Chaco diplomatic affairs came suddenly in June 1931. Earlier in the
month Eduardo Diez de Medina, Bolivian minister to the United
States, called attention to the fact that Bolivia was reducing her arms
purchases at a time when Paraguay had contracted an Argentine military
mission and was preparing to take delivery on two gunboats. When
asked to comment, Pablo Max Ynsfran, Paraguayan chargé d'affaires
in Washington, replied that Bolivia was reducing her arms shipments
because the Altiplano government was unable to pay for previous purchases. Ynsfran defended Paraguayan acts, claiming that his nation was
only modernizing its arms and could fortunately do so without falling
victim to crushing debt.[15] On June 22 La Paz sent a telegram to Asun-

[14] U.S. Dept. of State, *Foreign Relations, 1930*, I, 312.
[15] See Vicente Rivarola, *Memorias diplomáticas*, II, 63–64; and Argentina, Minis-

ción demanding a disavowal of Ynsfran's statement. Gerónimo Zubizarreta, Paraguayan foreign minister, refused, and Bolivia severed diplomatic relations with Paraguay on July 5, 1931.

Sensing a new opportunity to lure the contestants away from Washington, Foreign Minister Ernesto Bosch of Argentina offered his good offices on July 10 to settle the dispute.[16] Asunción acquiesced, but La Paz refused to accept any kind of formal mediation by the Argentine government. Informal discussions among the three parties did persist. Under pressure to make some kind of gesture, Bolivia decided to try the Washington peace table rather than its Buenos Aires counterpart. On July 24, 1931, Sánchez Bustamante, Bolivian foreign minister, officially suggested a nonaggression pact between Paraguay and Bolivia.

Francis White, assistant secretary of state and chairman of the Washington Committee of Neutrals, was extremely skeptical of the value of such a proposal. Yet compared with the possibility of Chaco conflict or Argentine supervision of negotiations, the nonaggression pact seemed better than no agreement at all. Official invitations were forwarded to both parties on August 6, 1931, and on September 18 the Committee of Neutrals announced that discussion of a nonaggression pact would begin in Washington on October 1, 1931.

Events soon proved otherwise. On September 25 a new clash of arms at Fortín Masamaclay (Agua Rica to the Bolivians) heightened tension between Asunción and La Paz. October 1 arrived and the Washington Neutrals still did not know whether the Bolivians would send a negotiator. With the imminent collapse of the proposed negotiations, White unveiled a new weapon. On October 16, 1931, nineteen American states sent identical telegrams to La Paz calling on Bolivia to send a delegate to Washington for negotiation of the nonaggression pact.[17] Taken by surprise the Bolivian government concurred, and the

---

terio de Relaciones Exteriores y Culto, *La política argentina en la guerra del Chaco*, I, 211–212.

[16] Rivarola, *Memorias*, II, 69; U.S., Dept. of State, *Foreign Relations, 1931*, I, 744–748. Rivarola (*Memorias*, II, 70) confirms that such discussions, albeit informal, continued through the assistance and with the knowledge of the Argentine Foreign Office.

[17] U.S., Dept. of State, *Foreign Relations, 1931*, I, 767–768. Plans for the special dispatch were laid in a circular telegram sent to all Latin American diplomatic posts

opening of the negotiations was set for November 11, 1931. After a two-year boycott, Bolivia grudgingly returned to the peace table.

On December 9 Bolivian representatives formally presented their views on a nonaggression pact. On January 18, 1932, the Paraguayans offered counterproposals and the customary deadlock ensued. The Bolivian reply on February 25 demanded that the delegation of Paraguay reconsider its position or Bolivia would terminate the negotiations. Paraguayan sensitivities were offended by what they interpreted as Altiplano audacity, and an immediate disavowal was demanded. Surmising that both sides were more intent on impressing nationalistic sentiment in their homelands than on reaching an agreement, White suggested a quasi-suspension of formal talks and a continuation of "oral exchanges of view."[18]

The assistant secretary of state had made a similar suggestion on February 5 and had carried on such "exchanges," independent of other committee members, since that time. It had been necessary, however, for him to meet with representatives of the two litigants separately, because permission for the Bolivian diplomats to engage in oral negotiations with Paraguayans was not forthcoming until April 7.[19]

Francis White's final effort to save negotiations came none too soon. Rumors of large arms shipments to the prospective belligerents and of military clashes in the Chaco and the Committee of Neutrals' inability to induce a settlement had stirred several South American states to action.[20] On March 16, 1932, Carlos Saavedra Lamas, the new Argentine foreign minister, initiated independent negotiations between Bolivian and Paraguayan representatives, purportedly aimed at reestablishing diplomatic relations. In addition, representatives of Argentina, Brazil, Chile, and Peru (ABCP group) met in Santiago, Chile, and

---

on October 16, 1931. Bolivian informal acceptance was forwarded through the United States minister in La Paz on October 17–18 (*ibid.*, pp. 766–767).

[18] U.S., Archives, RG 59, Decimal File 724.3415/1663, 1/19 to 12/18, Memorandums 2/5/32 to 3/8/32.

[19] See *ibid.*, Decimal File 724.3415/1773, 4/14, White, Memorandum of conversation with Enrique Finot and Eduardo Diez de Medina, April 7, 1932, p. 1.

[20] *Ibid.*, Decimal File 724.3415/1663, no. 10, Feely (La Paz) to Dept. State, Mar. 3, 1932, p. 1; and Decimal File 724.3415/6653, 5/19, White, Memorandum of conversation with Cruchaga Tocornal, Feb. 18, 1932, pp. 1-2.

organized an informal mediatory body. The ABCP states were temporarily prepared to cooperate with the Washington Committee of Neutrals in solving the Chaco embroglio, but not all the parties interested in a Chaco settlement favored ABCP intervention. When on April 15, White suggested a joint meeting between the two disputants, the ABCP representatives in Washington, and the Committee of Neutrals, Bolivia promptly demanded ABCP exclusion.[21]

Fortunately, when oral negotiations were begun attention was no longer focused on the contending delegations, and progress became relatively rapid. A draft nonaggression pact was presented to the litigants on May 7, 1932. On June 2, 1932, Paraguay presented a series of objections to the draft and, without mentioning specifics, demanded international guarantees.[22] Bolivian representatives informed White on July 5 that, barring minor revisions, they fully expected to sign the pact. In forwarding his personal observations to White, Secretary of State Stimson concluded that perhaps Paraguay "does not desire a pact of nonaggression."[23]

Whatever the validity of the secretary of state's speculations, dictation of the course of events already had passed from the hands of the negotiators. On June 15 a Bolivian military detachment attacked and occupied Fortín Carlos Antonio López. On July 7 Paraguayan delegates, citing Bolivian aggression, announced that they were withdrawing from the negotiations. The search for Chaco peace would continue, but the odds against success, always incredible, suddenly had doubled.

[21] *Ibid.*, Decimal File 724.3415/1711, no. 14, Feely (La Paz) to Dept. State, Apr. 16, 1932, p. 2.

[22] *Ibid.*, Decimal File 724.3415/1789, no. 35, Wheeler (Asunción) to Dept. State, June 2, 1932, p. 1. The official text of Paraguay's objections to the proposed pact is given in U.S., Dept. of State, *Foreign Relations, 1932,* V, 15–18. Post Wheeler, United States minister to Paraguay, stated that Higinio Arbo, Paraguayan foreign minister, had avoided discussing "any suggestion as to the possible character of a direct guarantee which Paraguay would consider adequate or desirable" (*ibid.*, p. 14). Upon receipt of Wheeler's dispatch, White telephoned Juan José Soler, Paraguayan representative, and asked him what kind of guarantee Paraguay desired. Soler announced that his government had not specified (U.S., Archives, RG 59, Decimal File 724.3415/1803 2/9, White, Memorandum of telephone conversation with Soler, June 3, 1932, p. 1).

[23] U.S., Dept. of State, *Foreign Relations, 1932,* V, 24.

The protocol of September 12, 1929, had been a victory for Bolivian diplomacy. Not only was Asunción castigated, but the status quo obtaining in 1907 had been unquestionably altered.[24] By signing the September 12, 1929, protocol Paraguay agreed to return Fortín Vanguardia to Bolivia and thereby accepted the commission's recognition that Vanguardia was Bolivian property. This judgment automatically negated the 1907 boundaries, since Paraguay promised to return to Bolivia a *fortín* in territory it had always considered Paraguayan. Moreover, any attempt to change the situation physically by capturing *fortines* would become a violation of the signed protocol.

From January to March 1930 Paraguay was struggling to recover some of its international prestige by rejecting Uruguayan proposals for implementing the September protocol. Acting Secretary of State Joseph P. Cotton sent the following message to the Uruguayan Foreign Minister: "Department sincerely hopes that a settlement between Bolivia and Paraguay will not be jeopardized by a squabble over wording."[25] Cotton, Stimson, and their coterie had been logical and dispassionate. They believed themselves justifiably perturbed by Paraguayan and Bolivian intransigence. Unfortunately, their worries were not soon to be alleviated. Both Bolivia and Paraguay were convinced of the innate justice of their causes. Neither peace nor *détente* was sought by the Chaco antagonists; what each really wanted was vindication. Ultimately it was unimportant if Bolivia obtained Bahía Negra, for La Paz might never have the financial resources to develop a port there. No one could estimate when Asunción would be able to overcome the navigational hazards that plagued the Paraguay River. What did matter was that after fifty years of provocation, mutual suspicion, and chronic agitation, neither Bolivia nor Paraguay was prepared to suffer a serious loss of face in the Chaco.

As early as January 1930 President Augusto Bernardo Leguía y Salcedo of Peru had informed the United States that the only solution

---

[24] *Ibid., 1929*, 1, 860. The September 12, 1929, protocol unquestionably altered the status quo despite statements in the protocol to the contrary ("this does not signify in any way prejudgment of the pending territorial or boundary questions"). See Maps 2 and 3. Fortín Vanguardia is located near Coordinates 19° 30'S., 58°10'W.

[25] U.S., Dept. of State, *Foreign Relations, 1930*, I, 323.

for the Chaco dispute was the drafting of a treaty that would be as equitable as possible; Bolivia and Paraguay would then be forced to accept it.[26] Implementing Leguía's suggestion would undoubtedly have earned the United States the condemnation of both the litigants and much of Latin America. In another sense, however, the United States had relatively little to lose; if the negotiations dragged on only to end in failure, the United States' prestige would plummet and the North American reward would be Latin American contempt as well as reproach.

Leguía's suggestion was not practical in 1929–1932. Those were the years of economic depression, the J. Ruben Clark memorandum, and increasing United States regret for the presence of Marines in Nicaragua and Haiti. But what can be said of the policy the United States was pursuing? Its major weapons in mediating the Chaco dispute had been moral force and reason. By the summer of 1932 the effectiveness of both was open to serious question. Moral pressure and reason failing, Washington had no intention of using military force in the Chaco dispute.

The only real alternative, then, was discreet disengagement and transfer of negotiations to a mediatory group that would take the steps Washington felt incapable of executing. But Stimson, Cotton, and their associates were unprepared to take such action. Instead they persisted in employing their inadequate weapons in a sincere effort to bring peace to an obscure part of the Americas. It is no surprise that they failed. The question remains, how prudent were they to persist?

[26] *Ibid.*, p. 329.

3. THE AMERICAN STATES AND
THE CONDUCT OF THE WAR

The war of Bolivia against Paraguay is an event which is already inevitable, but I am not afraid in respect to the possible results, because we are going to win it.

Colonel José Félix Estigarribia, later commander of the Paraguayan army during the Chaco War, February 1931

The problem of the Chaco for me, has no solution other than war . . . the Paraguayan soldier of today . . . is not a soldier at all, so that with three thousand Bolivians, I promise to take Asunción.

General Hans Kundt, commander-in-chief of the Bolivian army from October 1932 to December 1933

ᘐᘐᘐ

D ESPITE RECIPROCAL ANTAGONISM, persistent prov-
ocation, and mutual resolve against making concessions, the Chaco War
appears to have begun by accident.[1] Following the June 15 Bolivian
capture of Fortín Carlos Antonio López and its recapture by Paraguay

[1] No narrative of the conflict is attempted in this chapter. Comprehensive studies
of the military operations on both sides have been written by Carlos José Fernández
(*La guerra del Chaco*), David H. Zook, Jr. (*The Conduct of the Chaco War*), and
Aquiles Vergara Vicuña (*La guerra del Chaco*). For notes concerning the Bolivian
role in the Chaco combat of June 1932, see Appendix I.

on July 15, 1929, Bolivian forces proceeded to escalate the conflict by seizing the Paraguayan *fortines* of Corrales, Toledo, and Boquerón between July 26 and 31. Both sides spent the month of August mobilizing and feigning consideration of peace proposals. Full-scale conflict began in September with the Paraguayan attack on Boquerón.

Possessed of greater wealth, more weapons, and a larger reserve of manpower, the Bolivians felt assured of eventual victory, and had the Paraguayans not been greatly helped by the Argentines, the Bolivians would probably have given a more creditable performance. Victims of disastrous encirclement battles and broken military codes,[2] Bolivian armies were, however, steadily pushed back, suffering heavy losses in men and equipment. Ballivián, a key Bolivian fortress, was captured on November 17, 1934. The Bolivian army was then thrown into retreat, and jubilant Paraguayans concluded that one more victory would eliminate their opponents as a cohesive fighting force.

While casual observers awarded the Bolivians many paper advantages, even Benito Mussolini concluded that Altiplano Indians never would adjust to the low altitude in the Chaco.[3] The Duce's observations do not seem to have impressed Bolivian leaders, but perhaps the Bolivians should not be criticized too harshly since after the first heavy losses only Altiplano Indians remained to fight. These ill-starred inductees were marched down to Villa Montes, the main Bolivian base, and given neither opportunity to acclimate themselves nor adequate orientation. Many of them had no idea why they were fighting, and most of them had no idea where they were.[4]

It must not be assumed that all Paraguayans had visited the Chaco prior to the conflict, but their infantrymen needed neither coca leaf nor

---

[2] Carlos Pastore, interview, Montevideo, Uruguay, August 20, 1965. Dr. Pastore was chief of the Paraguayan Cryptographic Intelligence Section (Jefe de Sección Correo y Claves en el Estado Mayor del Chaco) during the Chaco War. He affirmed that Argentine officers taught the Paraguayans the technique of breaking the Bolivian military code. The United States minister also reported that in 1930 the Paraguayan army was successfully translating Bolivian radio messages (United States, National Archives, Washington, D.C., Department of State, RG 59, Decimal File 724.3415/956, no. 3, Hibbard [Asunción] to Sec'y State, Jan. 24, 1930, p. 3).

[3] Julio Díaz Arguedas, *Como fué derrocado el hombre símbolo*, p. 131.

[4] Alfredo Campos, *Misión de paz en el Chaco Boreal*, II, 40.

a long period of adjustment to fight effectively. Climatic conditions in the Chaco were not the same as those in Pilar or Encarnación, but the Paraguayan was no stranger to the tropical heat of the scrub forest and savannah. Utilizing forced marches through the bush to bring them to the rear of the Bolivian positions, the Paraguayan command was able to exploit the weakness of the Bolivian soldier, who was unable to take advantage of the terrain because he feared the forest and regarded it as an enemy.[5] Not until January 1935, when the Bolivians had been pushed back into the foothills of the Andes, did the Indian demonstrate his abilities as a stubborn fighter.

Furthermore, despite paper advantages of wealth and manpower, transportation and logistics proved to be insurmountable barriers to Bolivian success. Altiplano forces controlled no navigable rivers in the Chaco, but Paraguayan troops and supplies were shipped by water from Asunción to Puerto Casado and then west by railway. Paraguay was also the fortunate beneficiary of some 420 kilometers of Chaco railway, all of which ran inland from ports or railroads to the north and west. There was no railway trackage available to Bolivia in the Chaco.[6]

In fact, consideration of the Bolivian transportation situation makes it difficult to understand how La Paz could have expected to fight the war effectively. The distance from La Paz to Villa Montes was 1,260 kilometers. Even when compared to other poor railway systems in that part of the world, the La Paz–Villazón route was considered hazardous. The 419 kilometers between Villazón and Villa Montes were covered by one road, which as late as 1953 was often impassable due to flooding and landslide.[7] The supply line from Villa Montes to Fortín Arce, the most advanced position, ran over 600 kilometers of unpaved and often flooded road.

[5] Zook (*The Chaco War*, p. 149) felt the Bolivian soldier was ineffective when required to employ fire and maneuver tactics. Campos (*Misión de paz*, II, 78) concludes that the Bolivians concentrated on frontal attacks. Major Víctor Mérida of the Bolivian army (interview, Buenos Aires, Argentina, September 21, 1965) noted that the individual Paraguayan soldier was a fierce fighter, much better than his Bolivian counterpart at hand-to-hand combat, especially in forests.

[6] Campos (*Misión de paz*, II, 23) is quite succinct about the importance of the railway from Puerto Casado inland: "From here entered and left everything."

[7] Harold Osborne, *Bolivia*, p. 37. As late as 1954, the rail line from La Paz to Viacha to Uyuni to Villazón still suffered from occasional landslides.

Supplying the Bolivian army in the Chaco created an unanswerable dilemma. Additional troops required additional supplies, but the more soldiers sent forward the less room for supplies in the limited number of operational trucks. Moreover, many troops had to be employed in security functions along the vulnerable supply line. Ultimately it became clear that opportunities for the Bolivian army to make effective use of its manpower advantage would be severely restricted.

Water was often the most pressing supply problem for both sides. In general, offensives were undertaken only during the dry season when swamps became mere savannah again. As might be expected, the best months for offensive action, April through October, were also the periods when wells and streams dried up. To keep the troops functioning, potable water was shipped forward in trucks. Considering the distances, the condition of the roads, and the limited number of trucks, it is understandable that the number of troops that died of dehydration easily ran into the thousands.

It might be argued that problems of supply and transport are decisive in every war and that the side best able to cope with these difficulties will emerge the victor. However, Chaco terrain and climate, the abominable roads, the distances, and the primitive transportation facilities meant that logistical considerations exercised an abnormal influence over the outcome of the conflict. After reviewing the many battles and the brilliant tactical moves, one military commentator concluded that the really unsung heroes of the war were the road builders and repairmen.[8]

Probably the most decisive advantage enjoyed by the Paraguayans during the war lay in the quality of their commanders. The two leaders, President Eusebio Ayala and Colonel (later General) José Félix Estigarribia, worked well together, each relying upon the other to accomplish specific tasks. On the Altiplano, President Daniel Salamanca and the Bolivian officer corps fought a war among themselves that increased in acrimony as the Chaco conflict raged on. The Bolivian constitution made the president captain-general of the army in wartime, and

---

[8] Campos, *Misión de paz*, II, 77. Traveling through the Chaco after the war, Campos was most impressed by the branch roads built to supply *fortines*. These roads had been hacked by hand out of the brush.

Salamanca took his position seriously. He replaced commanders, ordered operations, and adopted new methods without consulting his
high command. The officer corps retaliated by openly criticizing Salamanca and plotting rebellion.[9] Salamanca replaced two generalissimos
(commanders-in-chief) during the war, and his attempt to remove a
third following the fall of Ballivián on November 17, 1934, was prevented by a military coup on November 24, 1934. Vice-President
Tejada Sorzano became the new chief executive, and he felt the wisdom
of maintaining good relations with Salamanca's vanquishers.

The division and disunity of Bolivian leadership made effective
prosecution of the war a dubious business, for only a united command
could have coped with the massive problems of transport and supply.
A divided command in which personal antipathies and ambitions made
collaboration uncertain could do little more than observe the deteriorat-
ing military situation and blame other Bolivians, thereby generating
more hostility and mistrust, less cooperation, and further deterioration.

Camped in front of Villa Montes at the turn of the year, the Paraguayan army had every reason to be exultant; if it could capture the
town, it would enter the petroleum fields of Camiri while simultaneously destroying the last major Bolivian forces east of the Altiplano.
Paraguayan troops attacked confidently in January and February 1935,
but they discovered a rejuvenated enemy. The Bolivians now had the
advantage of shortened supply lines, and the climate of the Andes foothills worked a wondrous resuscitation on the Indian soldiers. Over
1,200 kilometers from Asunción, the Paraguayans became the victims
of shortages and overextended supply lines. They suffered painful reverses and managed only with difficulty to maintain their original attacking positions.[10]

---

[9] U.S., Archives, RG 59, Decimal File 724.3415/2614, no. 466, Feely (La Paz) to
Dept. State, Nov. 9, 1932, pp. 1–2. Minister Feely reported to Washington that the
personal intervention of former President Ismael Montes was all that saved the
government from military coup in September 1932. Salamanca was so afraid of a
coup in September 1932 that he made arrangements to seek asylum in the United
States embassy. Feely confidentially granted Salamanca's request (*ibid.*, Decimal File
724.3415/2449, no. 108, Feely [La Paz] to Dept. State).

[10] Pablo Max Ynsfran, *The Epic of the Chaco: Marshal Estigarribia's Memoirs of
the Chaco War 1932–1935*, pp. 195–202. The third dimension, elevation, and a new

March 1935 witnessed the end of the Paraguayan offensives; Asunción was forced to admit that it no longer possessed sufficient strength to crush its opponent or to reach the oil fields behind Villa Montes. The Bolivian army now took the offensive, but its timid attacks and cautious advances failed to demonstrate either the energy or the resolution needed if the Paraguay River were to be reached. Peace became practical because both sides were nearing the limit of their capacities and the possible gains were not deemed commensurate with the calculated cost of making the effort. Under these conditions the generals felt no qualms about letting the diplomats replace them as chief policy makers.

After any war that does not end in annihilation of the enemy's military capacities the question most often asked is, "Who won?" Bolivia lost the Chaco but retained its petroleum treasure. Paraguay won the Chaco but did not reach the oil fields. Although the winner of the war is open to question, it is clear that the losers were the more than 80,000 killed before the armistice was declared on June 14, 1935.[11]

In writing about the Chaco War, numerous Latin American scholars and publicists have accused the Standard Oil Company of starting the conflict. Proponents of this viewpoint tend to ignore the long-standing feud between Bolivia and Paraguay for Chaco control; instead, they insist that the petroleum princes of New Jersey, operating in conspiratorial fashion, became the primary causative agents of the struggle by demanding a pipeline exit from Bolivia for their products. Such interpretation has gained wide acceptance in Latin America despite the fact that proof of Standard Oil's involvement has never been demonstrated.

---

element, cold weather, disrupted the ingenious tactical maneuvers that the Paraguayans had perfected in the Chaco forests. General Estigarribia commented, "we paid for our inexperience in mountain warfare" (*ibid.*, p. 196).

[11] Vergara Vicuña, *Guerra del Chaco*, VII, 682. Vergara Vicuña gives the number of Paraguayan dead as 30,000; Bolivians, 20,728 dead (p. 683). Zook (*The Chaco War*, p. 240–241) gives the number of war dead as 80,000, 52,397 being Bolivians. Diaz Arguedas (*Cómo fué derrocado*, p. 2) gives the Bolivian dead as 50,000. Since the official figure as to the total number of soldiers dead through all causes is not available, the estimate of 80,000 is based on evaluation of the figures listed above.

Furthermore, available facts suggest that the story is much more complex than advocates of this thesis admit.

In 1921 Standard Oil of New Jersey acquired the Richmond Levering and Braden Associates concessions in the Bolivian departments of Tarija, Santa Cruz, and Chuquisaca.[12] On July 27, 1922, an oil development contract was signed between Bolivia and Standard Oil. By 1927 the company had acquired rights to some nineteen additional concessions, but it rapidly reduced its holdings and concentrated its operations in the four fields of Bermejo, Sanandita, Camiri, and Catamindi. By 1928 eight wells were in operation, and in 1931 two small refineries were completed at Camiri and Sanandita. Oil production reached six thousand tons annually in the period between 1930 and 1932.

Depression-initiated price decline and increasing belligerency between Standard Oil and Argentina brought a reappraisal of the company's position in Bolivia. The 1919–1928 legal battle between the oil company and the state of Salta over the extent of the company's concession there had become an explosive issue in Argentine nationalist circles.[13] The creation of the Argentine national oil company (Yacimientos Petrolíferos Fiscales—YPF) in 1922 was followed by the rapid transfer of many Standard Oil agents and engineers to Bolivia. Having rejected a trans-Chaco oleoduct, the company sought permission from the Argentine government in 1925 to construct a pipeline

---

[12] Standard Oil Company of Bolivia, *Confiscation: A History of the Oil Industry in Bolivia*, p. 1. Refer also to Herbert S. Klein, "American Oil Companies in Latin America: The Bolivian Experience," *Inter-American Economic Affairs*, 18, no. 2 (Autumn 1964), 51–52. Klein implies that both the Levering and Braden interests were either agents for Standard Oil or prospectors hoping to make a quick profit. Standard Oil officially bought the Levering concession in March 1921 and the Braden holdings the following October. The price ostensibly paid for both concessions was $5,000,000. For this price Standard Oil received roughly 3,144,850 hectares. The Standard Oil Company of Bolivia was founded in November 1921. Taxes had to be paid on all the acreage held so that the company gradually reduced its holdings to about 1,000,000 hectares (Klein, "American Oil Companies," pp. 54–55).

[13] Historians seem to have ignored the struggle that took place in the Argentine state of Salta over Standard Oil's efforts to obtain more concessions. The only comprehensive source is Augusto Bunge (*La guerra del petróleo en la Argentina*, pp. 72–93). Admittedly an Argentine nationalist, Bunge cannot be considered an unbiased reporter of the facts. What he does make clear is that there is a connection between the creation of YPF and the Standard Oil–Salta land-concession struggle.

from Bolivia to a deep-water port on the Paraná River. It was perhaps coincidence, but in 1927 not only was Standard Oil's construction petition refused but also Argentina raised the tax rates on Bolivian oil so high that export became prohibitive. Stymied in its efforts to market Bolivian petroleum, Standard Oil capped the Bermejo wells in 1931, adjusted production to meet local needs, and began to ship equipment out of the country.[14]

Almost simultaneously the good relations between Bolivian political leaders and Standard Oil ended. Learning that the petroleum company had surreptitiously shipped seven hundred tons of oil out of Bolivia in 1925 by means of a temporary pipeline, President Hernán Siles demanded back taxes in July 1928 and set January 1, 1930, as the deadline for payment.[15] The matter reached the Bolivian Supreme Court, but neither Siles nor his successor, Daniel Salamanca, was able to obtain monetary satisfaction. Company officials also had a few complaints. During the Boquerón-Vanguardia crisis of December 1928 Bolivian army officers had requisitioned Standard Oil trucks, but the company's demand for reimbursement had gone unanswered.

The essential conflicts between Standard Oil and the Bolivian government centered around neither taxes nor trucks but, rather, around the production of oil. Bolivian leaders believed that the beginning of commercial oil production in 1927 heralded an era of easy prosperity. Standard Oil was expected to inaugurate full production and La Paz would watch the royalties pour in. Even prior to the depression in 1929, Bolivia was faced with rising expenditures and saddled with

---

[14] Ronald S. Kain ("Behind the Chaco War," *Current History*, 42, no. 5 [August 1935], 473) gives the Standard Oil cutback date as 1931. He is supported by Klein ("American Oil Companies," p. 55). The League report noted that "by 1934" Standard Oil had stopped exploiting the deposits "above the Argentine frontier." These would be the Bermejo deposits. The cessation was only temporary (League of Nations, *Dispute between Bolivia and Paraguay: Report of the Chaco Commission, May 11, 1934*, Political, C.154M.64.VII[1934], pp. 16-17).

[15] Both Klein ("American Oil Companies," p. 56) and Standard Oil of Bolivia (*Confiscation*, pp. 4–5) give different accounts of what occurred. It is certain that between July 1925 and April 1926, 704 tons of oil were transported by two-inch pipeline from Standard Oil of Bolivia's Bermejo No. 2 well across the Bermejo River to Standard Oil of Argentina's property. The case went to the Supreme Court of Bolivia in October 1932. Final decision was not handed down for almost seven years.

heavy debts, and its leaders had envisioned petroleum reserves as a means of solving these economic difficulties. Given Argentine opposition, a trans-Chaco pipeline represented the only other exit for Bolivian oil products. President Daniel Salamanca succinctly summarized the situation for the Bolivian Congress in August 1932: "Bolivia possesses great oil resources with numerous wells already bored. . . . Bolivia badly needs this revenue, and her oil fields are unable to produce any wealth. She cannot take this oil to the Argentine, since that country, in its own interest, bars the way with high protective duties."[16]

The Bolivian President's assessment of the situation should not be construed to mean that the petroleum producers were in agreement, because the Standard Oil Company certainly did not equate Bolivia's interests with its own. To meet governmental demands, oil production was increased to 20,000 tons in 1933–1934, and to 20,600 tons in 1935. On the other hand, the company announced in 1933 that its southeastern wells were dry; when La Paz expressed incredulity and threatened nationalization, the wells became productive again. That same year the company refused to refine aviation gasoline in its Sanandita and Camiri refineries. Embroiled in a losing war, President Salamanca had no time for legalistic rhetoric; the refineries were nationalized and operated by the state until the cessation of hostilities. In 1935, shortly after the conflict ended, Standard Oil engineers were detected clandestinely moving parts of a dismantled refinery into Argentina. The company's uncooperative attitude and the memory of military disasters made Standard Oil a natural scapegoat for resentful Bolivian nationalists. Spruille Braden, United States representative to the Buenos Aires Peace Conference, observed that "even making allowance for Bolivian exaggeration and prejudice, the Standard Oil Company does not appear to have handled its relations with the Bolivians very intelligently."[17]

Thus mention of the Chaco War in Latin America elicits an almost

---

[16] League of Nations, *Dispute between Paraguay and Bolivia. Statement of the Paraguayan Case Submitted to the Assembly by the Paraguayan Government, September 6, 1934*, Political, A.19.VII(1934), p. 41.

[17] U.S., Archives, RG 59, Decimal File 724.34119/949, no. 464, Braden (Buenos Aires) to Dept. State, July 26, 1937, p. 7.

universal response: the Chaco War was the Standard Oil war. Adherents of this view may be divided into two categories: those who hold that the war was really not a conflict between Paraguay and Bolivia but one between Standard Oil and Royal Dutch Shell, the latter having Paraguayan support; or those who believe that Standard Oil, in order to obtain a trans-Chaco pipeline and a port for petroleum export, instigated and financed military adventures. Supporters for the former thesis generally have been Bolivian and Argentine publicists,[18] since Paraguayans never have admitted that Royal Dutch Shell wielded significant influence in Paraguayan affairs. Furthermore, the available evidence indicates that Shell favored Bolivia if it favored anyone.[19] The best argument against the first hypothesis is that since 1938 all the efforts of American companies to obtain oil from the Chaco have ended in expensive failure.[20] Bearing this fact in mind, Standard Oil's 1931 contention that commercially valuable petroleum would not be found in the Chaco takes on augmented significance.[21]

The second proposition has more adherents and appears more plausible, especially in light of Argentina's 1927 refusal to allow Standard Oil to build a pipeline to the Paraná River. The company officially denied having any intention of building a pipeline to the Paraguay River,[22] but such a denial does not in itself disprove Standard Oil duplicity. The chief difficulty with the theory that would blame Standard

---

[18] Among the publicists mentioned are Ricardo M. Setaro, *Secretos de Estado Mayor*, pp. 51–53; Tristan Marof, *La tragedia del Altiplano*, pp. 147ff. Argentine authors included are Elío M. A. Cole, *El drama del Paraguay*, p. 105; and Raúl González Tuñón, "Argentine Realities," *The Living Age*, 359 (November 1935), 240. It is interesting that the three books mentioned were all published by the "Claridad" publishers of Buenos Aires.

[19] U.S., Archives, RG 59, Decimal File 724.3415/392, Haughton (La Paz) to Dept. State, Sept. 20, 1928, p. 1; and 724.3415/4883, Memorandum, Thurston (Asunción) to Dept. State, April 16, 1935, pp. 2–3. Thurston refers to a dispatch of 1927, no. 1186, Cathrell (La Paz) to Dept. State, Feb. 3, 1927, p. 1.

[20] See Appendix VI for further information.

[21] U.S., Archives, RG 59, Decimal File 724.3415/1331, no. 247, note from H. Thaw (director of Latin American Affairs), Aug. 11, 1931, attached to report of Horn (Asunción) to Sec'y State. On August 11, 1931, Thaw saw Thomas Palmer, Standard Oil representative. He reported that "he [Palmer] said they [Standard Oil] had no interests in the Chaco and did not believe there was oil there."

[22] U.S., Archives, RG 59, Decimal File 724.3415/2831, McGurk (director of

Oil's acquisitive demands lies in its assumption that a pipeline to the Paraguay River would be beneficial to Standard Oil. Aside from the difficulties involved in merely crossing the Chaco, the moot question is where the hypothetical pipeline would terminate. No harbor above Asunción possessed basic navigational aids, let alone adequate facilities.[23] Obtaining an outlet from Fuerte Olimpo northward would be useless, for the littoral up to ten miles from the riverbank is inundated four to six months of the year.[24] While serious flooding does not occur from Fuerte Olimpo south, the thesis of the pipeline advocates still is not realistic. Assuming that Standard Oil constructed both a trans-Chaco pipeline and suitable harbor facilities at some point south of Fuerte Olimpo, what was the possibility of an oil tanker reaching a Chaco port and returning downstream? Theoretically, boats drawing twelve feet of water sometimes can reach Asunción or Concepción, the latter being almost two hundred miles further up river. Unfortunately, this depth is insufficient to allow accommodation for even the smallest ocean-going tanker.[25]

Latin American Affairs Division), Memorandum of conversation with Campbell of Standard Oil, Jan. 1, 1933, pp. 1–2. Campbell stated that Standard Oil engineers had discarded the idea of a pipeline across the Chaco in 1921 as "unfeasible" (*ibid.*, p. 1). In 1925 Standard Oil engineers had recommended the route through Argentina that has already been mentioned.

23 *Ibid.*, Decimal File 724.3415/692, no. 3218, Schoenfield (Rio) to Dept. State, Special Report of Lieutenant Colonel Lester Baker, Aug. 28, 1929, p. 3. In addition, Baker's report added that at Fuerte Olimpo and Bahía Negra "ships tie to the bank with tree stumps as mooring posts" (*ibid.*).

24 *Ibid.* "All terrain along the river is under water six months of the year and dry as a bone the other six months." Further evidence comes from the Bolivians themselves (U.S., Archives, RG 59, Decimal File 724.3415/669, Division of Latin American Affairs Memorandum, Aug. 21, 1929, p. 2). Bolivian representatives in Washington (delegates to the Commission of Investigation and Conciliation) informed the State Department (which was busy preparing the peace formula presented on August 31, 1929) that Bolivia needed a port south of Fuerte Olimpo, because of the flooding that occurred to the north.

25 Hugo Ferreira Gubetich, *Geografía del Paraguay*, p. 1306. Captain Bozzano, formerly of the Paraguayan navy (interview, Asunción, Paraguay October 14, 1965), took issue with Ferreira Gubetich's conclusion. A Marine engineer trained at the Massachusetts Institute of Technology, Bozzano stated that boats drawing twelve feet

Some pipeline thesis advocates have concluded that navigational problems on the Paraguay River made oil-tanker operation impractical. The only possibility of transporting petroleum from a Chaco port lay in the employment of shallow draft barges. At some ocean port downstream petroleum then could be transferred to shore or pumped into waiting tankers. Such a position ignores not only the expense of building and operating a fleet of barges, but also takes for granted the ability of Standard Oil to obtain the necessary storage space and harbor facilities at some ocean port on the Paraná River or the Río de la Plata. The nearest deep-water ports were Santa Fé and Rosario (near the mouth of the Paraná) or Buenos Aires (on the Río de la Plata). These are all Argentine ports, and if Argentina would not allow Standard Oil to build a pipeline to a Paraná River port, it is hardly possible that Argentina would have allowed Standard Oil to construct facilities in one of these same harbors for exporting Bolivian oil. Argentina's refusal of a pipeline plan in 1927 made a second refusal much more logical. The credibility of such a conclusion is doubled if Argentine designs on Bolivian petroleum are considered.

---

of water could reach Asunción only seven months of the year. He added that the possibility of such a ship reaching Concepción was "awkward" and later, "impossible." Bozzano also maintained that a boat of 1200 tons (loaded) could reach Asunción under normal conditions, but that vessels of more than 500 tons (loaded) rarely could travel as far as Concepción. S. H. Steinberg (ed., *The Stateman's Yearbook 1965–1966,* CII, 1312) finds boats drawing twelve feet of water are able to reach Asunción and Concepción only during the high-water period (about four months during the year). Paraguay today owns three tankers, all between 1,100 and 1,700 tons (*ibid.*), but it is doubtful that they could reach Asunción if loaded with petroleum. Lieutenant Commander E. C. Talbot-Booth's (ed.) *Merchant Ships,* pp. 1916–1918, lists all the classes of ocean tankers built to 1939. In 1929, for example, Standard Oil took delivery on the *Esso Campana,* the *Esso Salta,* and the *Esso Formosa.* Specifically designed for Latin American service, these vessels (the smallest employed by Standard Oil as ocean-going carriers), were 3,100 tons GRT (Gross Registered Tonnage) and drew 14.5 feet, making their operation on the Paraguay River exceedingly unlikely. In addition, the United States Department of Commerce, Maritime Division (*A Statistical Analysis of the World's Merchant Fleets—1958,* p. 108), lists all ocean-going tankers before 1941 still in service. However, figures show that the average draft for tankers between 1,000 and 6,000 tons was fourteen to seventeen feet. Vessels of larger displacement naturally had an even greater draft.

Evidence suggests that some Latin American authors, in blaming the foreign capitalists (Standard Oil and Shell) for the war, were seeking a means of uniting and absolving divided Latin Americans. It should not be concluded that Standard Oil was totally innocent or that common cause has here been made with those authors who dismiss the oil question as a significant cause of the war.[26] Standard Oil paid the taxes it could not avoid, and Altiplano rulers used some of this money to buy weapons. But such cooperation proves neither that Standard Oil instigated the war nor that it acted as La Paz's primary fund raiser.[27]

The basic problem involved would appear to be age-old and incapable of long-term solution. With the intensification of an already bitter war, a rational consideration of the petroleum question became increasingly difficult to maintain. For Paraguayans, Standard Oil's tax money was aid to the Bolivian enemy; for Bolivians, Standard Oil's sullen cooperation was treason. Under any circumstances, meaningful dialogue between petroleum giant and technologically underdeveloped state is a herculean task because both parties employ different standards. Conditions such as those generated by the Chaco conflict meant that the petroleum company's repeated denials of either complicity or sabotage were ignored. Under these conditions, Standard Oil should have seriously considered remaining silent.

[26] Zook (*The Chaco War*, p. 80) and Harris Gaylord Warren (*Paraguay*, p. 294) are examples of United States authors who dismiss petroleum as an insignificant factor in the war. They are correct in that there appears to be no oil of commercial value in the Chaco.

[27] U.S., Archives, RG 59, Decimal File 724.3415/3857, no. 100, Des Portes (La Paz) to Sec'y State, June 12, 1934, p. 3. This report notes that a loan of £500,000 ($2,000,000) had been obtained from Swiss banks and taken over by the Chase National Bank of London; the credit of Simón I. Patiño, Bolivian tin magnate, was used as collateral. Another loan of $570,000 from the Chase National Bank of London is also noted (*ibid.*, Decimal File 724.3415/3910, no. 713, Des Portes [La Paz] to Sec'y State, July 3, 1934, p. 2). The possible connection exists because Standard Oil and the Chase National Bank are both organizations with heavy Rockefeller investments. However, more evidence than this would be necessary to prove Standard Oil complicity. Much more than $3,000,000 would have been needed to finance Bolivian military operations. For example, the above sum would cover only about 30 per cent of the Bolivian military contract with Vickers, Limited, signed in November 1926 (see *ibid.*, Decimal File 724.3415/119, no. 1219, Cathrell [La Paz] to Sec'y State, July 24, 1927, p. 1).

The United States and Argentina. As early as 1927 Argentina had displayed extreme anxiety lest the contesting states respond favorably to United States State Department arbitration and conciliation efforts. In 1928 the United States Department of Agriculture caused consternation in Argentine government circles by prohibiting the importation of meat, grapes, and alfalfa from the latter state. At the Sixth Pan-American Conference in 1928 Argentine representatives sneered at the rationalizations of Washington's representatives and led the attack of Latin American delegates against United States military intervention in Nicaragua. The Argentine delegation, led by Honorio Pueyrredón, further insisted that the proposed Pan-American Union convention include a declaration condemning barriers in inter-American trade. When his plan for an inter-American *Zollverein* was rejected, Pueyrredón withdrew from the conference while it was still in session.[28]

The United States neglected to send a delegate to the 1928 Pan-American Penal Conference in Buenos Aires, and Argentina failed to attend the Washington Conference of Arbitration and Conciliation during 1928 and 1929. Argentina declined to participate in United States–directed efforts to settle the Chaco conflict; instead Buenos Aires "assisted" by blandly denying its efforts to seize control of peace proceedings from the Washington Committee of Neutrals. Indeed, additional steps were undertaken to make it clear that the United States would do well to leave South America to Argentine auspices. Disdainfully, the Kellogg-Briand Pact was rejected by Argentina;[29] four years later, in 1932, Foreign Minister Carlos Saavedra Lamas unveiled a new pact aimed at making war illegal. In October 1933 Brazil, Chile, Bolivia, Mexico, Paraguay, and Uruguay were invited to affix their signatures to this product of Argentine diplomacy; the United States

---

[28] *New York Times*, February 15, 1928, p. 3; and February 17, 1928, pp. 23–24; and United States, Department of State, *Report of the Delegates of the United States of America to the Sixth International Conference of American States at Habana, Cuba—1928*, pp. 1–8. Pueyrredón was replaced by Laurentino Olascoaga.

[29] U.S., Archives, RG 59, Decimal File 711.3517/17, no. 79, Bliss (Buenos Aires) to Dept. State, Nov. 9, 1928, pp. 1–2. Bliss was informed by an Argentine official that the Kellogg Pact "did not offer possibilities of realizing universal peace which had always been Argentina's policy and ideal."

was ignored.[30] With Saavedra Lamas directing strategy, a vigorous attempt to replace the United States as *de facto* leader of the Americas had been set in motion.

The Chaco War nearly brought on a direct confrontation between the United States and Argentina. In 1929 the United States had attempted to conciliate a dispute in the Argentine sphere of influence after the latter's efforts had been unsuccessful. This interference increased Buenos Aires' resentment of the United States. Eventually, State Department proponents of inter-American solidarity were forced to conclude that successful mediation of the Chaco dispute depended heavily on Argentine cooperation. It should be no surprise, therefore, that both the negotiations leading to the cease-fire and the peace conference settling the dispute took place in the capital of the Republic of Argentina.

Argentina's Relations with Bolivia. The development of the Bolivian Oriente and the export of its products via the Río de la Plata have long interested Argentine economic planners. In 1894 the Ichazo-Costa Convention, calling for a joint study to determine the feasibility of constructing a railroad from northern Argentina into the Oriente, was signed. In 1907 the Villazón-Zaballos agreement provided for further study concerning the extension of a railroad into the Oriente. Neither of these agreements, however, received the sanction of the Bolivian Congress.

The discovery of petroleum in southeastern Bolivia quickened Argentine interest in the railway project and placed Horacio Carrillo, Argentine minister to Bolivia for over a decade, in a critical position; his views were to affect Argentine policy toward Bolivia for almost twenty years. According to the Argentine diplomat Bolivia needed an eastern exit but not on the Paraguay River; the escape of the Oriente from isolation could be effected only by means of the railroad. In *El ferrocarril al oriente boliviano*, Carrillo enthusiastically described Oriente agricultural and mineral wealth, carefully enumerating "all the riches which on the other side of Yacuiba wait for the coming

[30] A copy of the Argentine Anti-War Treaty of Nonaggression and Conciliation can be found in United States, Department of State, *Papers Relating to the Foreign Relations of the United States, 1933,* IV, 234.

of the train."[31] He insisted that a railroad and supplementary canal system on the Bermejo River would be a means of mutual enrichment: "The Argentine economic action [construction of railroads and canals along the Bermejo River] . . . irradiates normally on the sister and bordering nation in a logical and faithful form to which it has just claim, as similarly it attracts toward Argentina's as yet underdeveloped industries, the basic raw materials which Bolivia offers in quantity and quality."[32] Carrillo's prognosis of Oriente development leaves little doubt about which nation would be the junior partner in the arrangement. Equally significant is Carrillo's view that Oriente development represented the proper means of rejuvenating northern Argentina, an area where industry had languished since the independence era.[33]

Concerning Bolivian petroleum Carrillo was ecstatic, though apprehensive about Standard Oil control of the fields. He confidently predicted, however, that Standard Oil petroleum would have to reach deep-water ports via Argentine-controlled railway lines. Chile, and not the United States, was seen as Argentina's major competitor in Bolivia. As conditions then stood, the developed mineral wealth of Bolivia (tin and copper) flowed out of the Chilean ports of Iquique and Antofagasta.[34] Carrillo felt that a Chilean railway into the Oriente proposed by the Bolivia Railway Company, an Anglo-Chilean concern, would be the supreme calamity; he urged rapid action to cause the collapse of this company, claiming that if such a road were ever completed, "the economic absorption of Bolivia by Chile . . . will be inevitable."[35]

In 1922 the Carrillo-Gutiérrez Railway Convention was signed, but

[31] Horacio Carrillo, *El ferrocarril al oriente boliviano,* p. 6.

[32] *Ibid.,* pp. 21–22.   [33] *Ibid.,* p. 9.

[34] Argentina, Ministerio de Relaciones Exteriores y Culto, Archivo, Buenos Aires, *La conferencia de la paz del Chaco,* Box 20, Folio 38, *Comisión para el estudio de las medidas consignadas en los incisos 5 y 6 del artículo #1 del protocolo de paz del 6/12/35,* pp. 54–55; and special memorandum, April 28, 1926, *Los ferrocarriles de la Compañía Ferrocaria Boliviana y el interés argentino en la república de Bolivia,* Reservado no. 3574.

[35] Argentina, Archivo, *La conferencia de la paz del Chaco,* Box 20, Folio 38, *Los ferrocarriles de la Compañía Ferrocaria Boliviana,* pp. 61–62.

the Altiplano congressmen displayed no interest in ratification. The agreement was renegotiated and re-signed on November 19, 1923, but politicians in La Paz still seemed unable to rid themselves of indolence.[36] Despite this temporary setback, negotiations for an Argentine pipeline from the Oriente to the Paraná River began in 1928 and continued intermittently until Carrillo left La Paz in February 1932. On June 15, 1932, Dr. Juan C. Valenzuela replaced Carrillo as ambassador; his first instructions called for "the settlement of the major questions pending between the two countries."[37] A team of Argentine negotiators also arrived, and on July 1, 1932, a tentative agreement on petroleum exports through Argentina was reached; unfortunately for Buenos Aires, Chaco hostilities soon brought further discussions to a halt.

Although the Argentine representatives returned to Buenos Aires empty-handed, they waxed enthusiastic about the potential of rail and pipeline construction in the Oriente and urged that Chilean, British, and United States interests be excluded.[38] The Argentine Foreign Office now formulated a series of proposals and presented them to La Paz in 1934. By the end of the Chaco War, La Paz had not yet replied.

[36] Carrillo, _El ferrocarril_, pp. 14–18. The proposed railroad would be financed and administered by Argentines (Articles 3–5), and the Argentine government would have the right to make railway rates free of Bolivian governmental interference (p. 14). Article 8 gave the Argentine-built railroad title to all public lands that it might cross (p. 17). Article 15 allowed Argentina the right to construct branches to Sucre, Puerto Suárez, Cochabamba, and into "the interior of the Bolivian Chaco" (p. 18). The latter article is evidence that to obtain the desired railway rights, Argentina was prepared to recognize at least part of the Chaco as being Bolivian.

[37] Argentina, Ministerio de Relaciones Exteriores y Culto, _La política argentina en la guerra del Chaco_, I, 354.

[38] _Ibid._, pp. 356–369, no. 253, _Informe sobre la situación económica y financiera de Bolivia_, June 7, 1933, Emillio Rebuelto, ed. This report draws a number of significant conclusions:

1. Establishment of communications on the Paraguay River for Bolivia is of little or no importance; the population, petroleum, livestock, and agricultural products can only move effectively by rail or boat through northeastern Argentina.

2. On the Chaco War, the report states that "the more the problem is examined, the less justified appears the statement that the struggle . . . may satisfy or resolve a desire of an economic nature" (p. 360).

3. Argentina would even be prepared to ship oil to the Altiplano but only if the Antofagasta and Bolivia Railway Company gave up the monopoly it had over traffic between La Paz and the Pacific.

Argentine policy makers were still undaunted. In an interview with the United States ambassador on June 18, 1935, Ibarra García, Argentine under-secretary of foreign affairs, outlined his nation's outlook on the future of the Oriente. The Argentine diplomat denied that a Paraguay River littoral would be useful to Bolivia. The Argentine government's official view was that "southeastern Bolivia's resources would only be developed through the Río de la Plata."[39]

Bolivia's Relations with Argentina. Poor relations between Argentina and Bolivia seem to have been the rule rather than the exception. The Argentine dictator Juan Manuel de Rosas supported Chile in its war against Andrés de Santa Cruz, the Bolivian caudillo. Difficulties between La Paz and Buenos Aires over the Department of Tarija lasted for more than sixty years. In 1909 an Argentine arbitral decision unfavorable to Bolivia caused the temporary rupture of diplomatic relations between the two countries. Comprehending the fear of Bolivian officials that Argentina intended to take over the Oriente, Carrillo often tried to assure La Paz that Argentina had no imperialistic intentions in southeastern Bolivia.[40]

Carrillo's protestations notwithstanding, Bolivian officials believed they had two excellent reasons for opposing increased Argentine economic activity in the Oriente: Bolivia had suffered grievous territorial losses since 1825, and separatist tendencies in Santa Cruz had long plagued La Paz governments.[41] No road or rail system connected Altiplano and Oriente, and Bolivian officials feared that the rail and economic links between the Oriente and Argentina might lead to new revolts in Santa Cruz. Furthermore, shipment of Oriente raw materials to Argentina did not benefit the people of the Altiplano. Until a transportation system between the Altiplano and the Oriente could be installed the Bolivian government would receive only a minor share of the potential wealth resulting from Oriente development. Even with

---

[39] U.S., Archives, RG 59, Decimal File 724.3415/5030, no. 737, Weddell (Buenos Aires) to Dept. State, June 18, 1935, pp. 1–2.

[40] Carrillo, *El ferrocarril*, p. 82. For example, in a 1922 speech made in La Paz, Carrillo exclaimed, "my country, as you know, gentlemen, does not have any imperialistic aspirations."

[41] Argentina, Min. de Rel. Ext. y Culto, *La política argentina*, I, 354. For the history of separatist and independence movements in Santa Cruz, consult Enrique de Gandía, *Historia de Santa Cruz de la Sierra*.

the completion of a transportation network, the nonindustrial Altiplano would be unable to match the cost and quality of items manufactured in Argentina. Furthermore, the Argentines were not above applying pressure in order to gain their ends. When they raised the taxes on oil exported from Bolivia in 1927, they thwarted Bolivian plans to pay the national debts with petroleum royalties. This move, plus Argentine refusal to grant pipeline-building privileges to Standard Oil, were stiff blows to the Bolivian economy and created much anti-Argentine sentiment in La Paz.[42] The Oriente exit via Argentina was obviously the most advantageous route; but the Argentines had decided that Bolivian petroleum was to be kept off the Argentine market until Buenos Aires gained the commanding voice over its marketing and/or transport.[43] Thus, in 1935 Argentina found itself seeking entrance to the Oriente from a nation that believed Argentina had made Paraguayan victory possible.[44] Obtaining any concessions from a beaten and embittered Bolivia would require both a great deal of luck and some judicious arm-twisting.

Argentina and Paraguay. Argentina was indeed a carelessly disguised belligerent during the Chaco war. For a good part of the conflict Buenos Aires supplied Paraguay with intelligence, information, medicine, and military and financial assistance.[45] By May 1935 Para-

[42] Argentina, Archivo, Box 20, Folio 38, *Memorándum sobre informaciones y consideraciones*, p. 2.

[43] *Ibid.*, Box 20, *Estado Mayor General de Marina—Consideraciones de orden legístico y estratégico que efectan la solución del conflicto boliviano-paraguayo*, pp. 19–20. The Argentine report readily admitted that Oriente petroleum was of a better quality than that found in Argentina. In August 1932 Juan María Zalles, Bolivian foreign minister, charged that Argentina's discriminatory oil practices were guided by the latter's desire "to avoid the competition of Bolivian petroleum" (U.S., Dept. of State, *Foreign Relations, 1932*, IV, 157).

[44] U.S., Archives, RG 59, Decimal File 724.3415/2844A, White to Wilson, Feb. 2, 1933, pp. 1–2; U.S., Dept. of State, *Foreign Relations, 1932*, IV, 102–103. Argentina, Archivo, Box 20, Folio 38, Coronel Don Ernesto Florit, ed., included memorandum *La posible colaboración de la Argentina, para contribuir a descongestionar el problema de la guerra boliviano-paraguaya: Informe del Ministro Doctor Horacio Carrillo, del 9 de enero 1934.* Carrillo notes that the war had greatly accentuated anti-Argentine sentiment in Bolivia, for Bolivians were convinced that Argentina was aiding Paraguay (p. 88).

[45] Evidence of Argentine financial and military assistance to Paraguay during the Chaco War is well documented in the works of Vicente Rivarola, *Memorias diplo-*

guay, its resources exhausted, was virtually dependent upon Argentina for such items as gasoline and artillery shells.[46] Argentina cannot be said to have given its support strictly on moral grounds, and Paraguayan statesmen had no illusions on this score. In a private memorandum to Vicente Rivarola, Paraguayan minister to Argentina, President Eusebio Ayala stated that he considered the prime reason for Argentine support to be the latter's refusal to allow a river port for Bolivia. In granting military assistance to Paraguay in July 1932 Captain Pablo Casal, Argentine minister of marine, made it quite clear that Chaco defeat for Paraguay was not in his nation's interests: "All my classes have been developed on the basis of the friendship and alliance of Paraguay for the Argentine in case of conflict for us. . . . It is Argentina's distinct advantage to have Paraguayan official and popular good will for, in the eventual case of war between Brazil and herself, she counts upon Paraguayan assistance either active or passive. Argentina

---

máticas, II, 230, 237–238, 254–255; III, 57–58, 83–87, 102–104, 166–170. Rivarola was the Paraguayan minister in Argentina during the Chaco War and personally claims to have arranged loans of over 8,000,000 pesos. Bolivian writers have been very vehement and explicit about Argentine assistance to Paraguay during the Chaco conflict. See also Bautista Saavedra, *El Chaco y la conferencia de paz de Buenos Aires*, pp. 24–25; Eduardo Diez de Medina, *Problemas internacionales*, pp. 125, 213; and Rogelio Ayala Moreira, *Por qué no ganamos la guerra del Chaco*, pp. 345–349, 356. Ayala Moreira places the sum of Argentine loans to Paraguay at 6,000,000 pesos. Both specific and general evidence of Argentine assistance to Paraguay can be found in the U.S., Archives, RG 59, Decimal File 724.3415/2187, no. 103, Wheeler (Asunción) to Dept. State, Aug. 30, 1932, p. 2; Decimal File 724.3415/2863, no. 1552, G-2 Report from Chile, Wooten (Santiago) to Dept. State, Jan. 4, 1933, p. 1; Decimal File 724.3415/7844A, White to Wilson (Geneva), Feb. 2, 1933, p. 1; Decimal File 724.3415/3490, no. 13, Weddell (Buenos Aires) to Dept. State, Jan. 4, 1934, p. 1; and Decimal File 724.3415/5076, no. 4566, G-2 Report from Paraguay, Jan. 15, 1935, p. 1. Zook (*The Chaco War*, p. 20) establishes the sum of Argentine loans to Paraguay at 16,626,072 Argentine pesos.

Understandably, Paraguayans have been reticent on this subject. In a letter dated November 25, 1965, to this writer, Juan Isidro Ramírez made no mention of Argentine loans and insisted that the only military aid sent by Argentina was "old machine guns which were all ruined." When asked about the same subject in January 1935, President Ayala Moreira of Paraguay categorically denied that Argentina had given Paraguay any assistance during the conflict (U.S., Archives, RG 59, Decimal File 724.3415/4526, no. 6, Nicholson [Asunción] to Dept. State, Feb. 2, 1935, p. 2).

[46] Zook, *The Chaco War*, p. 232.

feels that in case of a general South American conflagration, Bolivia would naturally side with Brazil."[47]

The economic predominance that Argentine interests exercised in Paraguay also looms as a major consideration.[48] Victory for Paraguay heralded expansion in the Chaco by Argentine interests. Paraguayan defeat would put Argentine concessionaires at the mercy of Bolivia, not a pleasant prospect since La Paz might easily assume that these companies had aided their opponent. Paraguayan defeat was seen to place Argentina at a strategic and economic disadvantage without guaranteeing her the opportunity to obtain a share of Oriente wealth. Bolivian defeat, not Paraguayan victory, became vital.

Uruguay. Even before the conflict actually began, Uruguay had established its policy of "absolute neutrality,"[49] first announced by Foreign Minister Juan Blanco. Following the Paraguayan declaration of war on Bolivia, Uruguay, on May 12, 1933, became the first Platine state to issue a proclamation of neutrality. Despite this official display of altruism Uruguay did not make an unconditional commitment to peace. When the League of Nations called for an embargo against arms sales and transit to the belligerents in June 1934, Montevideo stated only that it would associate itself with such measures as the League Council decided to take provided they were agreed to by neighboring countries.[50] The other "neighboring countries" indicated

[47] Rivarola, *Memorias*, II, 164.

[48] While all companies paid the increased wartime taxes, some Argentine companies did more. Compañía Nicolas Mihanovich, whose headquarters were in Buenos Aires, allowed the Paraguayan government 500,000 Argentine pesos of shipping credit but withdrew the offer when reports of it became known (Rivarola, *Memorias*, III, 83, 92). Nicholson reported that the Argentine firm of Mate Larangeira Cía. donated 250,000 Paraguayan pesos to the Paraguayan government for the purchase of aviation equipment (U.S., Archives, RG 59, Decimal File 724.3415/3265, no. 83, Nicholson [Asunción] to Sec'y State, July 28, 1933, p. 3). An enclosure of September 1934 makes no definite charges but points out that the largest investor in the Chaco, Carlos Casado, was brother-in-law to President Agustín Justo of Argentina, and that both the Sastre and Mihanovich families "had many relatives in the Argentine Government" (U.S., Archives, RG 59, Decimal File 724.3415/42222, no. 1997, G-2 in Paraguay, Sept. 12, 1934, enclosure 1, p. 1).

[49] Uruguay, Ministerio de Relaciones Exteriores y Culto, Archivo, 1980/29: *Paraguay-Bolivia: La cuestión de límites*, 606, M-358, July 21, 1932.

[50] United States, Congress, Senate, *Munitions Industry: Chaco Arms Embargo*, prepared by Manley O. Hudson, Senate Committee Print 9, 74th Cong., 2nd sess., p. 13.

a similar degree of concurrence, and shipment of arms to Bolivia and Paraguay was, therefore, restricted only by the necessity of minimal surface compliance.

Uruguay manufactured no arms, but maritime companies based in Montevideo carried on a thriving business transshipping arms to Asunción from steamers that carried them into Uruguayan territorial waters. The volume of this traffic severely strained relations between Uruguay and Bolivia, but Uruguayan diplomatic sources stoutly maintained that they were unable to control it.[51] After all, business was business, and Uruguay was the best interpreter of what it meant by its self-imposed "absolute neutrality."

Peru. Peru also agreed to take part in the League Embargo of June 1934, but in its declaration it cautioned that any steps taken would be "conditional upon the steps taken by the Chilean government in the matter."[52] Peru did not manufacture arms, but she also took no significant steps to halt the flow of military equipment through Mollendo, the free port for Bolivia in Peru. Much to Paraguayan displeasure, a small number of Peruvian officers also served with the Bolivian army in the Chaco.[53] In September 1934 Peru simultaneously fattened its purse and bartered away the remainder of its neutrality by selling to Bolivia arms it had acquired to prepare for possible hostilities with Chile and Colombia.[54] Essentially, Peruvian conduct typifies that of the

[51] Evidence concerning this topic is abundant. See Uruguay, Archivo, 1980/29: *La cuestión de límites*, S-797887, 276/934, Aug. 20, 1934; Tenente Coronel Zubia (firmador [sic]) 1980/29, T–160/37, 323/934–3415, Sept. 27, 1934; Zubia to Ministro de Relaciones Exteriores, 1980/29, T-160/35, 324/934–3452, Sept. 27, 1934; Zubia (firmador [sic]), 1980/29, T-282050, 532/9345–3831, Nov. 14, 1934; Zubia (firmador [sic]), 1980/29, 343/34, 3904, Nov. 23, 1934; Zubia (firmador [sic]) and 1980/29/417, 34/34, Feb. 13, 1935. Concerning Uruguayan practices and arms transit shipping to Paraguay, the United States minister commented, "this traffic [arms transit shipping] is carried on openly in Uruguay, as the country has made its adherence to the arms embargo conditional to similar action by the other neutral countries adjoining the territory of the belligerents" (U.S., Archives, RG 59, Decimal File 724.2415/4515, no. 932, Dominian [Montevideo] to Dept. State, Jan. 17, 1935, pp. 1–2).

[52] U.S., Congress, Senate, *Munitions Industry*, prepared by Hudson, p. 12.

[53] U.S., Archives, RG 59, Decimal File 724.3415/5026, nos. 5026 and 5163, G-2 Report of Paraguayan Military Attaché, May 31, 1935, p. 1. At least three Peruvian officers served with the Bolivian army.

[54] Uruguay, Archivo, 1980/29, 268/934, De Santiago (Asunción) to Arteaga,

limitrophe states during the Chaco war: lip-service to peace and active concern for the national interest.

Chile. Except during January and February 1933 when Foreign Minister Miguel Cruchaga Tocornal seemed determined to force La Paz to adopt a more tractable attitude toward new Chilean-Argentine peace proposals,[55] Chile raised few obstacles to the transit of arms for Bolivia through the ports of Arica and Antofagasta. While acknowledging the League of Nations' embargo requests, the Chilean government referred to its 1904 free port treaty and declared itself disposed to cooperate provided such powers as Germany, Italy, and Japan did likewise. As the League never received statements of unconditional compliance from Germany or Japan, Chile had no need to construct an elaborate legal defense for allowing weapon transit to continue. On July 6, 1935, three weeks after hostilities had come to an end, Santiago flippantly announced to the world that it had never participated in the embargo.[56]

After 1933, in order to aid the faltering Bolivian forces and simultaneously relieve internal economic pressures, Chile allowed Bolivia to recruit Chilean army officers and hire laborers to replace workers called to the front. The Chileans profoundly hoped that Bolivia would obtain a littoral on the Paraguay River, for such an advance might divert

---

Sept. 15, 1934, p. 2. The Uruguayan minister reported that the arms had been sold to Peru by Japan, for Peru was preparing for possible war with Chile over Tacna-Arica. According to Gibson the arms had been purchased as a result of the Leticia embroglio with Colombia (U.S., Archives, RG 59, Decimal File 724.3415/4117, no. 218, Gibson [Rio] to Dept. State, Sept. 13, 1934, p. 3).

55 Bolivia, preparing her first Chaco offensive (January–February 1933), displayed a marked reluctance to consider new Chilean-Argentine peace proposals. Probably to pressure La Paz into line, Cruchaga Tocornal informed the British ambassador that after January 20 no armaments for transit to Bolivia could be landed at Arica. On February 2 a shipment of arms from Vickers, Limited, was seized. Both the British government and Vickers, Limited, representatives brought pressure on Chile. Cruchaga Tocornal soon realized his indiscretion, and on February 18 the weapons in question were forwarded to Bolivia (see U.S., Archives, RG 59, Decimal File 724.3415/2847, no. 19, Wheeler [Asunción] to Dept. State, Feb. 2, 1933, p. 1; and Decimal File 724.3415/2917, no. 1387, Culbertson [Santiago] to Dept. State, Mar. 3, 1933, pp. 1–2).

56 U.S., Congress, Senate, *Munitions Industry*, prepared by Hudson, p. 8.

Bolivian attention from the Pacific littoral lost to Chile in 1879. Santiago was painfully aware that Bolivian defeat might cause a westward
orientation of Altiplano ambitions.

In general Chile was opposed to Argentine diplomatic ascendancy
in Latin America, and Argentine support for Paraguay deepened
Chilean suspicions: "Chileans do not like Argentina to be considered
the leading South American nation, and are jealous of any action she
may take to assume such a position before the rest of the world."[57]
Initially, Chile appeared eager to work with Argentina in effecting a
Chaco settlement in which Latin American governments, rather than
Washington, played the decisive role. Subsequently, competitive rivalry between Foreign Ministers Saavedra Lamas and Cruchaga Tocornal,
plus Argentine prestige in having aided the victorious belligerent,
necessitated revision in the orientation of Chile's foreign policy. By
the time the Chaco Peace Conference opened on July 1, 1935, Argentina had become Chile's most dangerous rival.

Brazil. The sprawling giant extended friendship to all, and thus
Brazil played a relatively insignificant role in the Chaco War. Having
withdrawn from the League, Brazil promulgated its own arms embargo
in 1934 and participated in all the efforts of the limitrophe states to
negotiate peace. Between July and August 1933 Foreign Minister
Afranio de Mello Franco instituted his own peace offensive, but when
he could not obtain Argentine and Chilean cooperation he terminated
his maneuverings.[58] Foreign Minister José Carlos de Macedo Soares,
who assumed office in July 1934, did, however, figure prominently in
the final negotiations of May and June 1935. Yet only in October 1933
did Rio de Janeiro serve even temporarily as a seat for Chaco negotiations.

Bolivians preferred to believe that once hostilities began strong support would be forthcoming from Brazilian sources; the expected as-

[57] U.S., Archives, RG 59, Decimal File 724.3415/1043, 3850a-G-2-380, War Department to Dept. State, Jan. 27, 1930, p. 1.
[58] *Ibid.*, Decimal File 724.3415/3274, no. 4182, Thurston (Rio) to Dept. State,
July 20, 1933, pp. 1–3; Decimal File 724.3415/3311, no. 1528, Norweb (Santiago)
to Dept. State, Aug. 31, 1933.

sistance appears to have been limited chiefly to vague sympathetic expressions that did nothing to aid La Paz in its desperate efforts to halt the advancing Paraguayans.[59]

United States. The Chaco conflict provided numerous opportunities for United States manufacturers to sell millions of dollars worth of trucks, airplanes, and munitions, especially to Bolivia. Paraguay resented these sales and charged a United States–Standard Oil conspiracy after Bolivian soldiers were captured wearing United States World War I military uniforms.[60]

On May 28, 1934, President Roosevelt declared an embargo of arms sales to the belligerents.[61] At that time over $2,000,000 in equipment for Bolivia was on order or being completed, and exemptions totaling $615,000 were allowed. However, La Paz needed the weapons, North Americans desired the gold, and, despite official policy, smuggling was a perfectly natural means of circumventing troublesome laws. Equipment manufactured in the United States continued to reach Bolivia, but only the Curtiss-Wright Export Company and the Burns Shipping Corporation were officially charged and tried;[62] so much for the effectiveness of United States embargo enforcement.

A vital factor vitiating Washington's sincere efforts to terminate the

[59] See Afranio de Mello Franco, *Estudios de historia internacional recente.* This short work was published to refute charges made by two Bolivian diplomats, Luis Abelli and Enrique Finot, both of whom claimed that Bolivia had been led to believe that Brazil would support their Chaco position in July and August 1932.

[60] U.S., Archives, RG 59, Decimal File 724.3415/2837, no. 3, Wheeler (Asunción) to Dept. State, Jan. 30, 1933, p. 1; and Decimal File 724.3415/3304, Memorandum of Wilson, head of Latin American Affairs Division, Aug. 25, 1933, p. 1. United States army uniforms had been sold to Bolivia as war surplus goods by a contractor who had never bothered to remove the insignia. Wilson's memorandum absolved the United States and Standard Oil of supplying uniforms to the Bolivian army but does not disclose the name of the contractor.

[61] United States Commercial treaties with Bolivia (1858) and Paraguay (1859) did not permit the United States to prohibit export of arms unilaterally. The legal loopholes that the United States employed to declare the embargo can best be demonstrated in U.S., Dept. of State, *Foreign Relations, 1934,* IV, 290–292.

[62] U.S. v. Curtiss-Wright Export Corporation, *et al.,* 299, U.S. 304(1936). The defendants were found guilty (U.S., Archives, RG 59, Decimal File 724.3415/4058, no. 385 Weddell [Buenos Aires] to Dept. State [Report of Capt. F. D. Sharp], Aug. 16, 1934, p. 1). This report notes that despite the arms embargo, United States armament sales continued.

Chaco conflict was Standard Oil's operation in Bolivia. As early as 1928, United States field representatives had requested clarification of Standard Oil activities: Washington instead chose to ignore the matter. In 1933 Paraguayan and Argentine denunciations sent company officials hurrying to Washington in hopes of obtaining a federally sanctioned letter of absolution. State Department handling of the problem pleased no one and failed to end the controversy.[63] On May 30, 1934, Senator Huey Long of Louisiana charged in Congress that the Standard Oil Company was financing the Bolivian war effort. This sudden attack from an unexpected source caused consternation in the Department of State, where officials had been quietly denying such allegations since August 1933.[64] The senator's blast was presumably intended for the home audience, but its most permanent effects were achieved elsewhere. In gratitude for having revealed the "truth," the Paraguayan government renamed Fortín Loma Vistosa, Fortín Senador Long.[65] For other Latin Americans, too, the fact that this charge had been made by an important government official was proof enough; Standard Oil was guilty, and, by implication, so was the United States of America.

"Kingfish Huey's" venture into foreign affairs also seems to have affected markedly the direction of State Department policy. When in

[63] U.S., Archives, RG 59, Decimal File 724.3415/2813, McGurk (Latin American division), Memorandum of conversation with Campbell of Standard Oil, Jan. 17, 1933, p. 1. In an interview, Campbell, who represented Standard Oil in Washington, presented to McGurk a written defense by Standard Oil against charges that the company was financing the Bolivian war effort. Francis White, assistant secretary of state, attached a note to McGurk's memorandum of the meeting in which he recommended that if Standard Oil wanted any kind of press statement, "they must do it themselves."

On January 20, 1933, Campbell visited White (*ibid.*, Decimal File 724.3415/2818, White, Memorandum of conversation with Campbell, pp. 1–3) and requested a Standard Oil–Department of State communiqué to the effect that Standard Oil was not financing the Bolivian war effort. White refused but agreed to communicate to several United States ambassadors the crux of any particular memorandum the company might desire to forward. Standard Oil was to understand that any proposed memorandum would be sent as their material, not as State Department material.

[64] *Ibid.*, Decimal File 724.3415/3304, Memorandum, Wilson (head of Latin American Affairs Division), Aug. 25, 1933, p. 1.

[65] *Ibid.*, Decimal File 724.3415/2983, no. 85, Nicholson (Asunción) to Dept. State, July 5, 1934; and Decimal File 721.3415/5198, Unsigned memorandum to Wilson, Oct. 18, 1934, p. 1.

April 1935, Joseph C. Thurston, United States minister who was then leaving Paraguay, notified Sumner Welles of the scurrilous propaganda attacks linking Washington and Standard Oil as partners-in-crime, the assistant secretary casually referred the matter to Edwin Wilson, chief of the Latin American Affairs Division. Thurston had sought to obtain some kind of guidance for American officials faced with the problems of replying to such charges, but he received no help. Writing under Welles's name, on May 11, 1935, Wilson informed Thurston that the assistant secretary could offer no positive defense either for Standard Oil or against insinuations of United States government–Standard Oil Company collaboration. Furthermore, important peace negotiations were about to begin in Buenos Aires, and the Department adjudged it "distinctly preferable not to arouse any issue . . . which might have an effect upon the negotiations."[66] In short, the harassed diplomats were on their own, and Latin Americans could believe what they liked. As of May 11, 1935, Washington was more interested in Chaco peace than in defending its good name. It might also be added that, by this time, efforts to explain the United States role were deemed hardly worth undertaking.

On June 9, 1933, United States Acting Secretary of State W. Phillips, and Assistant Secretary Francis White forwarded a joint memorandum to President Roosevelt advocating the disbanding of the Commission of Neutrals: "After four and one-half years of patient endeavors in this matter, the United States can in this way get out of the matter peacefully and leave it to the League and the South Americans. In our opinion, we should not be a member of the League Commission [the League was preparing a special Chaco Commission dealing with the Chaco matter] because, if we do so, we will surely run into conflict with Argentina, which is not a neutral and has openly supported Paraguay. We do not want to get into trouble with Argentina on account

---

[66] *Ibid.*, Decimal File 724.3415/4883, Memorandum, Thurston to Welles, April 16, 1935; Decimal File 724.3415/4883, Attached letter, Welles to Thurston, May 11, 1935.

of American interests in that country. We have no interests in the Chaco."[67]

⌈The United States and the states bordering Paraguay and Bolivia ⌉ proclaimed their neutrality in the Chaco conflict. All spoke of inter-American solidarity while nurturing what they considered to be their basic interests. The Phillips-White memorandum is a case in point: the United States wanted Chaco peace, but the United States did not want a confrontation with Argentina. The United States had "no interests in the Chaco," so finally the United States liquidated its commitment to mediation.

The memorandum in question provides a key to the inability of both the United States and some of the neighboring states to end the Chaco struggle. Argentina and Chile considered as critical the possible results of a war between Bolivia and Paraguay. No peace mediation had the slightest chance of success unless it provided the ends envisioned for Argentina and Chile, as well as for Paraguay and Bolivia. The only other possibility was that military stalemate and gradual exhaustion of effort would force both belligerents and their erstwhile supporters to adopt accommodating attitudes.

Phillips and White reasoned prudently that the United States would lose more by attempting to conciliate the conflict; better to let more interested parties halt the carnage. No limitrophe nations wanted trouble with Chile or Argentina, for they apparently made similar decisions. But are not inter-American peace and the best interests of all American states identical? If actions are considered to be more revealing than words, the true inter-American law, at least during the Chaco ⌋ conflict, was every nation for itself.

[67] *Ibid.*, Decimal File 724.3415/3251A, Phillips to President Roosevelt, June 9, 1933, p. 2.

4. THE SEARCH FOR PEACE

> *Respect for law is a tradition among the American nations
> who are opposed to force and renounce it both for the solution
> of their controversies and as an instrument of national policy in
> their reciprocal relations. . . . Therefore, the nations of America
> declare that the Chaco dispute is susceptible to a peaceful solu-
> tion and they earnestly request Bolivia and Paraguay to submit
> immediately the solution of this controversy to an arrangement
> by arbitration or by such other peaceful means as may be
> acceptable to both. . . . The American nations further declare
> that they will not recognize any territorial arrangement of this
> controversy which has not been obtained by peaceful means nor
> the validity of territorial acquisition which may be obtained
> through occupation or conquest by force of arms.*

> The representatives of nineteen American republics
> assembled in Washington to the ministers of foreign
> affairs of Bolivia and Paraguay, August 3, 1932

T HE PLANS OF THE Washington Committee of Neu-
trals for a nonaggression pact entered the realm of irrelevancy when
Paraguay withdrew from negotiations on July 7. Accusations and
countercharges regarding the Bolivian assault of June 15 clouded the
atmosphere, and United States State Department strategists were uncertain of their next move. Hearing of renewed Chaco gunfire, Assis-

tant Secretary of State Francis White dropped nonaggression pact negotiations on July 22 and proposed instead that the Washington Neutrals be allowed to investigate the present disturbances. After recapturing Fortín Carlos Antonio López on July 15, Paraguay expressed an interest in the new proposal. Any Bolivian reply was lost in the roar of cannon when Altiplano troops retaliated for July 15 by seizing Fortines Corrales, Boquerón, and Toledo between July 26 and 31. Asunción's attitude cooled perceptibly, and on July 31 La Paz expressed a disinterest in any Chaco investigation. The first phase of White's war-prevention plan ended with Bolivia's insisting on August 1 that it was "entitled to a bank on the Paraguay River."[1]

In addition to the possibilities of Chaco conflagration, White was conscious of rumblings in yet another quarter. On July 25 White was informed by Argentine Ambassador Felipe Espil that Brazil had proposed joint Brazilian-Argentine mediation to prevent conflict. A special meeting including the ambassadors from Argentina, Brazil, Peru, and Chile was called in Santiago.[2] On July 26 Chilean ambassador to the United States, Miguel Cruchaga Tocornal, approached White with a plan calling for partnership between the ABCP (Argentina, Brazil, Chile, and Peru) powers and the Committee of Neutrals in Chaco litigation. But the assistant secretary wanted to maintain control of his docile mediation committee. His chilly reply was that any scheme calling for the enlargement of the Committee of Neutrals "did not seem applicable at this time."[3]

[1] United States, Department of State, *Papers Relating to the Foreign Relations of the United States, 1932*, V, 159–160.

[2] *Ibid.*, p. 144. The Brazilian foreign minister, Afranio de Mello Franco (*Estudios de historia internacional recente*, p. 8), admits (without specifying the date) that he forwarded to Buenos Aires certain proposals that were rejected by Argentina on July 25. Buenos Aires claimed that the Washington Committee of Neutrals was handling the job effectively. Mello Franco then notes his surprise when he received mediation proposals (July 28) from Buenos Aires (*ibid.*, pp. 7, 13–14). Argentina, Ministerio de Relaciones Exteriores y Culto (*La política argentina en la guerra del Chaco*, I, 374–375), relates that Saavedra Lamas forwarded peace proposals to the Brazilians on July 25, and that these were accepted in principle but rejected on July 29. It appears that Washington never learned of the Argentine proposals of July 25.

[3] U.S., Dept. of State, *Foreign Relations, 1932*, V, 146. White had reacted unfavorably to a similar inquiry by Peru on July 22 (*ibid.*, p. 143).

On July 27 White called in Felipe Espil and suggested that Buenos Aires take the initiative in presenting proposals to bring moral pressure on Paraguay and Bolivia. White suggested that "it would be well for the nations of this hemisphere to make a statement to Bolivia and Paraguay to the effect that law and order is a tradition of this hemisphere . . . that the nations of this hemisphere further advise both Governments that they will recognize no territorial settlements made by other than peaceful means, and that they will not recognize for any future arbitration . . . any territory acquired at this time . . . by force of arms."[4]

The assistant secretary insisted that the United States was not looking for a prestige victory and assured Espil that the United States government believed a statement could have more impact if it were to originate from Argentina or some other limitrophe state; but Espil was far from enthusiastic. White telephoned Robert C. Bliss, United States ambassador to Buenos Aires, and told him to seek authorization for Espil "to make the suggestion to all the nations of the continent for a collective telegram to Bolivia and Paraguay to the effect that any conquest by them would not be recognized."[5] Carlos Saavedra Lamas, Argentine foreign minister, responded on July 29 with a vague treatise, simultaneously offering ABCP mediation of the Chaco dispute and ABCP "adherence [to] and cooperation [with] the Committee of Neutrals."[6] Saavedra Lamas' manifesto suggested the possibility of double jurisdiction, although the methods to be used were not made clear in the rest of the declaration. Brazil refused to accept this plan, claiming that the Argentine draft "would respectively debilitate the Neutral Commission and transfer its power to the group of neighboring republics."[7] White feared that Saavedra Lamas intended to establish independent mediation and was relieved the following day when, at a meeting of the Washington Neutrals and the ABCP ambassadors, Espil called for a joint telegraphic statement against hostilities. The

[4] *Ibid.*, p. 147.
[5] *Ibid.*, p. 150.
[6] *Ibid.*, pp. 151–152.
[7] See United States, National Archives, Washington, D.C., RG 59, Decimal File 724.3415/1984, no. 73, Thurston (Rio) to Stimson, July 30, 1932, p. 1.

nine representatives agreed to a collective telegram, and Assistant Secretary White was commissioned to make the draft. The finished product, signed by representatives of nineteen American republics, was made public on August 3, 1932.[8] A representative example of the pietistic declarations of the period, it bore an unmistakable resemblance to the ill-observed "Hoover Doctrine"[9] and eventually joined it in the library of discarded policy statements.

Reaction to the collective telegram was superficially favorable. Julio A. Gutiérrez, Bolivian foreign minister, cabled, "Welcome to the doctrine that force does not confer rights."[10] Paraguay's reply seemed even more enthusiastic: "They [principles of the declaration] constitute the invariable standard of its international policy. . . . Paraguay feels honored in expressing her absolute adherence to that declaration."[11] Noble rhetoric aside, the replies must be judged in the context of past and ensuing developments. Gutiérrez praised the August 3 declaration but insisted that it could not pertain to the Chaco because that territory was Bolivian; Bolivia was, therefore, defending what was rightfully hers. Furthermore, Paraguayan delegates had returned to negotiate only after their army had retaliated for the June 15 attack by recapturing Fortín Carlos Antonio López. Asunción had ordered general mobilization on August 1, but despite its reply to the August 3 telegram, no order to halt or slacken the massing of troops and equipment was executed. Both Bolivian and Paraguayan replies were strategems that suggested adherence to lofty principles, while in reality they promised nothing concrete. President Salamanca would soon make this clear by condemning the action of the Committee of Neutrals as illegal interference in his nation's internal affairs.[12]

---

[8] For a complete copy, see U.S., Dept. of State, *Foreign Relations, 1932*, V, p. 159.
[9] For a copy of the "Hoover" or "Stimson Doctrine" as it is sometimes referred to see *ibid., Japan, 1931–1941*, I, 83.
[10] Ibid., *1932*, V, 162.
[11] *Ibid.*, p. 163.
[12] Argentina, Min. de Rel. Ext. y Culto, *La política argentina*, I, 392. In a speech to the Bolivian Congress (August 6) Salamanca declared: "The Neutrals, with our consent, exercise nothing more than good offices, granted under international law. Now they come forward in the role of teachers and judges, pretending to know our rights, exercising jurisdiction which we have not conferred upon them."

Francis White's plan for inter-American cooperation appeared to be maturing well, but within a week storm clouds had gathered. The August 3 declaration had been hailed in Buenos Aires as a triumph of Argentine diplomacy. Acclaimed by the Argentine press as the formulator of the August 3 declaration,[13] Saavedra Lamas was quoted as saying, "the principle, which was the essential part, was maintained in all its force, as an initiative of our own; but we preferred to have its material consecration made jointly by all the countries of America grouped about the Neutral Commission."[14] Ambassador Bliss hurriedly advised Washington to be forbearing since an unfavorable reaction would cause difficulties. Assistant Secretary White, on the other hand, felt that the issue should be faced directly. In the margin of Bliss's report he wrote, "Argentina was offered the initiative, but refused it. . . . When we succeeded, she then jumped in to try to take the credit."[15] On August 12 White drafted a cable for direct delivery to President Augustín P. Justo of Argentina concerning the origins of the August 3 declaration. Fortunately it was never sent.[16] Five days later White charged Bliss to inform the Argentine foreign minister that "if he [Saavedra Lamas] will play the game there will be plenty

---

[13] U.S., Archives, RG 59, Decimal File 724.3415/2072, no. 1740, pp. 4–5, Bliss (Buenos Aires) to Dept. State, Aug. 5, 1932. Bliss enclosed copies of *La Nación* for August 5, 1932, and *La Prensa* for August 4, 1932. *La Nación* called the nonrecognition principle a noble Argentine tradition that had now received definitive formalization. *La Prensa* stated that the August 3, 1932, declaration "materializes and interprets the Argentine point of view, the essential formulation of which was requested by our Ministry of Foreign Affairs with the promise on the part of the United States and of other neutral states that they would adhere to it."

[14] *Ibid.*, p. 5. In the interview with *La Prensa*, Saavedra Lamas vaguely admitted that Espil and White had discussed the matter of an all-American declaration on July 27, but he made no reference to subsequent events. *La política argentina* (Argentina, Min. de Rel. Ext. y Culto, I, 381), edited during Saavedra Lamas' sojourn as foreign minister, takes a different position. It declares the August 3 declaration to be a "formula proposed by Argentina that together with the concepts of Mr. Stimson, came to be incorporated in a plan which Under-Secretary White edited."

[15] U.S., Archives, RG 59, Decimal File 724.3415/2072, no. 1740, Bliss (Buenos Aires) to Dept. State, Aug. 5, 1932, p. 3.

[16] *Ibid.*, Decimal File 724.3415/2090, 1/14, Memorandum of telephone conversation with Bliss, Aug. 17, 1932, p. 2. It is possible that Stimson intervened to prevent this cablegram, which bypassed the Argentine foreign minister, from being sent.

of credit to pass around to everybody, and we will see that he gets his full share."[17] Not until August 19 was the assistant secretary able to circulate a memorandum among South American diplomats, conclusively demonstrating that the August 3 declaration had not been proposed by Saavedra Lamas.[18] The memorandum may have comforted White, but the course of events would soon make any position based on the August 3 declaration untenable.

The Bolivian attacks of July 26 through 31 had immeasurably aggravated the Chaco crisis. On August 2, the Washington Committee of Neutrals formally demanded suspension of hostilities on the basis of positions maintained by Bolivia and Paraguay on June 1, 1932. Three days later Asunción unconditionally accepted the Neutrals' program, but Foreign Minister Gutiérrez confidentially had informed United States Minister Edward F. Feely that "serious internal disturbances"[19] would result if Bolivia accepted a status quo based on June 1 positions. When La Paz refused to modify its stand, Asunción temporarily became the aggrieved party.

Active as the Neutrals had become, Saavedra Lamas kept pace. On August 6 he called a meeting of representatives of the ABCP powers, who established a separate commission to mediate the Chaco conflict. The declaration, signed by the four limitrophe states in Buenos Aires, called for ABCP unity in attempting to prevent war between Bolivia and Paraguay. It pledged collaboration with the Washington Neutrals but indicated that the ABCP powers would operate independently when necessary.[20] A competitor had entered the field, but no coalition of any kind could prevent Saavedra Lamas from acting alone whenever he chose to do so. On August 8 he proposed to United States Ambassador Bliss a conciliation formula calling for status quo based on presently held positions, observance of the status quo to be guaran-

[17] *Ibid.*, p. 4.
[18] U.S., Dept. of State, *Foreign Relations, 1932*, V, 182–183. See also U.S., Archives, RG 59, Decimal File 724.3415/1920, 13/14, White, Memorandum of conversation with Luis O. Abelli (Bolivian minister), Aug. 16, 1932, p. 2.
[19] U.S., Dept. of State, *Foreign Relations, 1932*, V, 58.
[20] For the full text of the agreement, see *ibid.*, p. 168.

teed by a "civil commission," and "agreement to resolve the fundamental question."[21]

Saavedra Lamas' proposals pointedly discarded the "nonrecognition of conquests" provision in the August 3 declaration. This change alarmed both Stimson and White; when White received Bliss's report, he telephoned Buenos Aires and ordered Bliss to inform the Argentine diplomat that too many peacemakers "could only muddy the waters." Saavedra Lamas made no immediate reply, but White and Stimson must have felt acute exasperation when they discovered on August 10 that the Argentine foreign minister was confidentially circulating a second formula calling for a thirty-day truce based on presently held positions. On August 11 Secretary of State Stimson addressed a joint meeting of the Washington Neutrals and the ABCP ambassadors. He promised the ABCP representatives all the Chaco information they might request: ". . . but the Neutrals desire this cooperation to be mutual . . . in order that there may be no crossing of wires, it is very essential that all work together."[22]

In an effort to establish room for diplomatic maneuver, Stimson stipulated the conditions that would enable the Neutrals to reconsider their August 2 position but left no doubt of his opposition to the recent proposals of Saavedra Lamas.[23] Stimson's scarcely veiled censure was not lost on Buenos Aires. On the following day Argentina's foreign minister took pains to impress upon Ambassador Bliss his intention of cooperating with Washington. Possibly to show his good

---

[21] U.S., Archives, RG 59, Decimal File 724.3415/1997, 70, Bliss (Buenos Aires) to Dept. State, Aug. 8, 1932, p. 2.

[22] U.S., Dept. of State, *Foreign Relations, 1932*, V, 172–173.

[23] *Ibid.*, p. 173; U.S., Archives, RG 59, Decimal File 724.3415/2001, 25, Stimson to Feely (La Paz), Aug. 11, 1932, p. 3. The special conditions whereby the Committee of Neutrals would allow Bolivia to continue occupying the *fortines* captured between July 26 and 31 follow.

(1) "Temporary cessation of hostilities with the understanding that *de facto* occupation did not alter the *de jure* situation.

(2) "Agreement to begin arbitration not later than September 15th.

(3) "Unless Bolivia and Paraguay are able to reach another agreement, the Bolivians must withdraw from those *fortines* captured by June 15, 1933.

(4) "Bolivia must agree to provide facilities for Neutral Commission representatives who are sent to the Chaco for investigatory purposes."

intentions, he intimated that Chile was preparing to circulate an independent peace proposal.[24] The State Department officially ignored Saavedra Lamas' protestations of loyalty, but possible subterranean initiatives by Santiago soon caused Washington to send searching telegrams to both Santiago and Lima. Governments in both capitals denied carrying on independent negotiations.[25]

Adherence to moral idealism had achieved nothing, and both antagonists were mobilizing; the Neutrals, therefore, quietly abandoned the August 2 position. On August 20 White confidentially inquired if Asunción would agree not to occupy the *fortines* captured between July 26 and 31, providing Bolivia would evacuate them. The official rebuff came on August 24 when President Ayala delivered an ultimatum: Bolivia must return the captured positions or Paraguay would retaliate. At this point pretense of inter-American cooperation utterly vanished. Saavedra Lamas began to circulate a new conciliation formula, and Chile immediately informed Washington of Saavedra Lamas' latest maneuver.[26] Having evened scores a bit, on August 31 Chile confidentially requested Paraguayan abandonment of the Committee of Neutrals and proposed an ABCP conference to solve the Chaco

[24] U.S., Archives, RG 59, Decimal File 724.3415/2043, no. 71, Bliss (Buenos Aires) to Dept. State, Aug. 12, 1932, p. 1; Decimal File, 724.3415/2013/52, Stimson to Bliss, Aug. 13, 1932, pp. 1–2. Saavedra Lamas denied that he was presently carrying on any negotiations with Paraguay or Bolivia. Stimson immediately wired his disbelief: "Dept. now understands that Argentina is discussing a direct settlement or at least an agreement by [sic] with Paraguay." The secretary of state declared that this report on Argentine perfidy was based on "reliable Paraguayan authority" (see *ibid.*, Decimal File 74.3415/1920, White, Memorandum, Aug. 11, 1932, p. 1).

[25] U.S., Dept. of State, *Foreign Relations, 1932*, V, 179–180, 181, 184.

[26] U.S., Archives, RG 59, Decimal File 724.3415/2140, Circular telegram from Castle (acting secretary of state), Aug. 25, 1932; also Decimal File 724.3415/2150, no. 79, Bliss (Buenos Aires) to Dept. State, p. 1; and Decimal File 724.3415/2156 1/2, White, Memorandum of conversation with Espil, n.d. Saavedra Lamas had mentioned (August 25) a vague scheme "suggested by Bolivia" to Bliss, but he had given no details. Proof that a new Argentine diplomatic maneuver was in the making came from the United States ambassador in Chile, William B. Culbertson. Cruchaga Tocornal "leaked" the news to Culbertson with the Argentine ambassador to Chile in the next room, waiting to discuss Saavedra Lamas' new proposal (*ibid.*, Decimal File 724.3415/2184, no. 187 Culbertson [Santiago] to Dept. State, Aug. 25, 1932, p. 1).

dispute; the Washington committee was to send one delegate to the conference.[27] Unfortunately for the Chileans, Francis White learned of the details for the proposal within twenty-four hours and acted quickly to stop the plan. Thoroughly vexed, Acting Secretary of State William Castle, Jr., dispatched orders that the ABCP powers were to be watched.[28] The zealous guarding of United States mediation prerogatives proved unnecessary. On September 3, the Chilean foreign minister met in Santiago with the ambassadors from Peru, Brazil, and Argentina and proposed a joint peace conference composed of ABCP powers and members of the Committee of Neutrals. The representatives accepted the feasibility of such a conference, but they could not reach agreement on its location.[29] By September 9 internal disagreement and mutual distrust had temporarily immobilized ABCP as an effective competitor.

Balancing its success in scotching "peace-talk piracy," the Department of State was forced to admit the growing weakness of the Washington Neutrals. While simultaneously proclaiming no retreat from the principles of the August 3 resolution, the Committee of Neutrals on August 29 formally requested La Paz and Asunción to accept a sixty-day truce based on present positions. Realizing who controlled the situation, La Paz halved the truce period, and the Neutrals acquiesced. Asunción, readying its first offensive, indignantly spurned all

27 *Ibid.*, Decimal File 724.3415/2154, no. 71, Culbertson (Santiago) to Dept. State, Aug. 26, 1932; and Decimal File 724.3415/2184, no. 187, Culbertson (Santiago) to Dept. State, Aug. 25, 1932.

28 *Ibid.*, Decimal File 724.3415/2191 no. 78, Castle to Culbertson, Sept. 1, 1932, p. 1; and Decimal File 724.3415/2214, White, Memorandum of conversation with Emilio Edwards Bello, Sept. 1, 1932. White denounced the Chilean move as "destructive intrigue" (*ibid.*, Decimal File 724.3415/2160, no. 74, Culbertson [Santiago] to Dept. State, Aug. 27, 1932, p. 1). The Chileans were not very upset by Washington's discovery. On September 3, Santiago presented a new proposal calling for a conference of ABCP powers and the Washington Neutrals. This proposal was never forwarded to Washington either (*ibid.*, Decimal File 724.3415/226, 146, Culbertson [Santiago] to Dept. State, Sept. 3, 1932, p. 1).

29 U.S., Dept. of State, *Foreign Relations, 1932*, V, 196–197; U.S., Archives, RG 59, Decimal File 724.3415/2223, no. 105, Wheeler (Asunción) to Dept. State, Sept. 2, 1932, p. 1; and Decimal File 724.3415/227, no. 197, Culbertson (Santiago) to Dept. State, Sept. 5, 1932, p. 2.

truce talks. The Neutrals were now back where they started but without their prestige.

Paraguayan forces began to attack Fortín Boquerón on September 9. The following day the Washington Neutrals forwarded a new peace formula to both sides. Talks dragged on, but by September 19 the situation at Boquerón had deteriorated, and Bolivia had agreed to a cease-fire. With victory so close, Asunción became intransigent. Reluctantly admitting that neither side would agree to a proposal believed acceptable to the other, on September 22 the Neutrals called for both a cease-fire and unconditional arbitration. The terms of the message indicated that the committee's patience was wearing thin: "The Commission of Neutrals will immediately send a delegation to the Chaco to verify the effective termination of hostilities, and inform the parties that if its delegation advises it that one of them has violated the engagement to terminate the struggle, the Commission of Neutrals will declare that such country is the aggressor, and will suggest that all the Governments of America withdraw their diplomatic and consular representatives from that country."[30]

The belligerents were unimpressed by this change in the mediators' attitude, but Saavedra Lamas now had an excuse to begin his assault. Having guided Argentina back into the League of Nations on September 30, the Argentine foreign minister believed he possessed the leverage needed to force the committee out of the Chaco litigation. The dispatch he forwarded to the Washington Neutrals on October 18, 1932, should have removed all doubts concerning the implacability of Argentine intentions. Charging the Neutrals with adopting a minatory attitude toward the belligerents, Saavedra Lamas lectured the committee on the fine points of international law: ". . . the Argentine Chancellery will not go along with the Commission of Neutrals in any act which extending beyond the limits of good offices and the moral influence and opinion of all the Continent, might approximate an intervention, even though it should be only a diplomatic one. . . . The Argentine Chancellery understands that the adoption of coercive measures can be based only on a Treaty accepted beforehand by the

[30] U.S., Dept. of State, *Foreign Relations, 1932*, V, 86–87.

countries to which it is to apply . . . a mere Declaration like that of August third is not sufficient to produce comminatory effects against third powers."[31] Saavedra Lamas had no doubt foreseen the reaction to his bombshell, but its effects were somewhat alleviated by Felipe Espil, Argentine ambassador. On October 22, Espil called on Assistant Secretary White to inform White that he "had changed the note considerably . . . for not to do so would have caused greater resentment."[32]

White tried to ignore the hostile tone of the document. Choosing to believe that the Argentine's attack was based on a misconception, White replied on November 4, "the proposal of the Commission of Neutrals to Bolivia and Paraguay on September 22 . . . was made in the interests of lasting peace. . . . The proposal was not a threat expressed or implied because . . . the proposal would first have to be accepted by the two countries in dispute, and they would accept it knowing in advance what action the Neutral Commission would take."[33] The assistant secretary then artfully defended the August 3 proclamation on the basis that it notified Bolivia and Paraguay that the American states would accept only a peaceful solution to the Chaco conflict.[34]

White's defense failed to elicit the desired cooperation. Indeed, the malicious nature of the Argentine reply indicated that Saavedra Lamas wanted the committee to terminate its Chaco mediation as soon as possible. Dated November 19, 1932, the lengthy document read in part:

My Government regrets that it does not similarly concur in the opinion expressed by the Commission of Neutrals when it attributes to its laudable work for peace . . . the same force and efficacy which an instrument might

31 *Ibid.*, pp. 204–206.
32 *Ibid.*, p. 208.
33 *Ibid.*, pp. 207–210.
34 The October 18 message was also read by other members of the Committee of Neutrals. Varela Acevedo, Uruguayan ambassador, reported that the note made clear that Argentina would not cooperate in the future with the Committee of Neutrals (Uruguay, Ministerio de las Relaciones Exteriores y Culto, Archivo, Montevideo, File 1980/29: *Paraguay y Bolivia: La cuestión de límites*, 510, Varelo Acevedo to Juan Carlos Blanco [Montevideo], Jan. 10, 1933, p. 1).

have which would lend effective operation to so noble a purpose . . . it is well known that the Commission of Neutrals lacks political power, not being an international person qualified to deliver itself authoritatively, but merely an assemblage of friendly countries . . . an assemblage however, the extent of whose action is rigorously limited to good offices. . . . My Government believes that the League of Nations has in this emergency a field of action indicated by the will of the parties themselves, who are signatories of the constituent covenant of the League, and . . . we are also in agreement that it [the League] can and ought to develop its action without finding an obstacle in regional or continental doctrines . . . which . . . have not had Argentine adhesion.[35]

Realizing that any rebuttal might bring on the very confrontation they were straining to avoid, neither White, Stimson, nor the commission ever replied.

By August the Chaco controversy had been brought before the League of Nations. Bolivia and Paraguay were nominally members of the League, and on August 1, 1932, both belligerents presented charges to the League Secretariat. Since past relations between the United States and Geneva had not been satisfactory, the League of Nations was in no mood to preempt negotiations. Prentice Gilbert, United States consul in Geneva, reported after a conference with Acting League Secretary Albert Dufour-Feronce on August 3, 1932, that "the League policy in this [Chaco dispute] is not to intervene or to take steps which might interfere with measures already taken by American states."[36] A confidential agreement was reached whereby the United States consul in Geneva would supply progress reports to the League secretary and the League would remain discreetly removed from the Chaco affair. The utility of this arrangement persisted until September 26, when a demand for action by League members led to

---

[35] U.S., Dept. of State, *Foreign Relations, 1932*, V, 218–219. This communication from the Argentine Foreign Office was not made public by the Department of State until the publication of this series in 1948. No formal response to this document was found in the United States Archives. The assistant secretary reported: "I will discuss with the Commission the answer to this note." There is no record of whether he did so or not (U.S., Archives, RG 59, Decimal File 724.3415/2558, White, Memorandum, Nov. 23, 1932, p. 1).

[36] U.S., Dept. of State, *Foreign Relations, 1932*, V, 222.

the creation of a "Committee of Three" to examine Chaco developments. This committee was chaired by Eamon de Valera of the Irish Free State and comprised de Valera, Salvador de Madariaga y Rojo of Spain, and José Matos of Guatemala. Two days later League Secretary Eric Drummond anxiously requested additional information on the progress of the Neutrals' efforts. Replying on September 30, Stimson unsubtly suggested that the "Gentlemen of Geneva" continue to view the Chaco conflict as a strictly western hemispheric quarrel. Stimson warned that if the League became "impatient and jumps into it [Chaco negotiations]," the League would receive "a severe rebuff."[37] As a sop to Drummond, he claimed, "it [the course of negotiations] seems to be entering a more satisfactory state."[38]

Eamon de Valera was not satisfied with Stimson's reply. He believed that the League should dispatch a military commission to the Chaco to bring about the belligerents' disengagement. De Valera pressured Drummond, and on November 3, the much-harassed League secretary informed the United States Consulate in Geneva that unless the Neutrals could show progress and exchange views with the Committee of Three, independent action must follow. Stimson still was in no mood to brook interference. On November 15 he cabled: "Patience is essential . . . the League has not been dealing with the matter, and apparently does not appreciate the difficulties."[39]

Geneva wanted a confrontation with Washington no more than Washington desired one with Buenos Aires. De Valera's committee halted their efforts so that the Committee of Neutrals would have yet another chance to establish an agreement. Presenting their final proposals on December 15, 1932, the Neutrals again summoned the telegraphic support of nineteen American states.[40] Within forty-eight hours, Paraguay had rejected the terms, and on December 20, 1932, Juan José Soler, Paraguayan representative to the Washington Neutrals, departed for Asunción.[41] He informed Francis White that his

37 *Ibid.*, p. 247.
38 *Ibid.*, p. 248.
39 *Ibid.*, p. 248.
40 *Ibid.*, p. 248. See pp. 127–129 for copies of the terms.
41 *Ibid.*, p. 130.

withdrawal was "no more than temporary," but White had reason to believe otherwise.[42] The Bolivian reply was at best ambiguous, because Bolivian plans for a Chaco counteroffensive were already taking shape. The coming of the New Year found the committee ignored by the ABCP powers but still unfavorably disposed toward League intervention in Chaco affairs. In a rather ungracious telegram on December 30, 1932, Francis White informed Geneva that the Committee of Neutrals' latest efforts to terminate hostilities had failed, but in the view of the State Department, "the nations of America working in common" were best suited to solve Chaco problems.[43] The assistant secretary's message suggested that the ABCP powers should now inherit the mantle of Chaco peacemaker, but he did not specifically mention them. In any event, the failure of the antagonists to accept the committee's final proposals and the Paraguayan representative's withdrawal meant that the committee had outlived its usefulness.

The Committee of Neutrals held no formal meetings between December 31, 1932, and May 12, 1933. On June 18 White called upon the body to liquidate itself. Mexico was already preparing to abandon the organization,[44] but Uruguay opposed dissolution. The United States had spoken, however, and the membership dutifully fell in line. The committee's final communiqué on June 27, 1933, made no attempt to conceal the bitter pique felt for Saavedra Lamas and the ABCP powers: "Experience has shown that if there is more than one center of negotiations, confusion and lack of agreement are the inevitable results. The Commission therefore feels that it can best con-

---

[42] U.S., Archives, RG 59, Decimal File 724.3415/2683, 7/11, Memorandum, Soler's letter to White, Dec. 20, 1932, p. 12. Wheeler, United States minister in Asunción, informed Washington that Soler's withdrawal was permanent (*ibid.*, Decimal File 724.3415/2716, Wheeler [Asunción] to Dept. State, Jan. 2, 1933, p. 1).

[43] U.S., Dept. of State, *Foreign Relations, 1932*, V, 258–259.

[44] Uruguay, Archivo, 1980/29: *La cuestión de límites* (1932–1945), 736–276, Varela Acevedo (Washington) to Juan Carlos Blanco, Jan. 31, 1933. The Uruguayan delegate reported that the Mexican ambassador to the United States had proposed the disbandment of the Washington Committee of Neutrals. In May 1933 the Mexican government also put out diplomatic "feelers" regarding the possible participation of Mexico in ABCP mediation activities (U.S., Archives, RG 59, Decimal File 724. 3415/3090, no. 93, Daniels [Mexico City] to Dept. State, May 11, 1933, p. 1).

tribute to peace on this continent by withdrawing from negotiations."
Reversing its previous statements, the committee concluded, "thus
negotiations can be centered in Geneva, if other peace agencies take a
similar attitude, allowing the League Committee to work with universal support for peace."[45]

This message suggests an historical precedent: the State Department previously had opposed League interference in the Chaco dispute.
Was the United States now advocating the settlement of an American
dispute by a non-American entity? Such a shift in policy was only
illusory. Francis White, for example, freely predicted that League
endeavors in the Chaco would fail. More significantly, the same day
the Committee of Neutrals ceased to exist, Acting Secretary of State
William Phillips telegraphed League Secretary Drummond through
the United States' consul in Geneva that under no circumstances would
the United States cooperate in any League-sponsored Chaco negotiations. Washington simply was making as gracious an exit as possible,
while intimating that Argentine diplomatic maneuvers had sabotaged
its efforts.

The Committee of Neutrals' attempt to prevent a holocaust in the
Chaco had always been a battle against heavy odds. For this reason
failure and final disbandment were not disgraceful. But after four
years of negotiations the prestige of both the committee and its sponsor
was at stake. As late as September 1, 1932, a modicum of dignity
could have been preserved, for general hostilities did not begin until
the middle of the month. Furthermore, a prestigious United States
could have resurrected the mediatory group at some later date. Instead
the Washington committee was allowed to continue long after good
will had become manifestly nonexistent, after Argentine hostility had
become blatant, and for ten months after the high principles proclaimed on August 3, 1932, had been abandoned. Thus the committee
was liquidated, but not before the belligerents presented their griev-
ances at other peace tables.

Paraguayan rejection of the December 15 terms and Juan José Soler's
departure unofficially signaled the Washington Neutrals' final failure.

[45] U.S., Archives, RG 59, Decimal File 724.3415/3290C, no. 118, Phillips to
Wilson (Geneva), June 27, 1933, pp. 1–2.

With the turn of the New Year, Saavedra Lamas officially took command of the negotiations.[46] Already he had made some progress in Asunción, but the enthusiasm for his proposals felt in that capital was not shared by the government in La Paz. If the Argentine diplomat were going to maneuver Bolivia to a peace table, he would need an ally; the role of Chile in the negotiations thus took on added importance.

The new Chilean foreign minister, Miguel Cruchaga Tocornal, also aspired to become chief Chaco peace broker. Cruchaga Tocornal was prepared to dicker with Saavedra Lamas about a joint proposal, but independently he set his own peace formula in motion in ABCP capitals. On January 17 Argentina unconditionally rejected Cruchaga Tocornal's independent initiative.[47] Since the Argentine and Chilean foreign ministers were now aware that neither could gain his ends without the other, joint negotiations proceeded on a more amicable basis, but ABCP agreement on terms came only after verbal modifications insisted on by Afranio de Mello Franco, Brazil's foreign minister, had been accepted.

On January 25, the new proposals were handed confidentially to the Paraguayan and Bolivian ministers in Buenos Aires. They would not be publicly proclaimed, however, until Saavedra Lamas and Cruchaga Tocornal had met in Mendoza, Argentina, on February 1 and 2, 1933. The terms of the so-called Mendoza proposals, agreed to on January 25, called for (1) a juridical arbitration of all outstanding Chaco claims; (2) the termination of hostilities; (3) the disengagement and withdrawal of military forces; and (4) the demobilization of forces and the return to peacetime troop strength.[48] On February 27 the belligerents finally replied; both agreed in principle, but both attached many reservations. When further negotiations were unproductive, the ABCP foreign ministers requested an unconditional sixty-

---

[46] U.S., Dept. of State, *Foreign Relations, 1933,* V, 215. On January 2, 1933, Saavedra Lamas read a memorandum to Bliss, United States ambassador, and stated that Paraguay's withdrawal meant that the good offices of the Washington Committee of Neutrals "were at an end."

[47] U.S., Archives, RG 59, Decimal File 724.3415/2780, no. 7, Bliss (Buenos Aires) to Dept. State, Jan. 12, 1933, pp. 1–2.

[48] See Argentina, Min. de Rel. Ext. y Culto, *La política argentina,* II, 27–29.

day cease-fire. The belligerents rejected this appeal, claiming ABCP had made no attempt to reconcile the Mendoza plan with their objections.

On April 21 and 22 the ABCP powers again submitted the Mendoza proposals and requested immediate reconsideration and cease-fire. On April 23 Paraguay dropped its reservations of February 27.[49] Three days later Bolivia lashed out, claiming ABCP pressure almost surpassed the bounds of good offices. Stung by Altiplano intransigence, Chile and Argentina replied on May 8. They angrily denounced Bolivian obstinacy as the cause for failure of the Mendoza proposals.[50]

Francis White had watched the ABCP powers repeat the failure of the Committee of Neutrals. He now approached Felipe Espil with a plan for an exchange of ideas between the ABCP and neutral powers. Espil forwarded this suggestion to Buenos Aires, but Saavedra Lamas indicated that he did not presently wish to cooperate with Washington. Replying on May 23, the Argentine foreign minister insisted that the Chaco conflict was the business of the League of Nations and that any action taken by American states would represent undue interference. After reading Saavedra Lamas' latest missive, White commented wryly, "Argentina had never wanted to cooperate with the Neutral Commission."[51]

The key to comprehending the diplomatic situation was a military one. The Washington Neutrals had been unable to pacify a victorious Paraguay. By March 1933, however, Paraguayan forces were on the defensive; Fortines Saavedra and Alihuata had been lost and Fortín Nanawa was under attack. Bolivia maintained the initiative but refused to agree to the proposals offered until the expected fall of Fortín Nanawa had occurred.[52] Both Cruchaga Tocornal and Saavedra Lamas

[49] *Ibid.*, p. 41. Margaret La Foy (*The Chaco Dispute and the League of Nations*, p. 55) claims that Argentine pressure made Paraguay more amenable. No other verification was discovered for this assertion.

[50] Argentina, Min. de Rel. Ext. y Culto, *La política argentina*, II, 53–57, 60–64.

[51] U.S., Archives, RG 59, Decimal File 724.3415/3150, Memorandum, White's conversation with Espil, May 23, 1933, p. 1.

[52] *Ibid.*, Decimal File 724.3415/3084, no. 4660, G-2 in Paraguay, April 4, 1933,

must have realized that neither belligerent would be particularly susceptible to reason or moral pressure. Other than one gesture by Chile, there is no evidence that the would-be peacemakers took significant steps to halt the flow of arms and supplies to the belligerents.[53] The situation is ludicrous when one realizes that both Paraguay and Bolivia eventually would have been reduced to fighting with sling-shot and bow and arrow had Argentina and Chile taken firm steps to interdict munitions shipments. The Mendoza affair taught that Buenos Aires and Santiago might formulate joint peace plans, but neither capital wanted peace at the expense of the party it was supporting. Under these circumstances, the termination of hostilities was unlikely no matter how, when, or where the mediation was carried on.

As early as January 1933 the Paraguayan Congress had considered declaring war on Bolivia. On February 24 President Ayala had been empowered to do so. Forty-eight hours after the May 8 Argentine-Chilean admission of failure, Asunción formally declared war. La Paz did not retaliate but instead appealed to the League. The Geneva peace practitioners now would be asked to solve a problem that American states had tacitly admitted to be beyond their capacity.

When Bolivia appealed for League intervention on May 12 the world peace organization accepted its charge, but with a great deal of anxiety. To mediate in the Chaco would mean that the League was, for the second time in one year, intervening formally in a purely

---

p. 1; Decimal File 724.3415/3125, no. 600, Feely (La Paz) to Dept. State, May 9, 1933, p. 2 (G-2, in particular).

[53] *Ibid.*, Decimal File 724.3415/3053, 3850, G-2, in Chile, no. 1632, Mar. 22, 1933, p. 1. Argentina and Chile had allegedly agreed to place arms embargoes on Bolivia and Paraguay if the Mendoza proposals failed. Earlier, Cruchaga Tocornal, Chilean foreign minister, had told United States Ambassador Culbertson that "the most important feature of the [Mendoza] Conference had been the implied decision to bring pressure on both belligerents by cutting off arms shipments." Cruchaga Tocornal apparently did attempt to bring pressure on Bolivia, but with the results noted in Chapter 3, note 55. In January 1934 Chile charged that Argentina had never brought similar pressure on Paraguay (see U.S., Dept. of State, *Foreign Relations, 1934*, IV, 47).

American dispute;[54] furthermore, the Chaco case would be the first in which one League member had officially declared war on another. On May 20, 1933, the League approved a series of preliminary recommendations to terminate Chaco hostilities. The proposals called for cessation of hostilities and withdrawal of the state of war, submission of the dispute to arbitration, and investigation of the dispute by a League committee leading to negotiation of a cessation of hostilities and preparation of an agreement. These demands were not acceptable to La Paz, and the League was forced to try another approach.[55] Finally, on July 3 the League established a Committee of Inquiry to visit the Chaco and make recommendations. The mediatory committee did not immediately leave Geneva, however, for on July 26 Paraguay and Bolivia sent nearly identical requests calling for another Chaco mediation by the ABCP powers.

As early as June 10 Saavedra Lamas had voiced displeasure with the manner in which the League was handling the Chaco affair, but it was Foreign Minister Afranio de Mello Franco of Brazil who proposed a new peace formula for the belligerents' consideration. Since Argentina and Chile seemed inclined to cooperate with Brazil, Geneva gladly passed the Chaco dispute back to American mediators. Simultaneously, Geneva took steps to avoid the double jurisdictional troubles that had plagued the Washington Neutrals. On August 3, 1933, the League resolved that it possessed the primary right of mediation, but it invited the "four limitrophe powers to intervene in its name."[56] The new ABCP initiative, apparently instigated by Afranio de Mello Franco, collapsed in September due to intergroup rivalry and Bolivian-Paraguayan intransigence. On October 1 ABCP mediation officially ended, but this did not prevent certain limitrophe powers from formu-

---

[54] The League also intervened to mediate the struggle between Colombia and Peru for possession of Leticia Trapezium.

[55] League of Nations, Official Journal, *Dispute between Bolivia and Paraguay. Appeal of the Bolivian Government under Article 15 of the Covenant*, Special Supplement 124, pp. 14–15.

[56] Argentina, Min. de Rel. Ext. y Culto, *La política argentina*, II, 125. The League further noted that it was the only international organization juridically obligated to arrange a settlement of the conflict (*ibid.*, p. 124).

lating still more peace proposals.[57] On October 11, 1933, Argentina and Brazil jointly presented a new peace plan to Paraguay and Bolivia. The proposals called for juridical arbitration of a zone in the Chaco by ABCP representatives and one unspecified party. A ceasefire was to follow Bolivian and Paraguayan acceptance of the terms. The plan generated no enthusiasm in either Asunción or La Paz, but the Brazilian and Argentine foreign ministers justified their action by stating that although ABCP mediation had officially ended on October 1, 1933, this latest effort was of a "private character" and as such was not an obstacle to League efforts.[58] Diplomats at Geneva were hardly impressed with the logic of this explanation, but the League officially took no action to preserve its prerogatives.

Not until October did the League Committee of Inquiry, established in July, sail for Montevideo; it arrived on November 3, 1933.[59] After visiting La Paz and Asunción between November 12 and December 23, a cease-fire was arranged and the committee returned to Montevideo. The Seventh Pan-American Conference still was in session, and it extended its assistance to the committee.[60] Such cooperation was at best a mixed blessing. President Gabriel Terra of Uruguay urged the committee to adopt his peace formula, while Saavedra Lamas insisted so strongly on his plan that Álvarez del Vayo, committee chairman, sought Cordell Hull's aid to fend off the persistent Argen-

---

[57] The comedy of errors that characterized the ABCP arbitration of July to September 1933 can be followed in U.S., Dept. of State, *Foreign Relations, 1933*, V, 354–362; and Argentina, Min. de Rel. Ext. y Culto, *La política argentina*, II, 127–137.

[58] See Argentina, Min. de Rel. Ext. y Culto, *La política argentina*, II, 140–141.

[59] League of Nations, Information Section, *The League of Nations from Year to Year*, 1933, p. 180. The committee membership was as follows: Brigadier-General A. B. Robertson (Britain), M. J. Álvarez del Vayo (Spain), General Freydenberg (France), Count Aldrovani (Italy), Major G. Rivera Flandes (Mexico). J. A. Buero, legal advisor to the League, was appointed secretary-general of the committee. M. Henry Vigier was his assistant. On November 3, Álvarez del Vayo was appointed chairman.

[60] Cordell Hull (*The Memoirs of Cordell Hull*, I, 330–331) claims credit for having brought about the cease-fire. Spruille Braden, interviewed on June 8, 1965, New York City, told a rambling tale of how a prize fighter's remembrances helped him to meet the right people and make the necessary arrangements.

tine.[61] On December 26 the committee summoned representatives from La Paz and Asunción to discuss terms.[62] Bolivia proved conciliatory, but Paraguay had just won a great victory at Campo Vía. Rejecting the League's offer on January 4, 1934, Paraguayan representatives blandly informed League representatives that they still believed in arbitration; Paraguayans only wanted the Hayes Zone, the Paraguayan River littoral, and "all the hinterland of the Chaco" recognized as Paraguayan.[63] On January 6 the truce terminated, and General Estigarribia's armies returned to the attack.

The League committee had angered and alarmed both Bolivia and Uruguay by abruptly transferring its activities from Montevideo to Buenos Aires on January 1 and 2. Álvarez del Vayo and his associates were preparing to return to Geneva when on January 20 the League Council decided that the definitive effort had yet to be made. Although it did not expect a favorable reply from either party, the committee presented the belligerents with slightly revised proposals on February 22, 1934.[64] Following renewed Paraguayan rejection on March 4 and conditional Bolivian acceptance two days later, the Chaco committee had a severe altercation with Saavedra Lamas and departed for Europe.[65] The final report of the Chaco committee was released on May

[61] U.S., Archives, RG 59, Decimal File 724.3415/3425 1/2, "Memorandum of Conversations Regarding the Chaco Dispute at the Seventh Inter-American Conference," by J. R. Butler Wright, Montevideo, April 30, 1934, p. 18. Following a personal visit by Hull to Álvarez del Vayo, the latter took J. Butler Wright aside and said, "I wish to heaven that the Secretary [Hull] would talk at length with Saavedra Lamas" (*ibid.*). Wright observed that "it is fair to assume that Argentina's desire to play the leading part in this settlement is one of the principal factors to which the President of the League Commission has so frequently referred" (*ibid.*).

[62] The Paraguayan delegation consisted of Gerónimo Zubizarreta (chairman), Colonel J. Manuel Garay, and Efraím Cardozo (secretary). The Bolivian delegation comprised Castro Rojas (chairman), Julio Gutiérrez, General Blanco Galindo, and Colonel David Toro (U.S., Archives, RG 59, Decimal File 724.3415/3455, 3/4, Memorandum of conversation between Sec'y of State and Dr. Castro Rojas, Dec. 21, 1933, p. 1).

[63] U.S., Dept. of State, *Foreign Relations, 1934*, IV, 37.

[64] See *ibid.*, pp. 52–53 for the League terms.

[65] Álvarez del Vayo and General Freydenberg were especially critical of Saavedra Lamas (Vicente Rivarola, *Memorias diplomáticas*, III, 95). The Argentine foreign minister had absolutely no use for the commission once he discovered that Álvarez

11, 1934. It concluded that neither side desired arbitration and that, left to themselves, the parties never would abandon their conflicting views. Perhaps in keeping with the character of the organization that created it, the report deliberately skirted basic questions: "The Committee prefers not to determine who is responsible for the failure of efforts which . . . it has had the honor of making."[66]

Among other things, the Chaco Committee of Inquiry failed to produce any concrete proposals of how to overcome the obstinancy of the embattled antagonists. When friendly mediation yielded no results, the League of Nations decided to employ tactics of a decidedly different nature. As early as November 1932 Great Britain had suggested the possibility of imposing an arms embargo on the Chaco belligerents. In February 1933 Britain and France cosponsored a similar proposal. On May 14, 1934, the League Committee of Three was requested to resume its examination of the question and "proceed to the indispensable consultations to permit of measures being taken."[67] As a result of this impetus and despite protests from both belligerents, some thirty-nine League members plus the United States and Brazil took legal action to prohibit arms sales to Bolivia and Paraguay by December 1, 1934.[68]

---

del Vayo had told the British minister in La Paz that a telephone call by President Justo to Asunción would do more to bring Chaco peace than any other mediational step (*ibid.*, p. 80). In a final interview Saavedra Lamas told Álvarez del Vayo that Bolivia was "finished" and that Paraguayan victory was inevitable (see U.S., Archives, RG 59, Decimal File 724.3415/2635, no. 209, Weddell [Buenos Aires] to Dept. State, Mar. 14, 1934, p. 2).

[66] League of Nations, *Dispute between Bolivia and Paraguay: Report of the Chaco Commission*, May 11, 1934, Political, C.154.M.64.VII(1934), p. 45. Count Aldrovani of Italy insisted on the "elimination of any reference in the report to the responsibility of the Argentine in the furnishing of material and encouragement of the conflict" (U.S., Archives, RG 59, Decimal File 724.3415/3662, no. 252, Gilbert [Geneva] to Dept. State, May 7, 1934, p. 1).

[67] League of Nations, Information Section, *League from Year to Year*, 1934, p. 46.

[68] Helen P. Kirkpatrick, "The Chaco Dispute," *Geneva Special Studies*, 7, no. 4 (June 1936), 30. Among the nations who agreed to undertake some kind of embargo action were the United States, Brazil, Great Britain, Switzerland, Austria, Canada, Denmark, China, Spain, Irish Free State, Chile, Peru, Uruguay, Mexico, Ecuador, Southern Rhodesia, Finland, Norway, Belgium, France, Italy, Netherlands, Czechoslovakia, Poland, Argentina, Yugoslavia, Panama, Guatemala, Latvia, Lithuania, Lux-

The call for an arms embargo again demonstrated the divergence between the ideals of states and their expedient intents. The Committee of Three produced a draft of the kind of embargo declaration it desired, but most members ignored it. At least ten states made their adherence to an embargo dependent upon similar acceptance by other states.[69] Norway, one of the states upon whose acceptance many contingencies were based, did not begin to enforce the embargo until December 1, 1934. Disappointed by the equivocal replies and the prolific reservations, sage League officials soon predicted that the arms embargo would not be effective.[70]

In the question of arms transit, all the limitrophe states made their action contingent upon that of other limitrophe states or attempted to relieve themselves of responsibility by citing League failure to halt arms shipments. On January 16, 1935, an authorized League committee ordered the embargo against Bolivia to be lifted. Ecuador and Venezuela took action but the other American states failed to comply. Evidence exists that arms shipments to both belligerents continued, despite signed pledges and the usual lip service given the support of international causes.[71] Not until December 24, 1935, was the embargo entirely dropped.

emburg, Sweden, Venezuela, Colombia, India, Australia, Soviet Union, Portugal, and Haiti.

[69] U.S., Congress, Senate, *Munitions Industry—Chaco Arms Embargo*, prepared by Manley O. Hudson, 74th Cong., 2nd sess., Senate Committee Print 9, pp. 9–10. The states who made the nature of their action contingent upon the action of other states were Australia, Belgium, Chile, Finland, France, Italy, Norway, Peru, Poland, and Czechoslovakia. A nation whose compliance was sought by several states who made their action contingent on others was Japan. Having withdrawn from Geneva in 1932, the Japanese government never agreed to cooperate with the League and passed no embargo.

[70] U.S., Dept. of State, *Foreign Relations, 1934*, IV, 254. See also U.S., Archives, RG 59, Decimal File 724.3415/4281, no. 1038, Special Memorandum of S. E. Grummond (Latin American Affairs Division), Oct. 12, 1934, pp. 2–3. Gilbert, United States consul in Geneva, had been advised by League officials that the embargo was more important in its "general implications."

[71] Manley O. Hudson (U.S., Cong., Sen., *Munitions Industry*, p. 18) specifically notes armament shipments through Belgian ports in November and December 1934. See also U.S., Archives, RG 59, Decimal File 724.3415/4390, no. 362, Gilbert (Geneva) to Dept. State, Dec. 21, 1934; Decimal File 724.3415/4467, no. 894,

The Chaco conflict presented a unique opportunity for an experiment in international cooperation, for neither belligerent had a way of manufacturing the needed arms.[72] Unfortunately, the embargo was declared during a time of world economic depression; some states were loathe to surrender a profitable means of shoring up weakened economies. If the League had been serious about stopping the arms traffic, the most effective means would have been to charge some power or group of powers with operating naval or military inspection teams at various European and limitrophe ports. Admittedly, the legal aspects of such a patrol would have given international lawyers unlimited material for contingent litigation. Nevertheless the alternative to an implemented embargo was the maintenance of a voluntary system that the world soon knew to be farcical. The embargo had been a gesture; unfortunately, gestures did nothing to end the blood bath.

On May 31, 1934, the Bolivian government requested the League Council to apply the procedure provided under Article 15 of the Covenant.[73] Subsequently, Bolivia entered a request calling for the Chaco dispute to be referred to the General Assembly. Paraguay expressed doubts about the possible application of Article 15 to the dispute. The question underwent examination by the Legal Committee of the Ordinary Assembly, which handed down a decision favoring Bolivia. Saavedra Lamas now called a halt to League proceedings on July 12 by producing a new set of peace proposals. The Argentine foreign minister's plan theoretically called for tripartite mediation, including Brazil and the United States, but he kept neither Geneva

---

Dominian (Montevideo) to Dept. State, Dec. 28, 1934, pp. 2–3; Decimal File, 724.3415/4596, no. 587, Thaw (Oslo) to Dept. State, Feb. 16, 1935, p. 2. Norway defended her armaments policy by arguing that not selling weapons would have resulted in "more unemployment," and "weakened resources for the national defense."

[72] U.S., Cong., Sen., *Munitions Industry*, p. 19; and U.S., Archives, RG 59, Decimal File 724.3415/3834, no. 64, Nicholson (Asunción) to Dept. State, May 26, 1934, p. 7. Both sources confirm that neither side manufactured sufficient arms or munitions to arm over 10 per cent of their armies.

[73] Article 15 of the League Covenant stated that if there arose between League Members any dispute that was not submitted to arbitration, then the matter would be submitted to the League Council. The Council would endeavor to effect a settlement. If such efforts proved unsuccessful, then the matter could be referred to the General Assembly.

nor his prospective partners informed of his positional shifts.[74] Saavedra Lamas terminated still another unsuccessful bid to become Chaco peace master on September 21, 1934, by abruptly informing Rio de Janeiro and Washington that Chaco matters were best handled in Geneva: "Neither Brazil nor the U.S. can ignore the fact that the contending powers are both members of the League, and they cannot be in the position of advocating the principle of non-fulfillment of international treaty."[75]

Nine days later, however, Saavedra Lamas informed the United States ambassador that while Argentina remained loyal to the League, he personally was convinced that Geneva's latest efforts "would fail."[76] The attempts for which Saavedra Lamas so confidently predicted failure had begun on September 7 when the League Council laid the Chaco matter before the General Assembly and established a new Chaco Investigating Committee. The committee presented a report and recommendations, both of which were unanimously accepted on November 24, 1934.[77] On that day the General Assembly appointed a twenty-two–member Chaco Advisory Committee to execute the recommendation it had just approved.[78] On December 10 Bolivia unconditionally accepted the League proposals. Paraguay, newly triumphant at El Carmen and Yrendagüé, raised strong objections.[79] On Decem-

---

[74] Macedo Soares, Brazilian foreign minister, charged Saavedra Lamas with not having conducted negotiations in good faith (U.S., Archives, RG 59, Decimal File 724. 3415/4015, no. 185, Gibson [Rio] to Dept. State, Aug. 16, 1934, p. 1). State Department officials considered Argentina's handling of affairs distinctly unsatisfactory (U.S., Dept. of State, *Foreign Relations, 1934*, IV, 177–178, 196–197, 200–204). A history of the July to September 1934 negotiations is found in *Foreign Relations, 1934*, IV, 143–209. As could be expected, Argentina (Min. de Rel. Ext. y Culto, *La política argentina*, II, 220–239) gives a distinctly more favorable impression of Saavedra Lamas' strategems.

[75] U.S., Archives, RG 59, Decimal File 724.3415/4164, no. 236, Gibson (Rio) to Dept. State, Sept. 21, 1934, p. 1.

[76] U.S., Dept. of State, *Foreign Relations, 1934*, IV, 91–92.

[77] For the peace formula unanimously approved on November 24, 1934, see League of Nations, Information Section, *League from Year to Year*, 1934, pp. 49–50.

[78] *Ibid.*, p. 50. The Committee consisted of representatives from Argentina, Australia, Great Britain, Chile, China, Colombia, Cuba, Czechoslovakia, Denmark, Ecuador, France, Irish Free State, Italy, Spain, Sweden, Turkey, Uruguay, Portugal, Poland, Mexico, Peru, Soviet Union, and Venezuela.

[79] Pablo Max Ynsfran, *The Epic of the Chaco: Marshal Estigarribia's Memoirs of*

ber 21 the Chaco Advisory Committee set its next meeting for January 14, 1935, and requested Asunción to send a final reply by that date. A confrontation hardly could be avoided, but the Advisory Committee tried desperately to do so. On January 14 a new date was fixed for Paraguay's reply. When Asunción's rejection subsequently was received, the Advisory Committee unanimously agreed to raise the embargo against Bolivia. Realizing that in effect it had been named aggressor in the conflict, Asunción dispatched angry telegrams to Montevideo and Buenos Aires. This move was precipitate, for Uruguay and Argentina, among others, already had decided against further punitive action.[80] Article 12 of the League Covenant forbade military attack by one member of the League against another member for at least three months after a League report. Since the November 24, 1934, report had been accepted unanimously, League members were prohibited from making war on a state that accepted League recommendations. Paraguay had ignored the Covenant and on February 23 resigned from the League. This step split the Chaco Advisory Committee, and the resulting internal dissension negated the possibility of successfully challenging Paraguay. The Advisory Committee might pass additional recommendations, but indications were that some of its members would in no way comply. The virtually immobilized committee met this new crisis by postponing its February 24 meeting until March 11.

With the war continuing and Paraguay ignoring Geneva's recommendations, the Chaco Advisory Committee now had to consider the

---

the Chaco War 1932–1935, p. 177. General Estigarribia had informed Ayala that as Paraguayan troops were advancing, "in these moments an armistice does not present any advantage to us."

[80] Uruguay, Archivo, File 1980/29, L-6460-Ro12-Guani (Geneva) to Montevideo, Jan. 22, 1935, p. 1. Chile, Argentina, and Uruguay voted in the Chaco Advisory Committee to raise the embargo on Bolivia, but none of the three nations acted to do so (*ibid.*, 1980/29, L-6460-R-012, Guani [Geneva] to Montevideo, Jan. 22, 1935, p. 1). In a special meeting (January 16) held at Geneva, representatives from Colombia, Cuba, Ecuador, Venezuela, Argentina, Chile, Peru, Mexico, and Uruguay agreed to oppose application of Article 16 of the Covenant against Paraguay. The United States Department of State also opposed all further sanctions (U.S., Archives, RG 59, Decimal File 724.3415/4492, Memorandum, Welles to Phillips, Jan. 7, 1935, p. 1).

application of sanctions authorized by Article 16 of the Covenant. At the March 11 meeting Chile and Argentina revealed they had been carrying on unreported negotiations with the belligerents and intimated that these talks might be the means of easing the committee out of its difficulties. Perhaps with a view toward impressing upon committee members their paucity of alternatives, Argentina's representative, José María Cantilo, again announced on March 11, 1935, his country's opposition to any further sanctions, arguing that the League's sanctions were political not juridical steps and thus not authorized by the Covenant.[81] Discussion continued for three days, but the Advisory Committee was pathetically unprepared to take drastic action. On March 15 the committee announced that it did not consider itself able to judge the actual notice of Paraguayan withdrawal, again called for the lifting of the arms embargo against Bolivia, made note of the new Argentine-Chilean conciliation effort, and summoned the League Assembly for May 20, 1935.

Having suffered their share of Chaco nightmare, League administrators deemed it propitious to take the offered escape route. Britain and France, alarmed by the oral effusions of Adolph Hitler, gave Argentina and Chile a free hand in return for support at Geneva against possible Nazi adventures.[82] On May 16 the League Council established a subcommittee to draft a report on the League's position concerning a mediatory group meeting in Buenos Aires sponsored by Chile and Argentina.[83] During the next three days the usefulness of the now-expendable Chaco Advisory Committee was effectively cut

[81] U.S., Archives, RG 59, Decimal File 724.3415/4620, no. 73, Blake (Geneva) to Dept. State, Mar. 12, 1935, p. 1.

[82] *Ibid.*, Decimal File, 724.3415/4839, no. 138, Gilbert (Geneva) to Dept. State, May 6, 1935, pp. 2–3. Gilbert stated, "There exists a tacit understanding that in return for their support in the matter of the German question, Great Britain, France, and Italy would accord Argentina and Chile a free hand in the League's disposition of the Chaco matter."

[83] *Ibid.*, Decimal File, 724.3415/4870, no. 182, Gilbert (Geneva) to Dept. State, May 16, 1935, p. 2. The Buenos Aires Mediatory Group had begun its deliberation on May 9. The League subcommittee consisted of Argentina, Chile, Spain, Mexico, Peru, Czechoslovakia, and Venezuela. Uruguay also was named but refused to serve, stating that it had "always believed" in leaving local matters such as the Chaco affair in the hands of those directly involved—the American states (*ibid.*).

The Chaco

The remains of Fortín Vanguardia after the Paraguayan attack of December 5, 1928.

Carlos Saavedra Lamas. Argentine minister of foreign affairs (1932–1938); President of the Chaco Conference of Peace (July 1935–February 1938).

José María Cantilo. Argentine minister
f foreign affairs; President of the Chaco
Conference of Peace after March 1938.

Felipe Espil. Argentine ambassador to
Washington.

Eduardo Diez de Medina. Bolivian
ıbassador to the United States (1927–
32); Bolivian delegate to the Chaco
ınference of Peace (1935–1937); Bo-
ian foreign minister (1938–1939).

Germán Busch. President of the Republic of Bolivia (1937–1939).

Courtesy of Pan American Union

Enrique Finot. Bolivian foreign minister (September 1936–May 1938);
Delegate to the Chaco Conference of Peace (May 1938–January 1939).

Courtesy of Pan American Union

General José Félix Estigarribia. Chairman of the Paraguayan delegation to the Chaco Conference of Peace after July 1938.

José Carlos de Macedo Soares. Brazil-
n foreign minister (1934–1937); Bra-
lian delegate to the Chaco Conference
Peace (1937).

Félix Nieto del Río. Chilean delegate
to the Chaco Conference of Peace (July
1935–February 1938).

Miguel Cruchaga Tocornal. Chilean
bassador to the United States (1927–
32); Chilean foreign minister (1933–
36).

Hugh Gibson. United States delegate
to the Chaco Conference of Peace (July–
October 1935).

Spruille Braden. United States delegate to the Chaco Conference of Peace (October 1935–October 1938).

Francis White. Chairman of the Washington Committee of Neutrals (1931–1933).

Cordell Hull. United States secretary of state (1933–1944).

Sumner Welles. United States assistant secretary of state (1933–1936); Undersecretary of state (1937–1943).

Antarctic Treaty of Peace, Friendship, and Boundaries at Buenos Aires, July 21, 1938

short.[84] The new subcommittee announced its support of the Buenos Aires mediators, and on May 20 the Special Assembly of the League followed suit. The assembly then instructed the Advisory Committee to follow developments, and all the representatives conveniently forgot that said committee had been adjourned without establishing a date for its reunion. Russia and Sweden created a stir over the question of whether the League retained primary jurisdiction in the Chaco dispute, but Britain and France quickly quieted the dissenters. Geneva went so far as to place the Chaco dispute on the assembly agenda for September 1935, but this was entirely a face-saving gesture. The truth had actually emerged much earlier. At a League Council meeting of June 20, 1935, the Argentine delegate had contradicted statements made by Bolivian and Chilean delegates by denying that negotiations in Buenos Aires were in any way connected with League procedures.[85] Moreover, in July 1935 when League officials had requested that an observer be allowed at the Buenos Aires Peace Conference, that erstwhile champion of League prerogatives, Saavedra Lamas, curtly refused to allow even one League representative near the peace table.[86]

In one sense, the League of Nations fared better than the Washington Committee of Neutrals: it never had to admit its impotency publicly. In another sense, the League's failure was much more serious. Both Paraguay and Bolivia were League members. Unlike the Washington Neutrals or the ABCP powers, Geneva's *de jure* primacy included a moral obligation to do everything possible to end the carnage. When Geneva passed the Chaco dispute to the Buenos Aires mediatory group in May 1935, it had no assurance that the new mediation would succeed or be carried on in accordance with League recommendations and principles. The League successfully jettisoned

[84] *Ibid.*, Decimal File 724.3415/4876, no. 187, Gilbert (Geneva) to Dept. State, May 17, 1935, pp. 3–4; and Decimal File 724.3415/4893, no. 196, Gilbert (Geneva) to Dept. State, May 21, 1935, pp. 1–2. The Chaco Advisory Committee voted to place the direction of its affairs in the hands of those committee members who would be represented at the Buenos Aires Mediatory Conference—namely Peru, Chile, and Argentina.

[85] *Ibid.*, Decimal File 724.3415/311 1/2, Memorandum, Dec. 10, 1935, p. 154.

[86] *Ibid.*, Decimal File 724.3415/77, 10, Gibson (Buenos Aires) to Dept. State, July 17, 1935, p. 1.

the problem, but in so doing abrogated a good deal of its remaining moral influence. Fortunately, it never again was asked to intervene in inter-American affairs.

The negotiation process that eventually terminated Chaco hostilities began inauspiciously on January 22, 1935, when Chile and Argentina reached agreement on new recommendations to be presented to the belligerents. Later during the month, Luis A. Podestá Costa of Argentina departed with proposals for Asunción. Paraguayan suggestions and modifications were received in Buenos Aires February 5. Nine days later Félix Nieto del Río, Chilean minister in Buenos Aires, traveled to La Paz. By March 25 Nieto del Río had reached a preliminary understanding on terms with the Bolivian leadership. Once again proposals were dispatched to Asunción, but the Paraguayans did no more than leave the door open for further offers.

Confirmation of Argentine-Chilean diplomatic activity and a vague peace formula were officially forwarded to Brazil, Peru, and the United States on March 23. On April 1, 1935, identical notes were presented to the United States, Brazilian, and Peruvian ambassadors in Santiago and Buenos Aires, inviting those states to join with Argentina and Chile in an effort to settle the Chaco dispute. The Argentine-Chilean missives optimistically stated that negotiations had reached "definite ripeness";[87] in fact, nothing concrete had been agreed upon by either belligerent. Speed and the appearance of progress were essential, however, for both Santiago and Buenos Aires were unalterably opposed to further interference from the League.

The latest Argentine-Chilean proposals were more favorably received by the belligerents because the military situation had deteriorated on both sides. Paraguayan attempts to reach the oil fields at Camiri or to capture Villa Montes in January and February 1935 had been repulsed with heavy losses. Both Paraguay and Bolivia rapidly were approaching exhaustion; for the first time the existing military conditions made peace a desirable alternative.

[87] United States, Department of State, *The Chaco Peace Conference*, Publication 1466, Conference Series 46, p. 46.

The United States dispatched conditional acceptance of the Argentine-Chilean proposals on April 6. Peru acted on April 8, but Brazil balked until May 2. The Argentine-Chilean proposals of March 23 had called for a simultaneous economic conference of neighboring states to which Brazil had not been invited. Not until both a joint letter of apology and the desired bid arrived was Rio de Janeiro mollified.[88] Uruguay frantically requested membership in this group of mediators, but Bolivian objections hampered Montevideo's quest for representation. Additional attempts by the United States and Bolivia to include former members of the Washington Neutrals were frustrated by Saavedra Lamas' objections.

On May 9 the mediation group, which comprised ABCP representatives Saavedra Lamas (Argentina), José Bonifacio de Andrada e Silva (Brazil), Félix Nieto del Río (Chile), and Felipe Barreda Laos (Peru), and United States delegate Raymond Cox, convened in Buenos Aires. On May 11 Uruguay received a formal invitation to join the other powers, and Eugenio Martínez Thédy then assumed the duties of mediator. Identical telegrams were dispatched to the foreign ministers of Paraguay and Bolivia inviting them to Buenos Aires for negotiations.[89]

On May 13 and 14 Tomás Elío of Bolivia and Luis A. Riart of Paraguay indicated their acceptances. Neither chancellor was asked to commit himself about proposals. Not until José Carlos de Macedo Soares, Brazilian foreign minister since July 1934, arrived in Buenos Aires on May 27 were terms formally laid before the belligerents. Between May 29 and June 2 Macedo Soares presented several peace plans, but all of these failed because of Paraguayan objections. Macedo Soares was unperturbed by these setbacks, but Saavedra Lamas believed the Brazilian had been shown sufficient diplomatic courtesy. Macedo

[88] For Brazil's official reply, see U.S., Archives, RG 59, Decimal File 724.3415/4735, no. 88, Gordon (Rio) to Dept. State, April 12, 1935, p. 2. Brazil claimed that Paraguay had called the attention of the Argentine government to the omission, but Argentina had done nothing about the matter; thus the omission was deliberate. Formal apologies were delivered to Brazil by Chile, Argentina, and the United States. On May 2 Brazil formally agreed to take part in the Buenos Aires negotiations.

[89] Argentina, Ministerio de Relaciones Exteriores y Culto, Archivo, *La conferencia de la paz del Chaco*, Box 4, "Actos Originales del Grupo Mediadores," 14, p. 6.

Soares was in the habit of holding informal meetings with Elío or Riart in his Buenos Aires residence. Saavedra Lamas now insisted that since Argentina was the host nation all discussions should take place in the commodious facilities of the Argentine Foreign Office. The other conferees assented. Macedo Soares' aspirations of becoming chief peace mentor thus were frustrated by Argentine adroitness.[90]

The basic issues between the belligerents continued to be those which had stalled peace endeavors for over two years. Before considering any arbitration, Paraguay demanded a cease-fire and sufficient guarantees of (1) international inspection of demobilization, (2) a pledge not to acquire new arms, (3) fixation of the armies at minimum levels, and (4) a solemn pact of nonaggression.[91] Bolivian representatives insisted that prior to a cease-fire the nature of the arbitration and a time limit on direct negotiation of the territorial question should be established. Seventeen proposed formulas had been presented and rejected by June 3. That date, however, marked the first day of real progress. Bolivia agreed to Paraguay's demand for guarantees in exchange for Paraguayan acceptance of *de jure* Chaco arbitration.[92]

The last barrier was the time limit for direct negotiations prior to the preparation of an arbitral *compromis*. On this issue Riart proved to be extremely evasive. On June 6 Argentine diplomats began to press Elío to drop his demand for such a time limit, but the Bolivian remained adamant. The foreign ministers of the two belligerents met for the first time on June 7, but no progress was registered. On the evening of June 8 a new proposal, which fixed the period of direct negotiations at 90 days with maximum extension to 180 days brought Riart into the open. The Paraguayan denounced the idea of a time

[90] U.S., Archives, RG 59, Decimal File 724.3415/4930, no. 150, Gordon (Rio) to Dept. State, June 4, 1935, p. 2. On June 2–3, Saavedra Lamas informed all the delegations by message that subsequently all diplomatic discussions would take place in the Argentine Foreign Office (Bautista Saavedra, *El Chaco y la conferencia de paz de Buenos Aires*, p. 63). The Argentine note and its approval by the other delegates was, according to the author, "a jar of cold water flung directly into Soares' face."

[91] Uruguay, Archivo, File 1980/29: *La cuestión de límites*, L.1043, 2/5, Eugenio Martínez Thédy (Buenos Aires) to Montevideo, July 2, 1935, p. 1.

[92] Argentina, Archivo, *Conferencia de paz*, Box 4: "Actos," June 3, pp. 22–23.

limit on direct negotiations as "useless."[93] He then produced a totally new proposition: the mediators themselves should decide when direct negotiations over the territorial question would end and when work on the arbitral *compromis* would commence.[94] The mediators were tired and irritable, and deadlock threatened to break up the mediation on this last important issue. Riart's suggestion struck a responsive chord among the delegates, but it was Saavedra Lamas who made the key declaration: "Argentina will not retire until the issue [settlement of the territorial question or submission of it to arbitration] is settled."[95]

Elío protested but the odds were now against him. To press for a time limit would intimate that the pledged word of Argentina's foreign minister could not be trusted. Under the circumstances, even if Elío were to gain his time limit, Saavedra Lamas would not forget the insult. It was Macedo Soares who pushed Elío into the trap by suddenly throwing his prestige behind Argentina's chief negotiator: "The deadline [on the period of direct negotiations] already exists since the Argentine Foreign Minister declares that he will not quit the Conference of Peace until arbitral *compromis* is agreed upon. It is evidently a deadline with the moral guarantee of a great Republic."[96] Elío still debated the issue, but the mediators would allow him only minor compensations. An argument developed over which international court eventually should assume jurisdiction over the territorial dispute. Again, Macedo Soares forced Elío's hand by announcing he was convinced that if the Bolivians accepted Saavedra Lamas' promise Riart would accept the Bolivian choice, the Permanent Court of International Justice at the Hague.[97] Riart lost no time in expressing his assent. Elío

---

[93] *Ibid.*, "Actos," June 8, p. 8.

[94] *Ibid.*, p. 13. Riart had prefaced these remarks by declaring that negotiation would be difficult, and therefore, "it is not possible to say that the work will be completed either in ninety or in one hundred days" (*ibid.*, p. 9).

[95] *Ibid.*, p. 14. The ensuing conversation suggests that Elío tried to ignore Saavedra Lamas' guarantee. The Argentine foreign minister's promise helped ensure an armistice but did much to harm future peace negotiations.

[96] *Ibid.*, p. 18. The moment of truth for Elío seems to have come when Macedo Soares insisted that Saavedra Lamas' guarantee solved the issue.

[97] *Ibid.*

also raised difficulties over the previously discussed issue of war responsibilities. Riart blocked this last sally by proposing that the issue be referred to the Hague if the peace conference failed to solve it. Faced with the Argentine foreign minister's promise and the Hague Court as an arbitrator of disputes, Elío capitulated. The historic session adjourned at 1:15 A.M. on June 9, leaving Barreda Laos of Peru and Podestá Costa of Argentina to re-edit the peace formula. The mediators reassembled and initialed the document at 3:15 A.M.

The formal signing of the protocol ending Chaco hostilities came on June 12, 1935, at noon, two hours before the Peruvian and Chilean foreign ministers reached Buenos Aires. Saavedra Lamas had foreseen its results; of the mediating states the only other foreign minister present was Macedo Soares, whom the Argentine already had deflated.[98] The signing of the protocol in Buenos Aires thus moved the Argentine chancellor halfway toward his goal of becoming Chaco peace master.

The paradox of the settlement would have rewarded any cynic. In June 1935 the Bolivian foreign minister accepted a pledge made by the Argentine foreign minister, fully realizing that the Argentine government had done much to make Paraguayan military success possible. Almost as ironic, the Paraguayan foreign minister signed a protocol that ended hostilities without specifically guaranteeing the Hayes Zone and the Paraguay River littoral for Paraguay. Had politicians in either country agreed to such proposals in 1932, they would have lost their jobs and perhaps their heads. With the cease-fire the American states hoped that the ancient hatreds had been dissipated. Yet no issues had been settled, and the main difficulties were still to come.

[98] U.S., Archives, RG 59, Decimal File 724.3415/4838, no. 69, Weddell (Buenos Aires) to Dept. State, June 7, 1935, p. 1. Cruchaga Tocornal had decided not to go to Buenos Aires since he felt that the mediation could not succeed (*ibid.*, Decimal File 724.3415/1346, no. 677, Braden [Buenos Aires] to Dept. State, May 6, 1936, p. 2). Spruille Braden later learned that Barreda Laos, the Peruvian ambassador, had insisted that the protocol be signed at 11:00 A.M., even though he knew that Carlos Concha, Peruvian foreign minister, could not arrive until after noon (*ibid.*, Decimal File 724.3415/5035, no. 758, Gibson [Buenos Aires] to Dept. State, June 14, 1935, p. 3). The United States plenipotentiary delegate reported that Saavedra Lamas definitely had no intention of waiting for either Concha or Cruchaga Tocornal.

The signing of the protocol on June 12 was followed by a cease-fire in the Chaco which began at noon on June 14, 1935, at Córdoba Meridian, exactly three years after Major Moscoso had attacked Fortín Carlos Antonio López. Concerning the forthcoming conference in Buenos Aires, United States plenipotentiary Hugh Gibson remarked sarcastically, "there seems to be little disposition to get to work on preparations for the peace conference, as all energies are being devoted to an elaborate program of entertainment and "self-gratulatory speeches."[99] Gibson's Anglo-Saxon temper may have been roused by Latin American preference for frolic, but the United States diplomat had missed the difficult dialogues of June 3 through 8. He could not fully appreciate that a war which had bedeviled international peacemakers had finally been terminated primarily through local efforts. Although Latin Americans probably were the only ones who could have ended the conflict, such barbed witticism was inappropriate on June 14, 1935. The gunfire had ceased and the prospect of final settlement beckoned. There was indeed cause for jubilation; unknown to the revelers, thirty-seven months would pass before settlement was reached and they would again have cause to celebrate.

It conceivably is possible that Gibson's lack of cheer was based on his view of the protocol itself. The document had been hurriedly drafted so that the cease-fire could be announced quickly and was, therefore, considered defective by the United States Department of State.[100] In addition to the cease-fire, the protocol sanctioned the opening of a peace conference that would (1) resolve questions arising from the execution of the security measures adopted in facilitating the cessation of hostilities; (2) promote the solution of the Chaco dispute by direct agreement and, if direct agreement were judged impossible, draw up an arbitral *compromis*; (3) arrange for prisoner exchange and repatriation; (4) establish a regimen of transit, commerce, and navigation that would take into account the unfavorable geographic position of both states; and (5) establish an international commission

---

[99] *Ibid.*, Decimal File 724.3415/4974, no. 81, Gibson (Buenos Aires) to Dept. State, June 14, 1935, p. 2.

[100] U.S., Dept. of State, *Chaco Peace Conference*, Publication 1466, p. 10.

that would render an opinion on the responsibilities of every order resulting from the war.[101]

Article II, which covers security measures, is seriously inadequate. Clauses a and c both speak of the "line of separation between the two armies,"[102] but clause d suddenly introduces "lines of separation."[103] Was this simply an oversight? Was there to be a neutral zone between the armies? The conference soon would regret that this matter had not been clarified in the beginning.

In Article III, clauses 3, 4, and 5, a "Neutral Military Commission"[104] was given the task of checking both military demobilization and new weapons expenditures by the belligerents. The manner in which the commission would simultaneously supervise troop demobilization and determine how much military equipment the former belligerents had purchased provides unlimited speculation. Only the limitrophe states could prevent military equipment from reaching the antagonists, and they made no such promises in the protocol. Breaking the agreement incurred no penalty, and no powers of enforcement were specified.

Concerning the vexing territorial question, the protocol established that the conference could not end until the arbitral *compromis* had been drawn up. But if the conference failed to obtain agreement by direct negotiations, it was unlikely that Paraguay and Bolivia would agree to any arbitral *compromis* the mediators might devise. Since the conference could not withdraw, what would happen if repeated efforts to reach an arbitral *compromis* failed? No matter what Saavedra Lamas had promised the conference could not last forever.

When Tomás Elío failed to obtain a deadline on the period of direct negotiations, the Bolivian delegation split. The rebellious members requested and received confirmation of Elío's policies from

---

[101] See Appendix II for the June 12, 1935, protocol.

[102] *Ibid.*, Article II, clauses a and c.

[103] *Ibid.*, Article II, clause d. See also Argentina, Min. de Rel. Ext. y Culto, *La política argentina*, II, 364–367, for a copy of the treaty in Spanish. The same difficulty appears, for in clauses a and c "línea de separación" is used, while in clause d, "líneas" appears.

[104] *Ibid.*, Article III.

President Tejada Sorzano; only then did they accept the protocol.[105] In less than one month's time the fears of the dissenters were proved valid. The instructions of the Paraguayan delegation to the peace conference read as follows: "Paraguay never will admit the escape of its triumph. . . . The Bolivians now speak of their fear that the arbitration will be avoided . . . that Bolivia wants to put the Chaco into discussion signifies, from our point of view, that it does not desire to put an end to the conflict."[106] Arbitration? Brotherhood? The Paraguayans had won a military victory, and they sought conference recognition of the *de facto* territorial situation. With no time limit on direct negotiations the Paraguayans conceivably could stall indefinitely, effectively vitiating arbitral *compromis* negotiations.

In Article IV both belligerents recognized the "declaration of the third of August 1932, regarding territorial acquisitions."[107] Such an idealistic assertion hardly could be considered applicable, since neither Bolivia nor Paraguay viewed itself as a territorial conqueror. Practically speaking, Paraguay held most of the Chaco and none of the peacemakers proposed to send troops to dispossess them. Finally, Article I, clauses 3 and 7, made the Permanent Court of International Justice at the Hague the final arbiter in case of deadlock on the territorial boundary and war responsibilities questions.[108] Bolivian representatives had fought a tenacious battle to gain this point; yet as of June 1935 the Bolivian Congress had neither ratified the adherence convention of the Court nor signed the optional clause whereby the Court exercised compulsory jurisdiction.[109] Until such ratifications

---

[105] Bautista Saavedra, *El Chaco y la conferencia de paz de Buenos Aires*, p. 126. Elío threatened to resign unless the protocol was accepted without change. Bautista Saavedra's account gives no indication that Elío had informed the delegation of Saavedra Lamas' promise (*ibid.*, pp. 123–126). Zalles, Aramayo, and Rojas telegraphed to La Paz, but Tejada Sorzano replied that the government had received sufficient guarantees.

[106] Paraguay, Ministerio de Relaciones Exteriores, Archivo de Relaciones Exteriores, *La conferencia de paz de Buenos Aires*, Carpeta 1, "Memorándum Reservado," pp. 9–10. A copy of this memorandum was supposedly given by Gerónimo Zubizarreta to Saavedra Lamas on July 7, 1935 (*ibid.*, p. 10).

[107] Article IV of the June 12, 1935, protocol.

[108] Article I of the June 12, 1935 protocol.

[109] In the special report (U.S., Archives, RG 59, Decimal File 724.3415/4032

were executed, there was no assurance the Court would consider Chaco litigation. The mediators chose to ignore this minor difficulty.

The June 12, 1935, protocol seems impregnated with the implicit belief that the proposed peace conference would rapidly settle matters, for no provision was made for new security measures once demobilization was completed. Such an omission is excusable only if the mediators believed the belligerents were exhausted and prepared to accept equitable arrangements. The difficulty with such a position is that the mediators of May and June 1935 were all aware of the failure of past mediations. Why then assume that the parties were now acting in good faith? The ultimate justification for the June 12 protocol was that despite its crippling weaknesses it provided the interested parties with an opportunity both to save face and to stop the bloodletting. The parties acted expeditiously. They also would come to regret their haste.

The Neutral Military Commission referred to in Article II of the protocol began to assemble in Buenos Aires on June 10 and received its instructions four days later.[110] Military representatives from four of the mediator states immediately departed for the Chaco. The cooperation of the opposing commands in regard to the separation of the two armies was initially excellent. By June 26 a line of markers or *hitos*, delimiting the forward positions of the two armies, had been

1/2, McGurk, Memorandum to Sumner Welles, Aug. 23, 1934, pp. 1–3) McGurk, chief of the Latin American Affairs Division, noted that the Paraguayan Congress had ratified the Hague Court statute on May 11, 1933 (the day after Paraguay declared war on Bolivia). It had also ratified the optional clause the same day. Not until August 1936 did the Bolivian government adhere to the Hague Court Statute. Since the act was performed by the revolutionary president (Colonel Toro had taken office by coup in May 1936) and not the Bolivian Congress, its legality was open to question (Paraguay, Archivo, Carpeta 30, "Notas remitidas—22 de Mayo—6 de Agosto, 1937," p. 129).

110 See Appendix III for the membership of the Neutral Military Commission (U.S., Dept. of State, *Chaco Peace Conference*, pp. 61–63). In addition to the June 12, 1935, protocol, an agreement was signed specifically empowering the Neutral Military Commission to begin work immediately. This added protocol also had to be signed by both congresses. On June 22 and July 2, because the time limit stated in Article III was deemed insufficient, the mediators met to increase the time the Neutral Commission would need to bring about an adequate separation of the armies (see *ibid.*, p. 57).

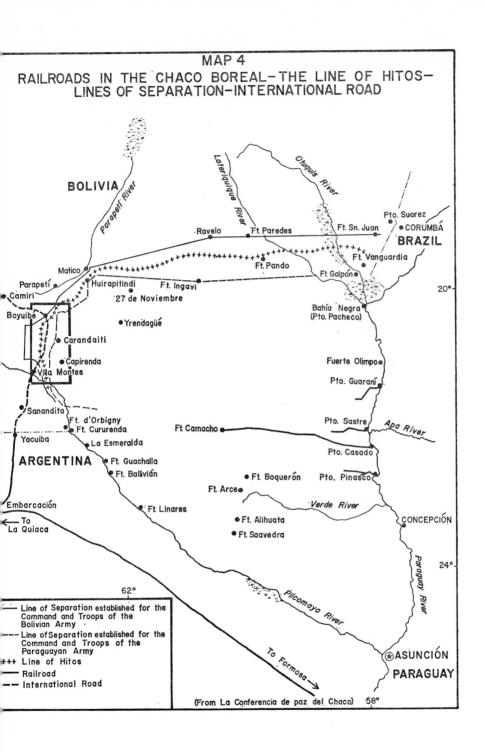

MAP 4
RAILROADS IN THE CHACO BOREAL–THE LINE OF HITOS–
LINES OF SEPARATION–INTERNATIONAL ROAD

BOLIVIA

Parapetí River

Lateriquique River

Otuquis River

Pto. Suarez

·Ravelo   Ft. Paredes   Ft. Sn. Juan   ● CORUMBÁ

BRAZIL

Matico ●   Ft. Pando   Ft. Vanguardia

Parapetí ●   Huirapitindi   Ft. Ingavi   Ft. Galpón●

● Camiri   27 de Noviembre

Boyuibe ●   Bahía Negra
(Pto. Pacheco)

● Yrendagüé

20°

● Carandaiti

● Capirenda   Fuerte Olimpo ●

Villa Montes   Pto. Guaraní ●

/ Sanandita

Ft. d'Orbigny   Pto. Sastre   Apa River

● Ft. Cururenda   Ft. Camacho ●

Yacuiba   La Esmeralda

Pto. Casado

ARGENTINA   ● Ft. Guachalla

● Ft. Ballivián   ● Ft. Boquerón   Pto, Pinasco

Ft. Arce ●

Embarcación   Verde River

● Ft. Linares

← To
La Quiaca   ● Ft. Alihuata   CONCEPCIÓN

● Ft. Saavedra

24°

62°

Paraguay River

Pilcomayo River

To Formosa →

⊛ ASUNCIÓN

PARAGUAY

---- Line of Separation established for the
Command and Troops of the
Bolivian Army

---- Line of Separation established for the
Command and Troops of the
Paraguayan Army

+++ Line of Hitos

—— Railroad

-- International Road

laid. Differences of opinion soon reached acute proportions because the commission desired to have both armies execute a withdrawal, thus creating a neutral "zone of separation" on both sides of the markers. Particularly in the central sector, between Villa Montes and Boyuibé, both commanders argued that vital national interests prohibited anything more than a token withdrawal. Only after several hectic bargaining sessions did both commands reach agreement.[111] On July 2, 1935, the Neutral Commission reported its success, thereby allowing the Chaco Peace Conference to initiate its labors auspiciously. The continued success of this commission would in future months be the only hopeful aspect of an otherwise darkening picture.

And what of the Chaco economic conference to which the Brazilians had vehemently demanded admission? Quite independently of Chaco negotiation a Pan-American Commercial Conference had been scheduled in Buenos Aires for May 26, 1935. The Chaco affair had not been included in the agenda, but at several reunions Paraguayan representatives expounded their views on area economic problems. The Pan-American Conference ended on June 19, its tangible contributions to

---

[111] The Department of State record (*ibid.*, p. 12) is unusually vague. *La conferencia de paz del Chaco* (Argentina, Archivo, pp. 81–121) gives a fairly complete picture of events. The three major problems faced were:

1. In the Villa Montes–Camiri section, the Bolivians were loathe to withdraw their forces, claiming that for them the political objective of the war was maintenance of control over the petroleum zone (*ibid.*, p. 106).

2. The Neutral Commission desired to establish a neutral zone on both sides of the line of markers laid June 26 (*ibid.*, p. 121). Estigarribia, the Paraguayan commander, denied that a neutral zone had been contemplated in the protocol (*ibid.*, p. 104).

3. On the last day of the fighting the Paraguayans had pushed across the international road (so-called Standard Oil Road to Paraguayans) in the sector between Villa Montes and Boyuibé. This road was the only one into the Oriente from the south or east and the Bolivians wanted the Paraguayans to withdraw from it (see Map 4). A last-minute Bolivian concession brought about a similar Paraguayan concession July 1, 1935, and so on July 2, 1935, the commission could report that the armies had been separated. Estigarribia later tacitly recognized that a neutral zone had been created on July 2, 1935 (*ibid.*, pp. 121–122). The only agreement that could be reached regarding the international road was that in the Villa Montes–Boyuibé sector the troops along the road on both sides would be under the command of a member of the Neutral Military Commission (*ibid.*, p. 118).

Chaco peace and progress undetectible. For over three years nothing more was heard about a Chaco economic conference.

On June 22 the mediator group issued formal invitations to the ABCP powers, the United States, and Uruguay to attend the Buenos Aires Peace Conference. Five days later Saavedra Lamas proposed that the conference open on July 1,[112] but on June 28 he telephoned Cordell Hull and announced that the conference would open on July 10![113] The Argentine foreign minister must have had a sudden change of heart, for the conference opened on July 1, as originally scheduled. The shooting war had ended; the struggle would continue by diplomatic means.

---

[112] U.S., Dept. of State, *Foreign Relations, 1935*, IV, 90–91.

[113] U.S., Archives, RG 59, Decimal File 724.34119/6, Carlos Saavedra Lamas to Cordell Hull, June 28, 1935, p. 2.

PART TWO

The Conference of Peace in Action

5. PROBLEMS OF DISARMAMENT, WAR
RESPONSIBILITIES, AND PRISONERS

*The idea . . . of continuing the investigation concerning the
responsibilities for the war . . . for reasons not referred to here,
was given up.*

República Argentina, *La conferencia de paz del Chaco*

*Everyone in Paraguay, from the President to the lowest
kitchen maid felt that Paraguay had won the war.*

Gerónimo Zubizarreta to Hugh Gibson

ᓵᓕᓕᓕ

O N JULY 1, 1935, the Chaco Peace Conference officially opened, and the following day, Carlos Saavedra Lamas was
elected conference president. On hand for these ceremonies as chairmen of their delegations, or posted shortly thereafter, were Carlos
Saavedra Lamas of Argentina, Félix Nieto del Río of Chile, José
Bonifacio de Andrada e Silva of Brazil, Felipe Barreda Laos of Peru,
Hugh Gibson of the United States, Tomás Elío of Bolivia, and Gerónimo Zubizarreta of Paraguay. By July 15 Luis Podestá Costa of the
Argentine delegation had been approved as conference secretary-general, José de Paula Rodrigues Alves had been named head of the Brazilian delegation, procedural rules of order had been adopted, several

plenary sessions had been held, and a number of committees were in the process of formation. The mediators then began the hard bargaining sessions characteristic of negotiated peace efforts.

No one was surprised when during the discussion of issues Bolivian and Paraguayan representatives almost invariably adopted diametrically opposed positions. What made Chaco peacemaking such a grim business, negating any sense of optimism, was the persistent intransigence of the spokesmen from La Paz and Asunción, who steadfastly resisted compromise solutions. Because of their rigidity the settlement of allegedly minor problems like prisoner repatriation took months, and intensive negotiation of the territorial question was delayed over two years.

The situation at Buenos Aires was further complicated by the unorthodox behavior of the conference president. Saavedra Lamas arbitrarily honored and broke procedural rules and left a trail of protesting delegates in his wake.[1] Repayment for such cavalier treatment was not long in coming. Late in July 1935, Saavedra Lamas produced a comprehensive formula for Chaco settlement. The provisions of the plan called for indemnification of Paraguay as victor in the war, United States government loans to Asunción and La Paz, extension of the Argentine railway system into the Bolivian Oriente, and Chilean cession of a Pacific Ocean port to Bolivia. On at least three occasions, Argentina's foreign minister informally presented his program, only to receive resounding rebuffs from the United States, Chilean, and Brazilian plenipotentiaries.[2] Henceforth, Saavedra Lamas treated his fellow mediators more tactfully, but his pro-Paraguayan bias remained unmistakable.

Not to be overlooked as serious barriers to a Chaco settlement were

[1] United States, Department of State, *Papers Relating to the Foreign Relations of the United States, 1935*, IV, 102–103, 106–107. Corroboration is also found in Bautista Saavedra, *El Chaco y la conferencia de paz de Buenos Aires*, p. 152. For a copy of procedural rules, see United States, Department of State, *The Chaco Peace Conference*, Publication 1466, Conference Series 46, pp. 58–60.

[2] See U.S., Dept. of State, *Foreign Relations, 1935*, IV, 100–101, 105–107; and United States, National Archives, Washington, D.C., Department of State, RG 59, Decimal File 724.34119/80, no. 18, Gibson(Buenos Aires) to Dept. State, July 23, 1935, pp. 3–6.

the capricious characters of many diplomats and the personal conflicts and animosities engendered by the arduous negotiations. Nursing
bitter memories of his May and June encounters with Saavedra Lamas,
Foreign Minister José Carlos de Macedo Soares of Brazil unsuccess-
fully schemed to puncture his Argentine counterpart's pride.[3] Félix
Nieto del Río carried on a private war with the Argentine foreign
minister while occasionally exercising a restraining influence on Tomás
Elío.[4] Never happy with his Buenos Aires assignment, Hugh Gibson
succeeded in having himself replaced, when on November 13, 1935,
Spruille Braden joined the mediators.[5] Most aloof was the Uruguayan
alternate, Pedro Manini Rios, who had been posted to the War Responsibilities Committee but who made himself conspicuous by his
frequent absences.[6] Saavedra Lamas occasionally shared his views of
other delegates, and while he respected Rodrigues Alves, his opinions
of Nieto del Río and Barreda Laos were distinctly unflattering.[7]

[3] U.S., Archives, RG 59, Decimal File 724.34119/20, no. 170, Gordon (Rio) to
Hull (copy forwarded to Gibson), July 6, 1935, pp.1–2; Decimal File 724.34119/20,
no. 121, Hull to Gordon (Rio), July 6, 1935, p. 2; Decimal File 724.34119/25, no.
119, Hull to Gibson (Buenos Aires), July 6, 1935, p. 1. Macedo Soares circulated
a note calling for Podestá Costa's replacement by Alan Dawson, Hugh Gibson's assistant. Cordell Hull, who suspected that Macedo Soares desired to even old scores
with Saavedra Lamas, informed Gibson that if Macedo Soares persisted in his course,
Gibson should inform Saavedra Lamas that no North American could serve as secretary-general of the conference.

[4] *Ibid.*, Decimal File 724.34119/321, no. 96, Braden (Buenos Aires) to Dept.
State, Dec. 7, 1935, p. 2. Elío was usually amenable to suggestions by Nieto del Río;
the Chilean had helped to form the conspiratorial group that had caused the removal
of the previous Bolivian foreign minister in April 1935.

[5] U.S., Dept. of State, *Foreign Relations, 1935*, IV, 117; U.S., Archives, RG 59,
Decimal File 724.34119/196A, no. 384, Hull to Welles, Sept. 26, 1935, p. 1. Cordell
Hull proposed Dana Munro as Gibson's replacement. Sumner Welles instead recom-
mended Spruille Braden. In an interview with Spruille Braden (New York City,
June 8, 1965) Mr. Braden remarked that Hugh Gibson was skilled in the ways of
European diplomacy but only faintly cognizant of Latin American methods and
procedures.

[6] U.S., Archives, RG 59, Decimal File 724.34119/99, no. 24, Gibson (Buenos
Aires) to Dept. State, July 27, 1935, p. 9. This committee passed a provision that
its members might be replaced by "technical advisors" if necessary. Gibson stated
that "this latter provision was obviously intended to allow Dr. Manini Rios to
continue his practice of spending five-day weekends in Montevideo."

[7] *Ibid.*, Decimal File 724.34119/295 1/2, no. 91, Braden (Buenos Aires) to Dept.

Beginning in August 1935, the question of prisoner repatriation became increasingly important, both as a problem demanding urgent consideration and as one the conferees believed they might solve. After months of bargaining, a protocol governing prisoner repatriation was signed on January 21, 1936. During February the conferees ordained vacations for themselves, but certain outside forces remained active. On February 17, Colonel Rafael Franco seized power in Paraguay and on May 31, Colonel David Toro did the same in Bolivia. Both new leaders threatened to renounce all previously signed protocols, but the governments of the mediator states reacted vigorously by unleashing a new weapon—joint diplomatic recognition—and thereby dissuaded the military presidents from executing any repudiation plans they may have nurtured.[8]

During July 1936 the conference reconvened, and on August 21, it declared the repatriation of prisoners completed. On August 25, Bolivia and Paraguay tentatively agreed to renew diplomatic relations. After a year of negotiation, the accomplishments of the conference seemed meager, but when personal conflicts, clashing national interests, and lack of precedents to guide the mediators are considered, perhaps the miracle is that anything was achieved at all.

With the signature of the protocol of June 12, 1935, a small detachment of military officers from several mediator states was placed under the command of General Rodolfo Martínez Pita of Argentina and flown to the Chaco. Acting under the terms of the protocol, these officers effected a cease-fire on June 14 and established a line (or lines) of separation between the contending armies. Joined in these duties by

State, Nov. 20, 1935, p. 2. Saavedra Lamas called Rodriguez Alves (Brazil) a "sincere, able man"; Barreda Laos (Peru) "unreliable, destructive"; and Nieto del Río (Chile) "doctrinaire . . . impulsive, unsound."

8 *Ibid.*, Decimal File 724.34119/76, no. 5416, G-2, April 23, 1936. This report notes that the Franco government intended to denounce both the June 12, 1935, and January 21, 1936, protocols. See also Uruguay, Ministerio de Relaciones Exteriores y Culto, Archivo de Relaciones Exteriores, Montevideo, File 1980/29: *Paraguay y Bolivia: La cuestión de límites*, no. 100, L.1195, Martínez Thédy (Buenos Aires) to Montevideo, May 29, 1936, p. 1; and 1980/29, no. 1, L.387, Martínez Thédy (Buenos Aires) to Montevideo, May 29, 1936, p. 1.

military representatives of other mediator countries, the so-called Neutral Military Commission reported to the conference on July 2 that it had completed its initial tasks. The commission then launched preparations for the supervision of the demobilization of the Bolivian and Paraguayan armies. On July 10 it forwarded to both commands the following schedule:

First Period (July 10–30, 1935): one-eighth of the total effectives of each army

Second period (July 31–August 9, 1935): two-eighths of the total effectives of each army

Third Period (August 10–September 8, 1935): three-eighths of the total effectives of each army

Fourth Period (September 9–30, 1935): two-eighths of the total effectives of each army.[9]

Check points were established at Paraguayan and Bolivian centers of demobilization, and the "cannon fodder" began to return whence it came.[10] Actual demobilization proceeded as follows:

First Period: Bolivia—10,815
               Paraguay—17,752
Second Period: Bolivia—26,047
               Paraguay—32,050
Third Period: Bolivia—49,490
               Paraguay—43,509
Fourth Period: Bolivia—54,105
               Paraguay—46,515

By September 30, 1935, Bolivia had demobilized 54,105 troops and Paraguay 46,515. Paraguayan demobilization was rapid because of the expense of maintaining a large standing army. Altiplano leaders be-

---

[9] U.S., Dept. of State, *Chaco Peace Conference*, pp. 13–14.

[10] Argentina, Ministerio de Relaciones Exteriores y Culto, *La conferencia de paz del Chaco*, p. 121. The places of demobilization for the Bolivian army were Caíza, Villa Montes, Santa Fe, Ravelo, Fortín San Juan, Laguna Camatindi, Invítiapi, and Uruiguá. For the Paraguayans, they were Fortín Galpón, Ingavi, Huirapitindi, Mandeyapecua, Carandaiti, Capirenda, Oruro, and Santa Teresita. Neutral Military Commission officers performed cross-checking activities at Cochabamba, Sucre, Tarija, and Santa Cruz (Bolivia); and at Puerto Casado, Puerto Pinasco, and Asunción (Paraguay). See Map 4.

lieved, however, that certain contingents were pro-revolutionary and, therefore, executed demobilization in a more cautious manner.

Among the neutral military commissioners, egos and differences in temperament further complicated an admittedly difficult mission.[11] Radio Illimani in La Paz pricked Paraguayan sensitivities with its provocative queries about Bolivian prisoners, while Asunción squeezed the utmost propaganda value from several minor incidents. Duty in the Chaco, however, was not without its benefits. On July 18 Generalissimos José Félix Estigarribia of Paraguay and Enrique Peñaranda of Bolivia were brought together, and both wine and emotions flowed. On August 6 La Paz summoned the Neutral Military Commission to sample Bolivian hospitality, and on September 16 the commission was invited to Asunción to savor Paraguayan pleasantries.

The Bolivian command announced on September 15 that in keeping with Article III of the protocol, its army had been reduced to 5,000 men. Two weeks later Estigarribia reported that his forces numbered 4,713 effectives. On September 30 General Rodolfo Martínez Pita reported to Buenos Aires that the commission's labors were virtually completed. The following day the Neutral Military Commission quit the Chaco, leaving Colonel José E. Trabal to remain as supervisor of security measures. In Buenos Aires the commission was feted by the conference and, following the submission of its report on October 18, passed into history.

The Neutral Military Commission's report was unanimously accepted by the conference, but for excellent reasons only part of it was published. Article III, clause 2 of the protocol called for the reduction of the two armies to a maximum of 5,000 men each. In its

<hr/>

[11] Alfredo Campos (*Misión de paz en el Chaco Boreal*, I, 108) speaks disparagingly of the North American Major John Weeks and severely criticizes his lack of facility with Spanish. Campos also considered the Chilean General Fuentes an "arrogant soldier" (*ibid.*, p. 107). Major Weeks is equally critical of his Uruguayan colleague: "General Martínez Pita . . . began to dictate and impress his personal ideas and those of the Minister of Foreign Affairs of his country [Argentina] from whom he had in all probability, received explicit instructions. The Uruguayan, General Campos, was apparently under the influence of the Argentine, but the Brazilian and Chilean members . . . took exception to this domineering" (U.S., Archives, RG 59, Decimal File 724.34119/5069, no. 19, Gibson [Buenos Aires] to Dept. State, July 25, 1935, p. 3).

conclusion the commission report stated that "the Military effectives of the Bolivian and Paraguayan armies have been reduced to less than 5,000 men."[12] The report admitted that it had been impossible to determine whether Paraguayan figures were correct but stated that "the Neutral Military Commission considers that the security measures contemplated in No. 2 of Article III have been met by both sides."[13] Evidence suggests a different conclusion. Nineteen years after this report was written, General Alfredo Campos, one of the neutral military commissioners, flatly contradicted the published report. He declared that internal difficulties necessitated Bolivia's giving legal force to the fiction that its army had been reduced to 5,000 men.[14] Campos avowed that the commission never had any means of determining the veracity of either the Bolivian or the Paraguayan declarations.

The Neutral Military Commission also was charged in Article III, clause 4, of the June protocol with seeing that the two parties made no new acquisitions of weapons "except for the amount indispensable for replacement."[15] The commission concluded that this security measure "has been tacitly carried out, since we have received no knowledge of the nonobservance of this clause on the part of the two governments."[16] Such a response raises an obvious question: did the commission expect either Asunción or La Paz to reveal its indiscretions? Even before the commission disbanded, Bolivia had begun to purchase new military equipment from the United States.[17]

In an unpublished addendum the Neutral Military Commission was

[12] U.S., Dept. of State, *Chaco Peace Conference*, p. 65.

[13] *Ibid.*

[14] Campos, *Misión de paz*, I, 232. The device employed by the Bolivians to void the spirit of the June 1935 protocol, was the creation of a "legion." The enlistment of legionnaires was simultaneous with demobilization.

[15] U.S., Dept. of State, *Chaco Peace Conference*, p. 65.

[16] *Ibid.*, p. 66.

[17] U.S., Archives, RG 59, Decimal File 724.34119/353 1/2, "Summary of Chaco Mediations and the Work of the Buenos Aires Peace Conference since December, 1935," Jan. 23, 1936, p. 30. Between October 10, 1935, and December 31, 1935, the Bolivians purchased $37,000 in military equipment from United States manufacturers. The United States government did not lift the embargo against Bolivian arms purchases until November 1, 1935. During the eleven-week period mentioned above, United States sources shipped $1,900 in ammunitions to Paraguay.

much more candid. This confidential supplement stated that determining whether either side had acquired excessive amounts of new military equipment was beyond the commission's capabilities. The commissioners simply interpreted demobilization to refer to manpower alone; with this reservation in mind, they concluded that the "demobilization of the armies has been completed."[18] These declarations were, however, unavailable to the public, which was led to believe that "the security measures, the execution of which was entrusted to the Neutral Military Commission . . . have been carried out in their entirety."[19] According to the protocol of January 21, 1936, Bolivia and Paraguay reiterated their willingness "to continue to honor . . . the stipulations relating to the measures of security adopted and clauses 2, 3, 4 of Article III of the protocol of June 12 . . . in their entirety."[20] Yet in June 1936 Majors Alves Bastos of Brazil and John Sharp of the United States, Chaco military observers assigned by the conference, reported that both Bolivia and Paraguay had more than 5,000 men under arms.[21] Such reports did not deter Paraguay from informing the conference in November 1936 that it adhered strictly to the protocol and had maintained its army at 4,551 men.[22]

Spruille Braden, United States plenipotentiary, was the first to openly question the wisdom of allowing ratified agreements to be blatantly disregarded. In February 1936 he introduced a plan calling for inspection of arms shipments destined for the former belligerents, periodic dispatches to the conference by states manufacturing and

[18] Argentina, Ministerio de Relaciones Exteriores y Culto, Archivo, Buenos Aires, *La conferencia de paz del Chaco*, Box 6, "Seguridades Expediente—1, 1935," p. 216. This report also criticized the diplomats for assigning to military men a task which the latter considered essentially political.

[19] U.S., Dept. of State, *Chaco Peace Conference*, p. 66.

[20] *Ibid.*, pp. 83–84.

[21] U.S., Archives, RG 59, Decimal File 724.34119/486, no. 188, Braden (Buenos Aires) to Dept. State, June 5, 1936, p. 2. The United States chargé d'affaires in La Paz reported that Lieutenant Colonel Hugo Honardt, chief of the First Section of the Bolivian General Staff, stated that Bolivia had five thousand men in the army and ten thousand men in the "legion" (*ibid.*, Decimal File 724.34119/490, no. 589, Muccio [La Paz] to Dept. State, June 12, 1936, p. 2).

[22] Paraguay, Ministerio de Relaciones Exteriores, Archivo de Relaciones Exteriores, Asunción, *La conferencia de paz de Buenos Aires*, File 28, no. 214, Coronel Franco to Carlos Saavedra Lamas, Nov. 27, 1936, p. 1.

shipping arms for the former belligerents, and maintenance of available data on these activities by the General Secretariat of the conference.

The United States delegate's recommendation was swiftly pigeonholed, but the mediators' consciences had been aroused. Circumstances now directed that the conferees take their first step to enforce the protocol's restrictions. In drawing up the "General Instructions for Military Observers Stationed in the Chaco Boreal," dated August 5, 1936, the mediators empowered the observers to take those steps necessary to assure "the fulfillment of the obligation undertaken by both countries not to make acquisitions of war material except in so far as may be indispensable for replacement purposes."[23] The following month Paraguay vetoed the attempt to put these instructions into effect. The mediators never again drew up instructions that would provide a means to discover whether the former belligerents were honoring their protocol pledges.

The blatant and undisguised resumption of the arms race between Paraguay and Bolivia finally forced the mediators into a corner. On July 12, 1937, the conference voted to investigate recent arms acquisitions and troop movements by both former belligerents. Juan Stefanich of Paraguay immediately moved to block the probe. Asunción's foreign minister glibly informed the mediators that "Paraguay has never committed, nor will it commit any act which implies, a violation of its international obligations."[24] The mediators' bluff had, in effect, been called. They quickly and quietly jettisoned the resolution. The Paraguayan foreign minister had, however, neglected to inform the other mediators that Juan Isidro Ramírez, Paraguayan delegation president, had already reported Paraguayan troop strength to Saavedra Lamas. Ten thousand men were stationed in the area—twice the legal limit. Since Ramírez' report was confidential, it is unlikely that Saavedra Lamas mentioned it to any other delegate.[25]

[23] U.S., Dept. of State, *Chaco Peace Conference*, pp. 99–101.
[24] Paraguay, Archivo, File 34, 29, Stefanich to delegation (Buenos Aires) for Saavedra Lamas, July 14, 1937, p. 267.
[25] *Ibid.*, File 30, no. 154, delegation (Buenos Aires) to ministry, May 22, 1937, p. 195.

Spruille Braden refused to let the issue remain suppressed. On November 22, 1937, the United States representative denounced the former belligerents for failure to observe the protocols on troop limitation and arms acquisition. He recommended that a special examining committee be set up to visit Bolivia and Paraguay. Saavedra Lamas announced his immutable opposition to the plan and claimed the conference secretariat had complete information on the matter. The Argentine foreign minister received strong support from both Chile and Peru. Delegates of the latter states declared an investigation unnecessary; their military attachés in Paraguay and Bolivia already had determined that both former belligerents were flagrantly violating the protocols![26] Braden then capitulated, for he knew that the other delegates were not prepared to face a test of strength on this question.

The problem of disarming the former belligerents was two-fold. First, the belligerents pledged, in keeping with the protocol of June 12, 1935, that they would demobilize their armies and refrain from new weapons purchases except as replacements. Second, it was up to the Buenos Aires mediators to make certain that Paraguay and Bolivia kept their pledges. Although a troop demobilization did take place, the Bolivians never reduced their forces to the limits agreed upon. In addition, both Paraguay and Bolivia began to make new arms purchases that far exceeded the replacement level.[27] The analogous fate of Spruille Braden's proposals of February 1936 and November 1937 further demonstrated that the conference would do nothing to enforce protocol disarmament provisions as long as it feared confrontation

---

[26] U.S., Archives, RG 59, Decimal File 724.34119/1132, no. 570, Braden (Buenos Aires) to Dept. State, Nov. 23, 1937, pp. 2–3.

[27] *Ibid.*, Decimal File 724.34119/1186, no. 618, Braden (Buenos Aires) to Dept. State, Jan. 20, 1938, p. 2. After conversations with Hochschild, Ellinger, and Chilcott, "all impressarios in Bolivian tin and copper," Braden reported that Bolivia had purchased (in 1937) £250,000 in military weapons from France and Czechoslovakia alone (*ibid.*, Decimal File 724.34119/1014, no. 493, Braden [Buenos Aires] to Dept. State, Sept. 9, 1937, p. 7). Paraguay had contracted from French sources a $2,500,000 loan (120,000,000 gold francs) that would be used to purchase French aviation equipment and materials so certain munitions henceforth could be manufactured in Paraguay. Campos (*Misión de paz*, I, 343) reports that in May 1937 Paraguay purchased $70,000 in war material from United States sources, supposedly to replace material that had apparently been sold to Spanish Republican forces.

would result. Bolivia and Paraguay thus could rearm and remobilize with impunity; by June 1938 troop strength and arms purchases on both sides had reached disquieting levels.

Perhaps the best excuse that the Buenos Aires conferees could give for ignoring this threat to their authority is an implied one. Since a military demobilization actually had taken place and neither of the former belligerents had openly renounced the disarmament clauses, the prestige and authority of the conference appeared publicly intact. The conference could still carry on its mediatory function and hold out the hope of eventual settlement. Such a situation appeared also to coincide with the interests of the antagonists. If, for example, either Paraguay or Bolivia publicly abrogated disarmament provisions and the conference failed to meet this defiance, the discredited body might collapse; renewed strife in the Chaco almost certainly would ensue.

In the final analysis Chaco peace rested not so much on signed pledges and moral guarantees as on the hope that memories of the 1932–1935 mutual bludgeoning would keep Paraguay and Bolivia from precipitous action. It should be noted that the western allied powers made a similar gamble with Germany after World War I, but they lost. The Chaco conferees had little more justification for taking such a risk, but they were to have better luck.

During the seventh plenary session of the Chaco Peace Conference on July 26, 1935, protracted discussion of the establishment of war responsibilities led to the selection of a five-member committee to handle the question.[28] Named to the committee were Manini Ríos of Uruguay, Edmundo da Luz Pinto of Brazil, Carlos Calvo of Bolivia, Vicente Rivarola of Paraguay, and Felipe Barreda Laos of Peru. Barreda Laos, who had previously voiced opposition to an investigation of war responsibilities, had purposely absented himself from the July 26 session and was much surprised to find himself a member of the projected committee. Perhaps the Peruvian only wished to retaliate for being selected; whatever his reason, at the first committee meeting on July 30 he suggested that the question of war responsibilities be

[28] U.S., Archives, RG 59, Decimal File 724.34119/99, no. 24, Gibson (Buenos Aires) to Dept. State, July 27, 1935, p. 609.

dropped. He insisted that if this issue were settled prior to the territorial question the conference would founder.[29] In taking this position, Barreda Laos exchanged heated words with Saavedra Lamas, ad hoc chairman of the committee, who insisted that the question of war responsibilities could be settled without affecting the boundary question. On August 2 the Peruvian renewed his arguments of July 30. The other members of the committee allowed Lima's representative to state his case and then approved a draft proposal to establish a war responsibilities tribunal. This measure, provisionally accepted by Bolivian and Paraguayan delegations, allowed both antagonists to select one judge from an American state and provided for a third magistrate, who as presiding official would have to be accepted by both Paraguay and Bolivia.[30]

All parties except Peru had established their loyal adherence to elevated moral and legal sentiments, when backsliding commenced. On August 13 Tomás Elío of Bolivia suddenly reported that his government was not prepared to agree to a war responsibilities investigation tribunal; further consideration of the issue was postponed. Meanwhile, negotiations on such vital issues as prisoner repatriation and territorial limits had become deadlocked. With the conference apparently staggering toward collapse, on September 14, 1935, Barreda Laos submitted a new proposal on war responsibilities to the delegations of the former belligerents. His plan called for a three-judge panel, the chairman of which would be a United States Supreme Court Justice.[31] At the eleventh plenary session six days later the Peruvian's plan was formally introduced and agreement concerted to the satisfaction of all the parties—except the United States, whose delegate had not been consulted before the proposal was made.

As early as July 24 Hugh Gibson had informed Washington that a Supreme Court Justice might be asked to sit as part of an international tribunal. The State Department had chosen to await the development of events. Caught unprepared by the sudden reemergence of the issue,

[29] Argentina, Archives, Box 1, " Acta de la primera sesión del 30 de julio de 1935: Comisión designada para el estudio del inciso #7," pp. 13–15.
[30] U.S., Dept. of State, *Chaco Peace Conference*, p. 20.
[31] U.S., Dept. of State, *Foreign Relations, 1935*, IV, 140.

the State Department made hasty inquiries to discover whether any Justice would accept the task. When Justices Hughes and Brandeis indicated their unavailability, Cordell Hull wired Gibson that probably no Supreme Court Justice would take the office. Wanting to avoid a flat refusal, Hull suggested that a judge of another category or an "eminent jurist of the United States"[32] might be quite willing to serve. Gibson submitted Hull's recommendations, but neither Bolivian nor Paraguayan representatives would consider a second-line jurist. On October 2, however, a formal resolution on war responsibilities was signed unconditionally by all the participants except the shifty Barreda Laos, who signed with strong reservation.[33] The delegates agreed on five points.

1. An international tribunal would be established to determine war responsibilities. The governments of Bolivia and Paraguay each should select a judge, and the third jurist would be a judge of the Federal Supreme Court or one of the highest courts of the United States of America.

2. The United States jurist would head the war responsibilities commission.

3. The international commission would be constituted no later than ninety days after October 2.

4. Each member of the commission would receive $1,500 monthly for as long as the commission existed. These salaries and all other charges would be paid by the disputants.

5. The dissatisfied party would be able to appeal the commission's decision to the secretariat of the Permanent Court of International Justice at the Hague.[34]

If a North American jurist headed the commission, the final decision rendered certainly would reflect his opinion and do nothing to enhance

---

[32] U.S., Archives, RG 59, Decimal File 724.34119/203, no. 223, Gibson (Buenos Aires) to Dept. State, Sept. 28, 1935, pp. 1–2.

[33] Argentina, Min. de Rel. Ext. y Culto, *Conferencia de paz,* p. 290. Barreda Laos claimed that there was a gross incompatibility in allowing a state both to function as mediator and subsequently to provide a jurist who would formulate a decision on war responsibilities. It should be remembered, however, that Barreda Laos had suggested the basis for the plan.

[34] U.S., Dept. of State, *Chaco Peace Conference,* pp. 95–98.

diplomatic relations between the United States and the party found to be the aggressor. The Department of State understandably was hesitant to accept this dubious honor.

Despite its anxieties, Washington soon was granted a suitable opportunity to rid itself of the spectre of war responsibilities. While in Asunción between December 21 and 24, 1935, Spruille Braden obtained President Eusebio Ayala's acquiescence to the suppression of the war responsibilities tribunal. Unfortunately, Ayala was not the only Paraguayan policy maker to be reckoned with. Gerónimo Zubizarreta, president of the Paraguayan delegation, was not pleased with his chief executive's decision. He forwarded an ultimatum to Asunción: suppression of the question of war responsibilities would necessitate the appointment of a new delegation president.[35] Article I, clause 1 of the January 12, 1936, protocol retained the provision calling for the creation of a tribunal to determine war responsibilities.[36] However, Zubizarreta's defiance hardly caused a stir in Washington. Department of State officials had noted that the coming of the new year signaled the invalidation of the October 2 agreement. If progress in peace negotiations continued, the issue of war responsibilities might be permanently laid to rest.

State Department desire to escape participation in deliberations concerning war responsibility was shared by at least two other mediator states. On November 2, 1935, Paraguay sought a member of the Argentine Supreme Court to serve as its representative on the international commission. Argentine eyes were fixed on Oriente petroleum, and Saavedra Lamas abruptly dismissed the request, declaring "the Argentine Government . . . does not desire to intervene in any form

---

[35] U.S., Dept. of State, *Foreign Relations, 1935*, IV, 197–198. Zubizarreta was a Paraguayan presidential aspirant (*ibid.*, p. 167). In October 1935 he had expressed his compliance with a proposal to by-pass war responsibilities investigations (*ibid.*, p. 153). Zubizarreta's dissent in December 1935 must, therefore, be seen as politically oriented. The concessions made by Ayala (December 21–24, 1935) could not be actively opposed without provoking serious dissension within the various elements of the Liberal Party. Zubizarreta's tenacity on the war responsibilities issue thus placed Ayala in a difficult position.

[36] See Appendix IV.

in the International Commission."[37] Paraguayan leaders next sought a jurist from Uruguay's highest court. Montevideo weighed this unsolicited request for six weeks before officially indicating on December 31 its implicit disinterest.[38] As Paraguay had no faith in Peru or Chile, President Ayala's concurrence with Braden's desire to scuttle the investigation of war responsibilities can be easily understood.

In a special November 1936 report, the Uruguayan delegation reviewed the question of war responsibilities and remarked, "the Conference, for its part, has remained silent in this respect fearing possibly, to disturb the course of the negotiations which are being carried on."[39] One need only recall that Barreda Laos had forecast this situation in July and August 1935. In Article IX of the July 21, 1938, treaty, both parties reciprocally renounced all responsibilities of every order and kind arising from the war.

The war responsibilities issue was pushed to the forefront primarily because negotiations on the territorial and prisoner repatriation issues seemed deadlocked; progress on some issue thus was deemed essential. When on August 13 Tomás Elío of Bolivia asked that the question of war responsibilities be set aside, the conference returned to the discussion of prisoners and frontiers. Negotiations on these issues again collapsed, and in September 1935 Barreda Laos consequently resurrected the question of war responsibilities. Had a definitive treaty been established before a former belligerent was named the Chaco aggressor, determination of war responsibilities at least could have been tolerated. Conversely, the promulgation of such a decision prior to the signing of a definitive treaty could have been catastrophic. At the very least, the belligerent found guilty might have abandoned the peace table. Given such alternatives the mediators saw no reason to invite trouble. This thesis is borne out by the October 2, 1935, agreement, which placed the ultimate responsibility to create a judicial tribunal not on

---

[37] Juan Isidro Ramírez, *La paz del Chaco: En defensa de la línea de hitos*, p. 216.

[38] *Ibid.*, p. 217. The Uruguayan Chancellery promised that if it underwent a change of heart, Dr. Furriol or Dr. Mariana Pereyra Núñez could be made available for service.

[39] Uruguay, Archivo, File 1980/29: Delegación de la República Oriental del Uruguay en la conferencia de paz del Chaco, Oct. 1, 1936, p. 23.

the conference but on Paraguay and Bolivia. Could two financially exhausted states, both nursing plans for rearmament, be expected to bear expenses for the proposed commission? Probably not, but henceforth only the former belligerents, not the Buenos Aires conferees, could be charged with being unsolicitous in the search for "justice."

Fundamentally the determination of war responsibilities must be seen as an effort to appease the moral appetites of the Americas. A just assessment of war responsibilities would have had to consider the part played in the conflict by the limitrophe states. However, since each limitrophe state was a potential party to the determination of war responsibilities via the provision of the jurist, nothing more than a limited investigation ever was realistically possible. The question was allowed to die quietly because ultimately it was simply too sensitive to be left to the impartiality of jurists.

While the June 12, 1935, protocol was being negotiated, Luis A. Riart, Paraguayan foreign minister, insisted that the exchange and the repatriation of prisoners were separate and distinct concepts. Tomás Elío of Bolivia took immediate and vigorous issue with these remarks. Rather than endure further jousting between nationalistic chancellors, the mediators wrote the following innocuous clause into the protocol: "To promote, when it is deemed opportune, agreement between the parties with regard to the exchange and repatriation of prisoners, bearing in mind the practices and principles of international law."[40]

---

[40] Appendix II, Article 1, clause 4 of the June 1935 protocol. The practices and principles of international law are hardly specific. The Hague Conventions of 1899 and 1907 discuss repatriation and exchange as separate entities. Almost nothing is said concerning exchange, and the commencement of repatriation (Article 20) is recommended "after the conclusions of the peace" (Carnegie Endowment for International Peace, *The Hague Conventions of 1800 (I) and 1907 (IV) respecting the Laws and Customs of War on Land*, No. 5, Division of International Law, p. 16). Neither Bolivia nor Paraguay ratified the 1899 treaty. Bolivia ratified the 1907 treaty; Paraguay signed but never ratified it.

The Geneva Convention of July 1929 (IV, section 2, article 75), holds that as soon as the belligerents enter some kind of armistice convention, "there shall normally come to be included therein provisions concerning the repatriation of prisoners of war." Neither party had signed this convention (see Manley O. Hudson, ed., *International Legislation*, V, nos. 230 and 303, 50, 200).

The determination of the "practices and principles of international law" was overshadowed by the realities of the situation. Riart blustered that Paraguay held nearly 29,000 prisoners whereas Bolivia held only 1,700 Paraguayans.[41] Instructions given the Paraguayan delegation to the conference left little doubt of Asunción's intentions: "Paraguay considers the return of all the prisoners would contain in this sense a danger, since it represents an entire army highly qualified for a new war. Paraguay understands that it ought to keep in its power these enemy forces. Once the peace is agreed upon, the prisoners will be returned."[42] In short, a vaguely worded protocol and a wealth of Bolivian captives were to provide the Paraguayans with the springboard for a smashing diplomatic victory.

Asunción's intentions were far from evident until the Prisoner Repatriation Committee met on July 23, 1935. The group comprised Tomás Elío and Bautista Saavedra (Bolivia), Higinio Arbo and César Vasconsellos (Paraguay), Luis A. Podestá Costa (Argentina), Félix Nieto del Río (Chile), and Hugh Gibson (United States) as chairman. Both Paraguayan and Bolivian delegates presented closely reasoned arguments to the other mediators and marshaled scores of historical and legal precedents to buttress their positions. Arbo and Vasconsellos claimed that exchange and repatriation of prisoners were distinct concepts. They listed forty-seven treaties terminating wars since 1800 and demonstrated that in forty of these, full repatriation of prisoners occurred only after a final peace had been signed.[43] Altiplano spokesmen maintained that the exchange and repatriation of captives were separate phases of the same action. They called attention to six treaties in which all prisoners had been exchanged and repatriated prior to the signature of a definitive settlement.[44] The legal logic of the Paraguayan argument was unassailable, but Chairman Hugh

[41] Argentina, Archivo, Box 4, "Actos originales del grupo mediador," June 8, 1935, pp. 26–27.
[42] Paraguay, Archivo, File 1, "Instrucciones para la delegación a la conferencia de Buenos Aires," July 1935, p. 25.
[43] Helen P. Kirkpatrick, "The Chaco Dispute," *Geneva Special Studies*, 7, no. 4 (June 1936), 36–37.
[44] For the full Bolivian argument and commentary on it, see Eduardo Diez de Medina, *Problemas internacionales*, p. 273 and *passim*.

Gibson pointed out that every instance cited by Paraguayan delegates dealt with "a war ended by the imposition of terms by the victor, but . . . in the present case, the cessation of hostilities was negotiated, not imposed, and the steps now underway leading to the formal termination of the war were relatively unprecedented."[45]

Gibson soon discovered how "unprecedented" the situation really was. On July 24, Saavedra Lamas curtly informed him that "all subsidiary questions" must be held in abeyance because successful negotiation on the prisoner issue was not in keeping with his master plan. Gibson ignored the Argentine foreign minister's demand and soon discovered that the Argentine-controlled Secretariat was making a deliberate effort to impede the progress of prisoner negotiations.[46] Tomás Elío next warned the United States plenipotentiary that internal difficulties precluded Bolivian acceptance of any repatriation plan before demobilization was completed. Paraguay's Zubizarreta continued to insist that little more than man-for-man exchange could even be contemplated. On August 3, Gibson saw both the Paraguayan delegation and Saavedra Lamas. He told them flatly that no prisoner settlement based on the precedents of international law was possible. Saavedra Lamas proposed an exchange of sick and disabled prisoners, and the Paraguayans immediately accepted. Gibson then suggested several changes in the plan, all of which called for the release of more Bolivian than Paraguayan captives; each of these changes the Paraguayans rejected.[47] On August 10 and 21, the Prisoner Repatriation Committee presented formulas calling for partial exchange and repatriation of captives. Gibson must have been convinced that neither proposal had even a remote chance of approval, because he departed for the solace of Rio de Janeiro before the last rejections were received in Buenos Aires.

With the beginning of September came the initial erosion of Para-

[45] U.S., Archives, RG 59, Decimal File 724.34119/89, no. 17, Gibson (Buenos Aires) to Dept. State, July 23, 1935, p. 5.

[46] U.S., Dept. of State, *Foreign Relations, 1935*, IV, 106; U.S., Archives, RG 59, Decimal File 724.34119/98, no. 23, Gibson (Buenos Aires) to Dept. State, July 24, 1935, p. 3.

[47] U.S., Archives, RG 59, Decimal File 724.34119/149, no. 45, Gibson (Buenos Aires) to Dept. State, Aug. 21, 1935, pp. 2–4.

guayan intransigence. Paraguay offered on September 14 to exchange some 203 sick Bolivian prisoners, but the representatives of La Paz announced they would accept only total repatriation. On October 28 the conference declared the Chaco War ended. This last act voided the security measures Paraguay so vigorously had demanded in June 1935. Mindful of its empty treasury and the burdensome cost of prisoner maintenance, Asunción now changed tactics. On November 2 the Paraguayan foreign minister dispatched special instructions to the conference delegation. Total repatriation of prisoners would be feasible if "the line of markers [*hitos*] fixed by the Neutral Military Commission will be considered as an international frontier between Bolivia and Paraguay up to the [signing of] the treaty of peace, and in consequence, all violation of said frontier . . . will constitute . . . a violation of the declaration of August 3, 1932, and an act of aggression."[48] The crafty Riart in one move had linked the repatriation and frontier security problems with Asunción's goal of legal recognition for the military frontier. The new Paraguayan diplomatic offensive was to be unleashed on still another front. In August 1935 Zubizarreta had hinted to Gibson that Paraguay would expect financial reimbursement for maintaining Bolivian captives. Riart now approved a full-scale raid on the Bolivian treasury and set the minimum acceptable figure at $500,000(U.S.). He further instructed the delegation to insert a clause in any new agreement stating that "direct agreement represented the best means of creating a stable and lasting peace."[49]

Zubizarreta and his associates fought hard, but the success of June 1935 was not to be repeated. On November 23 Zubizarreta reported that the unyielding opposition of the mediators made the acceptance of Paraguayan demands unlikely. On November 30 the mediators drafted a comprehensive proposal that both sides verbally accepted on December 2. The resolution provided for mutual maintenance of the nonaggression pledge, total repatriation of prisoners, renewal of diplomatic relations, and payment of a lump sum by La Paz to cover "the difference between the amounts expended by the two countries on the

[48] Paraguay, Archivo, File 6 (9), "Memorándum para la delegación nacional a la conferencia de paz," Nov. 2, 1935, p. 1.
[49] *Ibid.*, p. 2.

maintenance of prisoners of war."[50] The following day Zubizarreta virtually conceded defeat in a telegram to Asunción. Foreign Minister Riart, however, was not yet prepared to retreat. On December 5 the Paraguayan government officially rejected the terms offered three days before. On December 12 President Ayala informed the mediators that his acceptance would follow only when all Paraguayan demands had been met.

The possibility of confrontation and/or conference collapse appeared to be imminent. On December 17, Saavedra Lamas privately warned Zubizarreta that unless Paraguay accepted the formula laid down on December 2, the conference would issue a declaration blaming Paraguay for the collapse of negotiations and would take subsequent steps if necessary "to save its dignity."[51] In fact, monetary considerations already had decided the issue. The same day Ayala announced unyielding defiance, Riart instructed Zubizarreta to reduce the sum of 3,500,000 Argentine pesos that had been previously demanded for prisoner maintenance to 2,700,000 Argentine pesos.[52] Conceding that further obstinacy was suicidal for an almost bankrupt Paraguay, Ayala reluctantly chose discretion.[53] Saavedra Lamas then supplied the means to avoid serious loss of face; he insisted that Spruille Braden fly to Asunción to break the deadlock. By December 18 the United States representative had agreed to make the trip and arrived three days later leading a small delegation.[54]

[50] U.S., Dept. of State, *Chaco Peace Conference*, p. 18.

[51] Paraguay, Archivo, File 6 (17), no. 111, delegation (Buenos Aires) to ministry, Dec. 18, 1935, p. 91.

[52] *Ibid.*, File 6 (17), no. 103, ministry to delegation (Buenos Aires), Dec. 12, p. 88.

[53] Uruguay, Archivo, File 1980/29,23/9 Annexo (muy reservado), Santiago (Asunción) to Montevideo, Jan. 13, 1936, p. 6. President Ayala had privately stated to the Uruguayan minister that financial insolvency made the maintenance of the army almost impossible. He further admitted that the country had exhausted its monetary resources. Further evidence that Paraguayan economic difficulty necessitated capitulation on the prisoner issue is found in U.S., Dept. of State, *Foreign Relations, 1935*, IV, 183.

[54] U.S., Archives, RG 59, Decimal File 724.34119/334, no. 98, "Official Report Regarding Trip to Paraguay Made for Peace Conference by Prisoners Committee," Braden (Buenos Aires) to Dept. State, Jan. 10, 1936, p. 2. Braden's report credits Saavedra Lamas and Rivarola of Paraguay as having been instigators of the idea that

After some perfunctory resistance, Ayala dropped the former Paraguayan demands. He and Braden then worked out a five-point plan: (1) the conference would fix the amount to be paid by Bolivia for prisoner maintenance; (2) Paraguay would concede that the military frontier established by the Neutral Military Commission was in no sense a status quo line or a recognized frontier; (3) both Congresses would approve the new agreement since the security provisions of June 12, 1935, were no longer in effect; (4) Paraguay would not oppose the creation of a Neutral Military Commission to maintain security measures in the Chaco; and (5) Paraguay would agree to drop the investigation of war responsibilities.[55] Returning to Buenos Aires on December 24, Braden and fellow delegates still had much hard work ahead, but the battle had been won. Except for Zubizarreta's December dissent concerning war responsibilities, no serious revision of the December 22 formula was necessary. On January 21, 1936, a protocol was signed to provide for the reinstatement of security measures and the complete repatriation of prisoners. The Paraguayan Congress acted on February 8, and its Bolivian counterpart ratified the act the next day. The January 21 formal ceremonies provided Saavedra Lamas with a new opportunity to wax eloquent: "The War of the Chaco Boreal, with its bloody shadows and its innumerable sacrifices, has definitely ended."[56] Unfortunately, the war of words had hardly begun.

The mediators' defeat of the Paraguayan plan, intended simultaneously to solve the prisoner, security, and territorial questions using Bolivian prisoners as pawns, was in reality an act of self-defense. Had the conference acquiesced to Riart's clever maneuvering it would have totally discredited itself. The January 21, 1936, protocol demonstrated

a flying trip be made to Asunción. Uruguay, Archivo (File 1980/29,23/9, Annexo [muy reservado], Santiago [Asunción] to Montevideo, Jan. 13, 1936, p. 4) states that Zubizarreta picked Braden to go to Asunción because he was the most distinguished figure on the Prisoner Repatriation Committee.

[55] Argentina, Min. de Rel. Ext. y Culto, *Conferencia de la paz*, pp. 176–178. Point 4 is of interest. Paraguay would not support the creation of a new Neutral Military Commission, but it would not oppose it.

[56] Argentina, Ministerio de Relaciones Exteriores y Culto, *La política argentina en la guerra del Chaco*, II, 422.

that the June 1935 agreement was not to be construed as a victor's peace. By making the continuation of security measures dependent upon the closure of the conference rather than upon the settlement of final peace, the conferees unsubtly hinted that Asunción must adopt a more tractable attitude.

Internally January 21, 1936, was a black day for the Paraguayan Liberal Party. The intransigent attitude of Paraguayan diplomats temporarily welded the mediators together, while friction with Argentina over disputed territories along the Pilcomayo River robbed Asunción of the support that previously had emanated from that source.[57] Unfortunately, Braden's flying trip to Asunción failed to save the Liberal Party. Less than a month after the protocol was signed, the party was out of power and Colonel Rafael Franco was informing the Paraguayan people that weakness at the peace table had motivated his coup. The bluster of fledgling dictators often lacks veracity, but in this instance the accusation would appear to be substantiated.[58] Franco and his supporters were thus committed to a more militant defense of Paraguayan prerogatives than was the ousted party.

In the protocol of January 21, 1936, the mediators awarded Bolivia 400,000 Argentine pesos for prisoner maintenance and set Paraguayan costs at 2,800,000 pesos, a net gain for Paraguay of 2,400,000 Ar-

---

[57] U.S., Dept. of State, *Foreign Relations, 1935*, IV, 190. Both Argentina and Paraguay claimed certain territories along the Pilcomayo River. Paraguay's refusal to recognize the Argentine claim had caused a stiffening of relations between two otherwise friendly states in November and December 1935.

[58] Juan Stefanich, *El 23 de octubre de 1931*, pp. 205–206. Stefanich, Rafael Franco's foreign minister, attacked the January 21, 1936, agreement and denied that the Liberal Party diplomats had ever won any diplomatic victories over Bolivia. Juan Isidro Ramírez (*La paz del Chaco*, p. 29), classified the January 21, 1936, protocol as a brilliant Bolivian diplomatic stroke (see also Marco Antonio Laconich, *La paz del Chaco*, pp. 50–52). Laconich not only denounces the Liberals for agreeing to the January protocol, but also views the protocol as providing Paraguay with only paper guarantees (Uruguay, Archivo, File 1980/20, no. 140/9 [Confidencial], Martínez Thédy [Buenos Aires] to Espalter, Mar. 23, 1936). Colonel Abraham Schweizer of the Argentine army was dispatched to Asunción to question Franco and discover the attitude of the new government. The Paraguayan maintained (March 4, 1936) that he opposed the former government because it had signed the June and January protocols (*ibid.*, p. 2).

gentine pesos.[59] Since Paraguay never had forwarded to the conference accurate estimates of the number of prisoners held, how could prisoner maintenance be reckoned? The 1899 and 1907 Hague Conventions, as well as the 1929 Geneva Convention, state that prisoner maintenance is the duty of the state holding the captives.[60] Asunción had utilized the prisoners in labor gangs and authorized their employment as agricultural workers.[61] Although profiting from this labor, the Paraguayans now demanded and received reimbursement for maintenance. The January 21, 1936, protocol is carefully worded, but it cannot hide the fact that Chaco mediators sanctioned an arrangement whereby Bolivia ransomed its prisoners from Paraguay, an act hardly in keeping with international law.[62] Ever so dimly one recalls the

[59] Kirkpatrick, "Chaco Dispute," pp. 40–41; see also Appendix IV, Article VIII. This sum was also stipulated as £132,231/8/1. In American dollars (1936 exchange rate 1 £ = $4), the amount was roughly $529,285. Recall that Riart had ordered Zubizarreta to accept no less than $500,000.

[60] Carnegie Endowment, *Hague Conventions of 1899 (II) and 1907 (IV)*, Chapter II, Article 7, pp. 10–11. The 1929 Geneva Convention, Part I, Chapter I, Article 4 reads: "The determining power is required to provide for the maintenance of prisoners of war in its charge" (Hudson, ed., *International Legislation*, V, 26). The Paraguayans had informed Bolivia as early as the fall of 1932 that La Paz would be expected to pay costs for any prisoners Paraguay might capture. See David H. Zook, *The Conduct of the Chaco War*, p. 114; and Eduardo Arze Quiroga, *Documentos para una historia de la guerra del Chaco: Seleccionados del archivo de Daniel Salamanca*, I, 134.

[61] Uruguay, Archivo, File 1980/29, 318/935, Santiago (Asunción) to Espalter, Aug. 28, 1935, p. 2. The Uruguayan legate in Asunción reported that some Paraguayans had obtained the services of as many as one hundred Bolivians for use as agricultural workers. These laborers were to be paid by the state, which was also to receive at least a share of the produce.

After the battle of Boquerón, Major Mérida managed to escape capture. When apprehended some months later, he claims to have hidden his identity. In Paraguayan custody for roughly twenty-one months, Mérida reported that he and other Bolivian prisoners helped pave some of the streets of Asunción (interview, former Major Víctor Mérida, Buenos Aires, September 21, 1965).

[62] Pizarro Loureiro, *La conferencia de paz del Chaco*, pp. 23–25. Loureiro is perhaps the only author to have made a study of this question. He charges that the payment for prisoners was definitely opposed to international law.

Mr. Braden stated that the sum paid for the cost of prisoner maintenance was ransom and a violation of international law. He recalled that all the delegates understood that unless Paraguay received a payment the prisoners would have remained in Paraguayan custody. Describing the payment as prisoner "maintenance costs" *(gastos*

August 3, 1932, resolution and its opening line: "Respect for law is a tradition among the American nations."

On February 3 the conference adopted a resolution that created the Special Repatriation Commission, named Colonel Ernesto Florit of Argentina its commander, and empowered it "to deal with all details concerned with the reciprocal return of prisoners of war."[63] In March the commission inaugurated its labors.[64] Sharp disagreement both within the commission and with Paraguayan military officials consumed almost as much time as it eventually would take to exchange the bulk of the prisoners; not until April 29 was the repatriation plan agreed upon. Seven executive committees were formed to conduct inspections,[65] and actual prisoner repatriation began on May 2. The last of some 2,485 Paraguayans reached Asunción on June 13, while the final contingent of 16,939 Bolivians departed that city on July 6.[66]

Initially a crucial problem for the Special Repatriation Commission was the determination of how many prisoners of war each side actually held. In March the commission had requested the records of the former belligerents concerning number of prisoners held. On May 31 the Bolivians complied, but Paraguayan leaders supplied nothing more than unofficial estimates. When the commission posted a Bolivian officer to executive committee 5 assigned to Asunción, the Franco

---

efectuados) was the best means of covering up legalized ransom (interview, Spruille Braden, New York City, June 8, 1965).

[63] U.S., Dept. of State, *Chaco Peace Conference*, Article I of the instructions of the conference to the Special Repatriation Committee, p. 87.

[64] According to Article IV of the January 21, 1936, protocol, repatriation should have begun no later than March 9, for Bolivia had ratified the protocol on February 9. Repatriation actually began on May 2, 1936.

[65] For membership of the Special Repatriation Commission see Appendix III. Commission executive committees 1 (Asunción) and 2 (La Paz) began operation on April 7, 1936. On May 12 and 14, committees 1 and 2 became committees 5 and 6 (Argentina, Min. de Rel. Ext. y Culto, *Conferencia de paz*, pp. 242, 256–257).

[66] These are adjusted figures of the final commission report of May 17, 1937. Similar figures are found in *Conferencia de paz* (Argentina, Min. de Rel. Ext. y Culto, p. 224). See also Argentina, Archivo, Box 17, "Listas nominales de prisioneros paraguayos: 1936," V. The first-named prisoner on the list of Paraguayans was Irineo Díaz, a captain. The first Bolivian prisoner to be repatriated was Arnoldo Durán, a sergeant (Argentina, Archivo, Box 17, "Listas nominales de prisioneros bolivianos—1936," I–IV).

government refused the Altiplano military representative entrance into Paraguay. The Febrerista[67] government further endeared itself to commission officials by surreptitiously releasing seventeen Bolivian officers prior to the initial repatriation.

Most important, the commission could do little to regulate the modes of transportation the former belligerents chose to provide. The proposed aerial repatriation of seriously wounded prisoners never materialized. Paraguayan prisoners were moved by railroad along a route from La Quiaca to Formosa in Argentina and then by boat to Asunción.[68] Some Bolivian repatriates were packed into barges and moved up the Pilcomayo River to Villa Montes "without toilet facilities or water."[69] Bolivians usually were shipped by boat to Formosa and then entrained for Bolivia via the Formosa-Embarcación-Yacuiba route. Trucks from the latter point took most of them to Villa Montes. The railway repatriation scheme looked excellent on paper but collapsed on application. Efforts to provide prisoners with rations at stopovers and transfer points created havoc. One commission observer reported that "the food was cold from hours of standing and full of dust and dirt, and soiled by stray dogs sniffing at it."[70]

Bolivian officials viewed the repatriation program with steadily increasing irritation. They believed the number of reported prisoners incredibly small. The repatriates they saw were even more alarming. Of the first 7,907 Bolivians who returned, 2,247 were afflicted with skin disease, dysentery, or venereal disease.[71] On July 8 Salinas Aramayo, secretary-general of the Bolivian delegation, charged that Paraguay still detained thousands of Bolivian prisoners; the conference therefore should remit part of the 2,400,000 pesos being held for payment. On July 10 the Franco government unilaterally announced it had released all prisoners formerly held; if any prisoners remained

---

[67] A "Febrerista" is a follower of Colonel Rafael Franco, whose successful coup occurred on February 17–18, 1936.

[68] For a pictorial presentation of the route followed, see Map 4.

[69] U.S., Archives, RG 59, Decimal File 724.34119/536, no. 223, Braden (Buenos Aires) to Dept. State, Memorandum of Lt. Colonel Lester Baker (U.S. representative to the special Repatriation Commission), July 23, 1936, p. 2.

[70] *Ibid.*, p. 3.

[71] *Ibid.*, p. 3.

in Paraguay they were free to leave. The same day Bolivia again charged that Paraguay had not repatriated all the prisoners. On July 20 Lieutenant Colonel José Rivera of Bolivia reported at least forty-one prisoners still detained on Paraguayan soil.[72] Two days later the commission resolved to maintain executive committees in La Paz and Asunción, in effect contradicting the Paraguayan announcement of July 10.

On August 3, 1936, the Special Repatriation Commission sent its full report to the conference. The document was extremely critical of Paraguayan security provisions: "Paraguayan authorities at no time had the effective and complete control of the aggregate of prisoners captured by their military forces."[73] The report branded as ridiculous any assertion that all Bolivian captives had been accounted for or repatriated. "It is practically impossible to know, even in approximate form . . . the total number of Bolivians captured by the Paraguayan forces . . . the total of Bolivian prisoners dead, the total of Bolivian prisoners dispersed in Paraguayan territory."[74] Conversely, the report credited the Bolivians with providing sufficient records and statistical information to allow mathematical verification of Paraguayan prisoner repatriation.

On August 4 Bolivia filed a protest with the commission, claiming continued Paraguayan detention of Bolivian captives. Two days later

[72] *Ibid.*, Decimal File 724.34119/539, no. 220, Braden (Buenos Aires) to Dept. State, "Information Submitted by Lt. Colonel José Rivera respecting Prisoners Remaining in Paraguay," July 22, 1936, p. 3. Rivera's listing:
(1) 7 Bolivians held as material witnesses in a detention camp riot and murder
(2) 1 Bolivian jailed for homicide
(3) 1 Bolivian held in an insane asylum
(4) 1 Bolivian confined to a leper colony
(5) 5 Bolivians who had been checked but who had never appeared for repatriation
(6) 25 Bolivians who had come forward for repatriation after the last contingent had departed.
    Colonel Rivera reported that "there is not one person in Paraguay. . . who is not convinced that there are Bolivians scattered throughout the territory" (Argentina, Archivo, Box 20, Varios, no. 2, "Estudios-Reglamentos-Resoluciones e informe final de la Comisión Especial Repatriación," Sección D, "Exposición del *Tcnl.* Rivera a la Conferencia," July 20, 1936, p. 8).
[73] Argentina, Min. de Rel. Ext. y Culto, *Conferencia de paz*, p. 226.
[74] *Ibid.*, p. 229.

the Paraguayan minister of war and marine replied that the only Bolivians remaining in Paraguay were those who desired to stay. For the first time since Colonel Rafael Franco had seized control in Asunción, a Paraguayan government and the conference appeared on collision course. This time, however, the mediators were in the midst of delicate negotiations concerning Chaco security measures. They deemed a reopening of the prisoner question totally undesirable. To satisfy Bolivian public opinion, two commission executive committees would continue their operation and Paraguay would receive the full sum agreed upon in the January protocol. There still remained, however, the unreleased and potentially dangerous August 3 commission report. On August 19 the mediators unanimously resolved that "the conference will dictate a final resolution,"[75] the details of which would be conveyed to Colonel Ernesto Florit, commission chairman. Two days later, in a circumspect declaration, the Chaco mediators implied that prisoner repatriation had been completed.[76] That same day the commission published a separate resolution that strongly suggested that it had received irrevocable orders: ". . . it is now incumbent upon us to state that repatriation had been virtually concluded and liberation completely accomplished with regard to both Paraguay and Bolivia."[77] The conference applauded, the Paraguayan treasury swelled, and the commission suppressed the August 3 report.

During the next four months, despite mounting Paraguayan annoyance, Bolivian representatives filed six requests for investigation with the commission executive committee stationed in Asunción. By December 12, 1936, 13 Paraguayans and 150 additional Bolivians

[75] Paraguay, Archivo, File 22, no. 71, Acta de la conferencia, Aug. 19, 1936, p. 149. In other words, the conference had decided that the commission must not put out a resolution that (if based on the August 3 report) might contradict a conference resolution. Barreda Laos would appear (from the transcript) to have been the guiding genius behind the proposal.

[76] U.S., Archives, RG 59, Decimal File 724.34119/564, no. 233, Braden (Buenos Aires) to Dept. State, Memorandum, Aug. 15, 1936, p. 4. The United States plenipotentiary reported that repatriation could not be completed, but "within a given period, say 10 days, repatriation could be considered terminated and the 2,400,000 pesos paid to Paraguay."

[77] U.S., Dept. of State, *Chaco Peace Conference*, p. 103.

had been discovered and accounted for.[78] On March 4, 1937, the conference resolved to end the search for repatriates. The commission was reconstituted on May 5, and the two executive committees in La Paz and Asunción submitted reports. Twelve days later the commission submitted its final report to the conference. On June 2, 1937, the Chaco Peace Conference declared "the repatriation of Bolivian and Paraguayan prisoners positively terminated."[79] The mediators were almost right. On August 3 two more prisoners were exchanged. Finally, on September 15, 1937, a Bolivian soldier named Manuel Cuba was turned over to Bolivian authorities by Paraguayan officials.[80] Was Cuba the last of the many? Perhaps, but the termination of repatriation had been officially announced three months before; there positively could be no reconsideration of the question now.

In its final report, dated May 17, 1937, the Special Repatriation Commission reported that Bolivia had captured 2,578 Paraguayans during the Chaco War and issued certification on their disposition; the commission could only report incomplete statistics on Bolivians held in Paraguay.[81] There was to be no subsequent conference report on prisoners, but certain questions remained: How many prisoners did Paraguayan forces actually capture during the Chaco War? How many Bolivians died or escaped before the commission initiated its tabulations? Various sources give some indication (see table). In the opinion of this author, about twenty-three thousand Bolivians were captured by Paraguayan forces during the Chaco War. Perhaps three thousand managed in some fashion to escape detention and an equivalent number probably died in concentration camps. Such reasoning suggests that

[78] Argentina, Min. de Rel. Ext. y Culto, *Conferencia de paz*, p. 275. Of the thirteen Paraguayans discovered, seven returned to Paraguay while six remained in Bolivia. The complete total of Bolivians found between August 4 and December 12, 1936, came to 150. Eighty-nine of these returned to Bolivia, 61 chose to remain in Paraguay.
[79] *Ibid.*, p. 280.
[80] Paraguay, Archivo, File no. 32, Santos-Muñoz to Ramírez, Sept. 5, 1937, p. 17.
[81] See Appendix V for the official commission figures. Argentina, Archivo, Box 15, Acta 8, "Comisiones especiales-Repatriados," May 17, 1937, p. 32. The figures for those who died in captivity (*fallecidos*) and those who escaped (*evitados*) were obtained by Captain Dent Sharp (U.S. Army) from unnamed Paraguayan authorities.

TABLE
Estimates of Prisoners Taken in the Chaco War*

Source	Total Troops Captured	Total Troops Escaped	Estimated Number of Prisoners Dying in Captivity
Captain Dent Sharp,	(approx.)		
U.S. Army	18,980	2,000	1,097
Lieutenant Colonel Lester	(approx.)		
Baker, U.S. Army	18,980		
Ayudantía General			
Sección Histórica,	23,850		
Commando en Jefe de			
las FFAA de la Nación			
Coronel Vergara Vicuña	21,629	4,264	
Captain David H. Zook	21,000		4,264
Roberto Calvo	20,134	2,000	1,097

* The figures listed by Captain Sharp are taken from U.S., Archives, RG 59, Decimal File 724.34119/564, no. 233, Braden (Buenos Aires) to Dept. State, Memorandum, Aug. 15, 1936, p. 3. Captain Dent Sharp, United States Army, confidentially obtained the figure of 18,890 Bolivian prisoners held from the Paraguayan Ministry of War in October 1935. On July 8, 1936, Salinas Aramayo, secretary-general of the Bolivian delegation, quoted Captain Sharp as listing 2,000 Bolivians as having escaped, with 1,097 as having died in captivity. It is not clear whether the latter figures were part of the October 1935 report of Captain Sharp (see *ibid.*, Decimal File 724.34119/594, 247, Braden [Buenos Aires] to Dept. State, Aug. 28, 1936 [Minutes of Chaco Peace Conference Session of July 8, 1936], p. 12).

Lieutenant Colonel Baker's figures are found in Argentina, Archivo, Box 20, Varios no. 2, "Estudios-Reglamentos-e informe final de la comisión especial repatriación," Sección D, Map of Lt. Col. Lester Baker to conference, July 28, 1936. Baker accepts Sharp's figures of 18,980, but insists that it "did not take into account the many who had escaped or who were not counted."

The third estimate is taken from Paraguay, Ejército, *Guerra del Chaco, Partes del conductor,* Ayudantía General, Sección História e Imprenta, p. 267. The figure listed is the definitive figure arrived at by the Paraguayan Army Historical Section.

Coronel Aquiles Vergara Vicuña (*La guerra del Chaco,* VII, 683) makes his estimates from figures used by the Bolivian General Staff's Historical Section. The colonel makes no individual breakdown; he lists 4,264 Bolivians as either having escaped or else having died in prison.

The fifth estimates come from Zook, *The Chaco War,* p. 240.

The final estimate is made by Roberto Querejazu Calvo (*Masamaclay,* p. 459). Calvo also wrote descriptively about the intolerable conditions inside Paraguayan detention camps (*ibid.*, pp. 461–465).

conditions in Paraguayan prisoner-of-war camps hardly were conducive to survival.

In summary, it would appear that the entire negotiation of prisoner repatriation had been conducted in a cynical atmosphere. Did not the blood of the Bolivian dead in Paraguayan camps cry out for acknowledgement? The diplomats at Buenos Aires apparently thought otherwise, and the successive Bolivian governments seemed to realize that vehement protest would not make the dead live again. Moreover, the Franco government, in power only since February 1936, was not responsible for the security and sanitation conditions that had prevailed for over three years in Paraguayan detention camps. It can be argued that the threat of exposure might have made the Febreristas more tractable in negotiation, but it also could have brought their withdrawal from the conference. Even had the threat of exposure been employed successfully against the Febreristas, public admission of any notable concessions easily might have produced another coup. Any succeeding Paraguayan government would have had to adopt a more intransigent position toward Chaco mediation simply to protect itself.

The Buenos Aires Peace Conference had been called primarily to effect a final solution of the Chaco question. Only if mediation were kept alive could either a settlement be achieved or Chaco cease-fire maintained. Given such alternatives, the mediators hardly can be criticized because they chose not to provoke further controversy. Considering the other possibilities, their indifference was virtually a matter of necessity.

6. THE PETROLEUM AND
SECURITY QUESTIONS

Bolivia is one of the American States whose petroleum wealth, . . . is under the control of the Standard Oil Company, or that which is the same thing, the United States of America. The richest and finest wells in the world, according to statistics . . . are those of that country [Bolivia] in the region of the Chaco.

Carlos Santiago to Juan José Arteaga, June 1934

The Neutral Zone existed only during the ninety-day truce; thereafter the opposing armies were left a scant 150 meters apart, and the Paraguayan troops remained in control of a section of the road, under a modicum of supervision by two neutral military observers who had no effective authority, but who nevertheless, did help to maintain the status quo in the Chaco.

Spruille Braden

Disaster and badly divided, the mediators struggled from September 1936 to January 1938 to create a security plan acceptable to both antagonists. Although the mediators ultimately found themselves stymied, numerous events that would have a critical effect on future negotiations occurred during this period. Between

December 1 and December 23, 1936, the Inter-American Conference for the Maintenance of Peace met in Buenos Aires to strengthen the security system of the Americas. In keeping with the character of events, it was not the conference but friction between Carlos Saavedra Lamas and Cordell Hull that most significantly affected the course of Chaco litigation.[1]

Hull had presented a draft convention calling for the establishment of a permanent consultation committee charged with "arranging efficient methods of consultation in order to act with dispatch in an emergency."[2] When the American secretary of state found that the Argentine foreign minister was adamantly opposed to his plan for hemispheric security and could not be persuaded to cease his opposition, relations between the two cooled perceptibly.[3] This antagonism resulted in a shift in United States diplomatic policy. At the Chaco Peace Conference, Saavedra Lamas had announced himself opposed to the initiation of negotiations on the territorial question. When Spruille Braden sought instructions in May 1937, Hull allowed Braden to push for immediate action on the territorial question.[4] For the first time since 1932 the State Department had sanctioned a move calculated to bring a collision with the Argentine Foreign Office. For most of 1937 the United States, Chilean, and Brazilian representatives were unified in trying to force Saavedra Lamas to adopt procedures they believed imperative. Unable to dissuade or disrupt this informal coalition, the Argentine foreign minister openly supported Paraguay and systematically stalled negotiations.

On March 15, 1937, the government of Colonel David Toro of

---

[1] J. Lloyd Mecham, *The United States and Inter-American Security 1889–1960*, pp. 124–127.

[2] *Ibid.*, p. 126.

[3] Saavedra Lamas announced his opposition to the proposal (see Cordell Hull, *The Memoirs of Cordell Hull*, I, 499). In an effort to gain Argentine support, a number of meetings were held. At one of these "sharp words were exchanged" (*ibid.*). Hull no longer respected Saavedra Lamas, and the latter did not bother to attend the departure of the United States secretary after the conference ended.

[4] United States, National Archives, Washington, D.C., Department of State, RG 59, Decimal File 724.34119/836, no. 406, Welles to Braden (Buenos Aires), May 17, 1937, p. 1; Decimal File 724.34119/836, Duggan to Welles, State Department Memorandum, May 1, 1937, p. 9.

Bolivia, which had replaced that of Tejada Sorzano on May 31, 1936, became the first in Latin America to nationalize the properties of a North American petroleum interest. Since Bolivia had neither the personnel nor the equipment to develop the appropriated properties, this act brought a long-smoldering contest into the open. While 1937 passed in fruitless discussions among Chaco mediators, Argentina and Brazil fought a silent but savage struggle in La Paz over the economic development of the Bolivian Oriente.[5]

The frustrating dickering was complicated by internal unrest. Fourteen months after Lieutenant Colonel Germán Busch had led the May 1936 revolt that ushered Colonel Toro into power, Busch pushed Toro aside and made himself Bolivia's new *jefe*. In Paraguay Liberal Party adherents regained power on August 15, 1937, and sent Colonel Rafael Franco into exile. Spruille Braden had hoped that the Liberals' return to power would herald a breakthrough in negotiations. Gerónimo Zubizarreta, however, viewed the concessions of December 1935 as responsible for the February 1936 debacle, and at Buenos Aires Paraguay remained intransigent. Between September 1936 and January 1938 the conference reached its nadir. A realistic assessment of its future role revealed only two alternatives: illegal adjournment or settlement through direct negotiation. Prospects for the latter were far from encouraging.

The war's end found the Paraguayan army on the western edge of the Chaco but short of the oil fields at Camiri. Failure to reach these established sources of wealth did not daunt the Paraguayans. After spending some time as part of the Neutral Military Commission, Major

---

[5] *Ibid.*, Decimal File 724.34119/1008, no. 481, Braden (Buenos Aires) to Dept. State, Oct. 4, 1937, pp. 3-4; Decimal File 724.34119/1026, no. 631, Memorandum, Butler to Duggan and Welles, Jan. 28, 1938, pp. 3–6; Paraguay, Ministerio de Relaciones Exteriores, Archivo de Relaciones Exteriores, Asunción, *La conferencia de paz de Buenos Aires*, File 28, no. 165, delegation (Buenos Aires) to ministry, Nov. 21, 1936, p. 78. "There exists between Brazil and Argentina a great rivalry . . . in respect to the railway and project which each of these countries has with a view toward the economic development of the Bolivian Oriente. . . . It is a certainty that Bolivia has suffered alternately strong pressures both from Brazilian diplomacy as well as that of Argentina concerning the opposing projects."

John Weeks, United States military attaché, wrote, "from conversation with Paraguayan officers, it is evident that they believe that they
occupy territory containing oil, and they expect to retain this occupied
territory."[6] The military struggle allegedly had been fought to preserve Paraguayan sovereignty over the Chaco; Paraguayan diplomats
now sought to insure for their nation a share of the prospective petroleum riches.

The actual situation concerning oil deposits in the western Chaco
was far from clear. Not until June 1936 was Spruille Braden able to
make an authoritative report. He informed the State Department that
both Standard Oil and Argentine Yacimientos Petrolíferos Fiscales
(YPF) were in agreement: ". . . based upon their respective geological and engineering studies, and even a certain amount of drilling
. . . oil does not exist in the area to the east of the line of *hitos*. Authorities further state that were it to be found, it [oil] would be at
such great depth as to make it entirely uneconomical for exploitation.
In so far as possible, this information will be conveyed to Paraguayan
officials in an attempt to lessen their desire to retain this western section
of the Chaco."[7] Braden's conclusions failed to disturb the Paraguayans.
They had begun to drill in the Chaco even before hostilities ended
and were determined to strike oil.[8] Their efforts were conspicuously
devoid of success, but not until December 25, 1936, did Foreign
Minister Juan Stefanich indicate a possible reorientation of his nation's position. Rejecting a series of territorial offers by a special conference committee, Stefanich insisted that Paraguay must have either

---

[6] U.S., Archives, RG 59, Decimal File 724.34119/507, no. 197, Braden (Buenos
Aires) to Dept. State, June 23, 1936, "Memorandum of Major John Weeks," Enclosure 1, p. 2.

[7] *Ibid.*, pp. 1–2, main body of the report.

[8] Justo Pastor Benítez, *Estigarribia: El soldado del Chaco*, p. 104. Prior to June
1935, the Paraguayans had drilled some ninety-five wells searching for petroleum
(U.S., Archives, RG 59, Decimal File 724.34119/507, no. 197, Braden [Buenos
Aires] to Dept. State, June 23, 1936, "Memorandum of Major John Weeks," Enclosure 1, p. 1). On the Bolivian side of the line of the *hitos*, in what had been part of
the neutral zone, Altiplano troops guarded three capped wells. Dry wells had been
found by the Paraguayans near Machareti. Asunción cannot, therefore, be criticized
for believing that it held territory rich in petroleum.

oil or sufficient compensation.[9] The possibility that Asunción might accept this undefined alternative represented the first concrete step toward ultimate solution of the territorial question.

The foreign minister's stand did not indicate that all Paraguayan diplomats were preparing to renounce posthaste their quest for petroleum. Juan Isidro Ramírez, conference delegation head under Rafael Franco, continued to believe in the possibility of a Chaco bonanza. On January 18, 1937, he urged Stefanich to undertake an extensive subsoil study in the Machareti-Nancorainza-Tigüipa area.[10] In May 1937 Emiliano Rebuelto, Argentine government engineer, informed Ramírez that extremely deep wells would have to be drilled to obtain petroleum in the western Chaco.[11] In August Ramírez recommended that Carlos Emilio Crémieux, a Swiss-born Argentine national, be allowed to explore for petroleum near Machareti.[12]

The final Paraguayan effort to locate petroleum came in November and December 1937. A team of French engineers, working for the Compagnie Française des Pétroles, was hired to investigate several possible drilling sites in the western Chaco. On January 15, 1938, Bolivian officials at the conference protested this latest Paraguayan move, arguing that by granting contracts Asunción was expressing sovereignty over a disputed territory. Ten days later a Paraguayan representative tardily admitted to Spruille Braden that his nation had

---

[9] Juan Stefanich, *La diplomacia de la revolución*, pp. 23–24; and *El 23 de octubre de 1931*, pp. 210–211. Definite territorial proposals were submitted to Stefanich on December 25, 1936. The Paraguayans rejected both offers, but agreed that the more liberal one might serve as a basis for future negotiations (Stefanich, *El 23 de octubre*, p. 211).

[10] Paraguay, Archivo, File 29, no. 27, delegation (Buenos Aires) to ministry, Jan. 8, 1937, p. 189.

[11] *Ibid.*, File 30, no. 154, delegation (Buenos Aires) to ministry, Aug. 22, 1937, p. 193. Petroleum engineer Emiliano Rebuelto reported to Ramírez that petroleum in the Paraguayan-held sectors of the western Chaco might be difficult to reach because the further away from the cordillera one went, the deeper it was necessary to drill for oil. The Bolivians held the highlands, and Paraguayans were on the plain.

[12] *Ibid.*, File 30, R-225, delegation (Buenos Aires) to ministry, Aug. 13, 1937, p. 27. Crémieux was to be paid 2,500 Argentine pesos for his work. Crémieux stated that he had worked for Standard Oil and thus knew where to look for petroleum near Machareti. The Franco government fell on August 16, 1937. Very probably Crémieux neither carried out his investigation nor received his stipend.

indeed hired French engineers to search for oil in the western Chaco. No doubt the North American diplomat made the proper expressions of grave concern, but for almost a month Braden had been aware of the final conclusion of the Compagnie Française des Pétroles oil investigation: no large petroleum deposits were to be found in the Paraguayan-held areas of the western Chaco.[13] On December 30, 1937, Braden had spoken with the Paraguayans, who still insisted that they must receive territorial compensation elsewhere if they were to give up their most advanced positions in the Chaco, because these positions abutted rich oil fields. On January 4, 1938, however, Braden was able to report that Paraguayan delegates at last were prepared to admit that if petroleum reserves existed to the east of the line of *hitos* they were "commercially unimportant."[14] Braden felt that progress was at last possible because the Paraguayans doubted that the western areas were really valuable.[15]

The shift in the Paraguayan attitude was of inestimable importance, for if the western Chaco did not contain the supposed oil wealth, the position intimated by Stefanich in December 1936 became tenable. Paraguay could retreat in the western Chaco, lose no petroleum, and still expect some kind of compensation. Bolivia never would have accepted a territorial agreement that failed to open the Villa Montes–Boyuibé road or allowed the Paraguayans to threaten the Camiri and adjacent oil fields. Asunción's willingness to withdraw in the western Chaco was then a key factor for a definitive settlement.

The tragedy of the situation is that these decisions were so long in coming. For several years three speculators, Berger and Bullock, in company with Hirsch, the Paraguayan consul in Amsterdam, had

[13] U.S., Archives, RG 59, Decimal File 724.34119/1158, no. 594, Braden (Buenos Aires) to Dept. State, Dec. 28, 1937, "Chaco Mediation: French Banks Investigate Paraguayan Economy," p. 3. The report also added that no further explorations could be made because the engineers' parent company (Compagnie Française des Pétroles) "did not wish to disturb the friendly relations existing with the Standard Oil Company in other parts of the world" (*ibid.*).

[14] *Ibid.*, Decimal File 724.34119/1169, no. 604, Braden (Buenos Aires) to Dept. State, Jan. 4, 1938, p. 2.

[15] The final report of the French engineers had probably been made known to the delegation by Asunción in early January (*ibid.*, Decimal File 724.34119/1172, no. 606, Braden [Buenos Aires] to Dept. State, Jan. 7, 1938, p. 2).

elaborated the legend that the western Chaco was a petroleum *el dorado*.[16] Both Berger, who doubled as head of the Paraguayan national petroleum service company, and Bullock had obtained oil exploration rights to large sectors of the Chaco. How much this trio's activities hindered Chaco negotiations cannot be estimated, but these prospective petroleum magnates did not initially inculcate a cupidity for "flowing gold" in the Paraguayan psyche. Likewise, neither should Paraguayan actions be judged out of the context of events. Both Brazil and Argentina were displaying inordinate interest in Bolivian oil properties, and their representatives sat among the supposedly disinterested Chaco mediators.

When the sound of gunfire ceased, Paraguay held two solid bargaining points: a host of Bolivian captives and control of the international road between Boyuibé and Villa Montes. Bolivia, at the other extreme, approached the peace table hat-in-hand. If La Paz were going to gain any advantages, some means of currying the favor of the mediating states had to be discovered. The first Bolivian attempt to employ a persuader failed miserably. Exceedingly disgruntled after five weeks of verbal combat in Buenos Aires, Tomás Elío prepared a scheme to obtain a favorable territorial settlement. Bolivian representatives presented President Gabriel Terra of Uruguay with a plan suggesting that his nation act as sole Chaco mediator and confidentially promote a settlement on the basis of the Ichazo-Benítez Convention of 1894.[17] For performing this service and, incidentally, for double-crossing the mediators in Buenos Aires, Uruguay would receive "all the petroleum that its refineries would need."[18] Such enticement failed to convince Montevideo that this Bolivian gambit might not prove

---

[16] *Ibid.*, Decimal File 724.34119/1172, no. 606, p. 2; and also Decimal File 724.34119/1158, no. 592, Braden (Buenos Aires) to Dept. State, Dec. 28, 1937, "Chaco Mediation: French Banks Investigate Paraguayan Economy," p. 2. Neither report states how long the partnership between Berger, Bullock, and Hirsch had been spreading propaganda, or whether its members were naturalized Paraguayans or aliens. No direct evidence exists that Hirsch was involved in territorial speculation.

[17] Paraguay, Archivo, File 4, no. 22, delegation (Buenos Aires) to ministry, Sept. 3, 1935, p. 1. See Map 1 for the territorial boundary drawn in the Ichazo-Benítez Convention of 1894.

[18] Paraguay, Archivo, File 4, no. 22, p. 1.

exceedingly imprudent. Through diplomatic channels Terra informed Gerónimo Zubizarreta of the Bolivian offer. The Paraguayan's reaction was decidedly unfavorable; thus ended Bolivia's first attempt to convert petroleum favors into territorial advantages.

Fortunately for La Paz, interest in Bolivian petroleum deposits had never died in certain quarters. With the end of the Chaco hostilities Argentina was again in a position to proceed with its persistent efforts to grasp control of Oriente petroleum. A special committee had been formed to study the economic problems of the Chaco; its report was completed in November 1935. Among the conclusions reached, that of the Argentine naval general staff is most incisive: "Today, we have to import, as has been stated many times, an enormous amount of oil for the people of the Republic. Today, we import from Mexico and Peru, countries distant and uncontrollable; tomorrow, we ought to replace that importation with the Bolivian product . . . with the intention not of ending the traffic [with Bolivia], but of counterbalancing in quality and quantity our oil properties and the increasing necessities of the future."[19] Concerning the general development of the Oriente, the bulky report concluded that "the Argentine communication routes are destined to develop the Bolivian Oriente, and absorb its commerce."[20]

The ascent of Enrique Finot to the Bolivian Foreign Office in September 1936 marked the initiation of a new round of territorial bargaining with petroleum as bait. The following month Saavedra Lamas dispatched Horacio Carrillo to the Altiplano where Finot and Saavedra Lamas' emissary discussed the possibility of Argentine petroleum operations in the Oriente.[21] In November 1936 the Bolivian govern-

[19] Argentina, Ministerio de Relaciones Exteriores y Culto, Archivo de Relaciones Exteriores, Buenos Aires, *La conferencia de paz del Chaco*, Box 20, no. 38, Estado Mayor General de Marina, "Consideraciones de orden legístico y estratégico que afectan la solución del conflicto boliviano-paraguayo." This report is a part of *Memorándum sobre informaciones y consideraciones relacionadas con los problemas inherentes a las vinculaciones exteriores de Bolivia*, November 1935, pp. 19–20. The final report of this commission was not found in the foreign office archive of any other nation, and apparently never was issued to the other mediators.

[20] *Ibid.*, *Memorándum sobre informaciones*, p. 22.

[21] U.S., Archives, RG 59, Decimal File 824.6363 ST 2/68, no. 60, Norweb (La Paz) to Dept. State, Sept. 19, 1936, pp. 1–2. Norweb knew of the Carrillo offer

ment and Standard Oil amicably settled a long-standing dispute concerning allegedly illegal oil shipments.[22] Suddenly the Toro government announced on December 21, 1936, the formation of a national petroleum company, Yacimientos Petrolíferos Fiscales Bolivianos (Bolivian National Oil Company). But where were the oil properties that the fledgling petroleum concern would utilize? On March 15, 1937, Standard Oil discovered that the government had expropriated its entire operation in Bolivia.[23] Foreign Minister Finot presented United States officials with an extremely plausible explanation of the exigencies that necessitated such drastic action: "It had been obvious from the beginning of the Chaco controversy that the United States would not take issue with the Argentine. Chile is altogether too weak to stop the Argentine, and Brazil is too absorbed with its internal dissensions to thwart Argentine imperialism. The only recourse left to defenseless Bolivia under the circumstances is to placate the Argentine by making available the Bolivian oil resources coveted."[24]

---

because Foreign Minister Finot had presented the information to the local manager of Standard Oil in La Paz: this man had informed Norweb. The initial payment to Standard Oil was to have been £300,000.

[22] Refer to Chapter 3 of this work for background of the dispute between Standard Oil and the Bolivian government. See also United States, Congress, Senate, *Hearings* before a Special Committee Investigating Petroleum Resources, American Petroleum Resources in Foreign Countries, Senate Resolution 36, 79th Cong., 1st sess., p. 248. In November 1936 President David Toro signed a decree authorizing the return to the company of a bond that had been posted as a guaranty. The Toro government certified that the company had complied with the obligations for which the money had been deposited.

[23] For a study of the reasons for the seizure, see Herbert S. Klein, "American Oil Companies in Latin America: The Bolivian Experience," *Inter-American Economic Affairs*, 18 (Autumn 1964), 47–72. For the Bolivian defense, see René Gutiérrez Guerra, "Bolivia and the Standard Oil Company," *Bolivia: A Survey of Bolivian Activities*, 7, no. 3 (March–April 1939), 20–37. In a letter dated March 29, 1960, Robert G. Caldwell, political affairs officer for the United States in Bolivia, 1937–1939, wrote to Professor Robert B. Davies. Professor Davies forwarded the letter to the author on July 15, 1966. In the letter, Caldwell charges that the real reasons for the seizure of Standard Oil properties by the Bolivian government were the bitterness of the Bolivians because Standard Oil had not helped Bolivia during the Chaco War with loans and military equipment and disappointment because oil operations in Bolivia seemed to be subordinated to those in other places, especially Venezuela.

[24] U.S., Archives, RG 59, Decimal File 824.6363 ST 2/135, no. 22, Conversation, Norweb with Bolivian Foreign Minister, Norweb (La Paz) to Dept. State, May

Argentine-Bolivian discussions recommenced in earnest; in April 1937 the prospective construction of the Yucuiba–Santa Cruz railway was announced. So certain did it appear that Argentina soon would obtain its desired ends that Standard Oil representatives began preliminary efforts to save their Bolivian properties in Buenos Aires rather than in La Paz.²⁵ Argentine success had one other significant result: it aroused the apprehensions of its traditional competitor. In haste Brazil now inaugurated bargaining sessions in La Paz regarding the construction of a Corumbá–Santa Cruz railway.

May through September 1937 were not productive months for Chaco peace talks, but on the Altiplano and elsewhere two ancient rivals fervently courted the Bolivians. In July 1937 José de Paula Rodrigues Alves, Brazilian conference delegate, personally sought from the Bolivian minister of mines and petroleum assurance that the Brazilian railway project would be accepted.²⁶ In August, after a special Bolivian commission had arrived in Buenos Aires to establish economic pacts, Bolivian conference delegate David Alvéstegui told Spruille Braden, "Argentina is, to all intents and purposes, formally committed now, and I don't think they [*sic*] will be able to withdraw."²⁷ Bolivian assurance meant Brazilian displeasure. Rodrigues

5, 1937, p. 4. Assistant Secretary Butler argued that "the general petroleum situation in Argentina, Brazil and Bolivia is involved and that the Chaco negotiations are a factor in the case" (*ibid.*, Decimal File 824.6363 ST 2/103, Memorandum, Butler to Duggan, Welles, Beaulac, and Feis, April 3, 1937, p. 1).

²⁵ *Ibid.*, Decimal File 824.6363 ST 2/93, no. 189, Norweb (La Paz) to Dept. State, Mar. 29, 1937, pp. 1–2. Fred Schultz, vice-president of Standard Oil of Argentina, had decided "after conversing with various officials and private individuals in La Paz" (*ibid.*, p. 1) to take his case to YPF and attempt to convince the Argentine officials that "it would be difficult for it [YPF] profitably to work the Bolivian fields as their potential production has been exaggerated" (*ibid.*, p. 2).

²⁶ *Ibid.*, Decimal File 724.34119/949, no. 464, Braden (Buenos Aires) to Dept. State, pp. 2–4. Braden arranged for confidential talks to be held between Rodrigues Alves; Baldivieso, new Bolivian minister of foreign relations; and Colonel Rivera, minister of mines and petroleum. Rodrigues Alves argued that an oil and railway agreement between Bolivia and Argentina was "handing all the petroleum wealth in southeastern Bolivia to Argentina" (*ibid.*, p. 4).

²⁷ *Ibid.*, Decimal File 724.34119/1008, no. 481, Braden (Buenos Aires) to Dept. State, Aug. 31, 1937, p. 3. Braden, in his "neutral" status, informed Alvéstegui that he thought the Brazilian route to be the better. Alvéstegui countered by stating that

Alves telegraphed Mario de Pimentel Brandão, Brazilian foreign minister, to tell him that Saavedra Lamas purposely was stalling the conference until the signature of rail and oil conventions would pull the Oriente into Argentine orbit. Brazilian efforts to influence Bolivia were increased, and in October a preliminary agreement for Brazilian construction of a railroad between Santa Cruz and Corumbá was signed. Horacio Carrillo and Saavedra Lamas had, however, already gained the upper hand in negotiations; on November 19, 1937, a railroad and petroleum traffic convention between Bolivia and Argentina was signed.[28] Brazil's only hope then lay in convincing the ruling junta of Colonel Germán Busch that a Brazilian treaty offered more advantages.

The agreements signed November 19, 1937, provided Saavedra Lamas with a new opportunity to bask in glory, but the Argentine foreign minister had achieved only a Pyrrhic victory. Part of the proposed Yacuiba–Santa Cruz railway would have to pass through

---

once the Argentine agreements were signed, Buenos Aires would be forced "to side with Bolivia and insist upon Paraguayan withdrawal eastward from their present positions in the Chaco" (*ibid.*).

[28] *Ibid.*, Decimal File 624.3531/27, no. 1821, Weddell (Buenos Aires) to Dept. State, Nov. 30, 1937, pp. 1-3. This treaty provided for the following activities.

1. Entry into, storage in, and transportation through Argentina of Bolivian petroleum would be permitted.

2. Bolivian petroleum in transit through Argentine territory would be subject to no taxes.

3. The Argentine government would control all reservoirs and tank cars used in connection with the transport of Bolivian petroleum.

4. Bolivian petroleum and by-products destined for Argentine or foreign markets would be transported exclusively on Argentine state railways.

5. 300,000 tons of petroleum would be imported annually into Argentina from Bolivia, but the oil must be sold to YPF. The proposed agreement caused new difficulties between Argentina and the United States (see *ibid.*, Decimal File 624.-3531/27, Memorandum, Welles conversation with Argentine Ambassador Espil, Nov. 27, 1937, pp. 1–2). The under-secretary of state pointed out that Argentina was contracting to ship and/or buy petroleum from a nation that as yet did not legally control the wells, the case still being under litigation. He manifested his certainty that Buenos Aires did not wish to commit an act the United States would consider unfriendly. Ambassador Espil maintained that the provisional treaty was a "desirable and useful arrangement" (*ibid.*, p. 4) and that "no immediate danger" existed because the treaty could not be ratified until the Argentine Congress met in February (*ibid.*).

territory then occupied by Paraguayan forces.[29] The latter's retreat could be obtained only if there were a Bolivian-Paraguayan territorial agreement in the western Chaco. Saavedra Lamas, convinced that a final treaty would not be agreed upon at the Peace Conference, told Major Carlos Mauriño, Argentine military attaché in La Paz, to approach Colonel Busch with a secret proposal to negotiate peace outside the conference framework; to his chagrin, Brazilian military intelligence learned of his plans and of the secret mission of Major Mauriño.[30] Saavedra Lamas then made another blunder. The Paraguayans had vigorously protested the November 1937 Argentine-Bolivian economic pacts. In an effort to soothe a suspicious Asunción, Saavedra Lamas began to negotiate a new Argentine-Paraguayan commercial treaty. But tactics of accommodation were not successful on this occasion; La Paz immediately registered indignation over Argentine dealings with Asunción.

Saavedra Lamas' position was badly undermined by events that occurred at the end of January 1938. Major Carlos Mauriño flew to Buenos Aires to report that Brazil and Bolivia were on the verge of signing an oil and railway agreement. Mauriño declared that Busch and a few others wanted a treaty with Buenos Aires, but that the majority of the ruling junta viewed the November 19, 1937, convention as a one-way ticket into the Argentine pocket.[31] Busch also had complained to Mauriño about the "coldness"[32] of Argentine policy toward Bolivia. Saavedra Lamas, experienced interpreter of diplomatic jargon, fully comprehended the Bolivian president's reference to climatic conditions: if Argentina wanted the recently signed rail and

---

[29] The Paraguayans soon realized this fact (see Paraguay, Archivo, File 39, no 27, delegation [Buenos Aires] to ministry, Dec. 10, 1937, p. 391).

[30] U.S., Archives, RG 59, Decimal File 724.34119/1114, no. 554, Braden (Buenos Aires) to Dept. State, Nov. 3, 1937, p. 2; see also Decimal File 724.34119/1139, no. 580, Braden (Buenos Aires) to Dept. State, Dec. 17, 1937, p. 2. The United States delegate reported the Mauriño mission in detail but does not explain how the Brazilians obtained their information.

[31] Paraguay, Archivo, File 39, no. 50 (*confidencial y reservado*), delegation (Buenos Aires) to ministry, Jan. 29, 1938, p. 324.

[32] *Ibid.*

petroleum conventions ratified, it must induce a Paraguayan retreat in the western Chaco.

The Argentine foreign minister braced for a final effort. On January 28, the Chaco mediators agreed to give Saavedra Lamas one week in which to conduct private negotiations between Paraguay and Bolivia. Horacio Carrillo was hastily dispatched to La Paz with new promises while the foreign minister dealt with Zubizarreta himself. Saavedra Lamas' final peace plan called for Paraguayan withdrawal from the Villa Montes–Boyuibé road and retreat far enough eastward to provide for the construction of a railroad route; compensatory territorial cession by Bolivia to Paraguay in the northern Chaco; and recess of the peace conference, thereby permitting Bolivia and Paraguay to settle their problems through mutual negotiation.[33]

Even before Carrillo departed for the Bolivian capital, Spruille Braden had been informed that the Busch government would not accept the scheme. Presented with Saavedra Lamas' proposals, Gerónimo Zubizarreta promptly rejected them, telegraphing Asunción, "we are going to express to Dr. Saavedra Lamas that our country will not accept the fragmentary method of defining the boundaries of our western territories and that it would be useless to work on a partial settlement of the question."[34]

Carlos Saavedra Lamas' failure to become Chaco peace master would also have decisive effects on Argentine prospects in the Oriente. On February 25, 1938, the Gutiérrez-Brandão railway treaty was signed,[35] giving Bolivia an opening to the Atlantic through Brazil and granting Rio de Janeiro potential entry to the Oriente petroleum region. The climax came on March 15, when the Bolivian government

[33] U.S., Archives, RG 59, Decimal File, 724.34119/1219, no. 634, Braden (Buenos Aires) to Dept. State, Feb. 8, 1938, pp. 1–3.

[34] Paraguay, Archivo, File 39, no. 50 (*confidencial y reservado*), Jan. 29, 1938, p. 325.

[35] Philip L. Green, "Bolivia at the Crossroads," *Bolivia: A Survey of Bolivian Activities*, 8, no. 3 (March–April 1941), 14–15. The agreement set the projected cost of the Corumbá–Santa Cruz line at £1,732,509. Brazil was to put up £1,000,000 unconditionally, for she owed Bolivia this sum (and more) according to the terms of the 1903 Treaty of Petrópolis.

ratified the treaty with Brazil but ignored the November 19, 1937, agreement signed in Buenos Aires. The possibility of Argentine monopoly in the Oriente was permanently destroyed, although La Paz would continue to need Argentine technical assistance in order to operate the former Standard Oil properties. Thinking of the future, Buenos Aires continued to supply the required help;[36] finally in June 1945, a treaty calling for an Argentine railroad into the Oriente was ratified by both countries.

The effect on the Chaco Peace Conference of the struggle between Brazil and Argentina for control of the Oriente should not be under-estimated. The experience of December 1935 had proved that united pressure exerted on Paraguay could make that state yield. The Brazilian-Bolivian agreement did not deny Argentina a share of Oriente petro-leum, but it did ease Brazilian fears of Argentine hegemony in the area. Paradoxically, therefore, the Argentine setback removed the grave obstacle that had cast a long shadow over Chaco negotiations. Add to these factors the departure of Saavedra Lamas as foreign minister, and the prospect of Brazilian and Argentine cooperation in a con-certed drive for Chaco settlement became real.

The Brazilian-Argentine Oriente rivalry heralded a race for elusive and costly goals. The expense of building a railroad to Santa Cruz was not great for Argentina, but the necessity of constructing branch lines and accessory highways eventually would have to be faced. Sec-ondly, there would be comparatively little local traffic because the Yacuiba–Santa Cruz route ran through sparsely settled country. Only

---

[36] U.S., Archives, RG 59, Decimal File 824.6363 ST-2/298, Attached memoran-dum to Briggs and Welles from Donovan, undated, 1939, p. 1. The Department of State had evidence that Bolivia was receiving aid from the Argentine YPF in the confiscated oil fields despite the fact that the final disposition of the Standard Oil–Bolivian litigation had yet to be made (the Bolivian Supreme Court did not render a final decision until March 8, 1939). Donovan suggested that Argentine actions were motivated by a desire to have Bolivia reconsider the 1937 rail and oil agree-ments. Donovan would appear correct. In an unsigned memorandum (Argentina, Archivo, Box 6, Expediente XII, "Asuntos Varios — 1938 — FOLIO," Sept. 21, 1938, p. 1) an unnamed agent was sent "to instruct the Legation in La Paz in order that it carry out discreet and confidential labor among the members of the [Bolivian] government . . . in the sense of saving Argentine interests . . . assuring the con-struction of our railroad from Yacuiba to Santa Cruz."

after millions of pesos had been spent on additional drilling and pipelines would oil exploitation become really profitable. The enthusiasm of Carrillo and Saavedra Lamas notwithstanding, where was Argentina to obtain the needed finance? Brazilian plans were no less visionary. The proposed Corumbá–Santa Cruz route ran six hundred kilometers across a veritable no man's land. The possibility of profit rested solely on the hope that "at some future date, arrangements will be made to secure at least part of the oil."[37] Assuming this opportunity presented itself, no one in Rio de Janeiro could reasonably predict when the funds necessary for exploitation would be available. In allowing Brazil, and eventually Argentina, access to the Oriente, Bolivia cleverly reaped internal development benefits and inadvertently helped to reinforce the balance of power among Latin America's leading nations.

Despite the baffling ambiguities of the protocol of June 12, 1935, the Neutral Military Commission, whose task it was to create a regimen of security in the Chaco, had announced on June 15, 1935, its intention of dividing the antagonists by creating a "zone of separation"[38] between them. On July 2, 1935, the armies had been declared "separated." In its October 18, 1935, report to the mediators, the commission had recommended that the zone of separation be continued and that an international police service be established to maintain the separation of the two armies. Bolivia had readily agreed with

[37] U.S., Archives, RG 59, Decimal File 824.6363 ST 2/177, no. 54, Scotten (Rio) to Dept. State, Sept. 30, 1937, p. 2. The Bolivian diplomat, Eduardo Diez de Medina (*De un siglo al otro*, p. 360), stated that a major reason Bolivia ratified a rail and petroleum pact with Brazil was that it hoped the latter nation would finance "petroleum exploitation on the Parapetí River." For a summary of petroleum activities in Bolivia and Paraguay since 1938, see Appendix VI.

In June 1945 a Bolivian-Argentine railroad agreement was finally ratified by both congresses. Construction of the 550-kilometer Yacuiba–Santa Cruz route was begun in 1945 and completed in 1949. The Brazilians initiated rail construction in 1948. In January 1955, the 625-kilometer Corumbá–Santa Cruz line was completed.

[38] Argentina, Ministerio de Relaciones Exteriores y Culto, *La conferencia de paz del Chaco 1935–1939*, pp. 81–121. The zone itself was as much as ten kilometers across in some places, and in its environs could be found Indian villages and three capped oil wells (*ibid.*, p. 143).

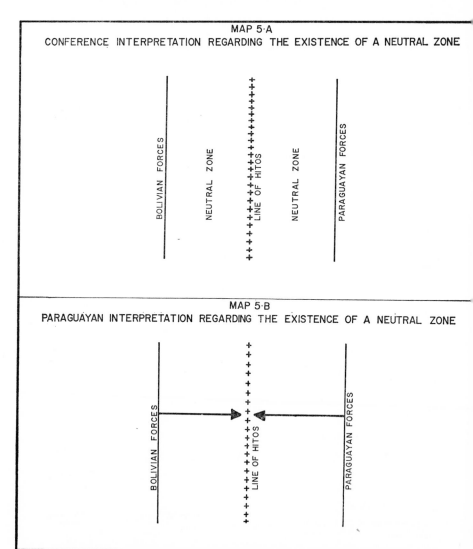

MAP 5·A
CONFERENCE INTERPRETATION REGARDING THE EXISTENCE OF A NEUTRAL ZONE

MAP 5·B
PARAGUAYAN INTERPRETATION REGARDING THE EXISTENCE OF A NEUTRAL ZONE

Article II, clauses a and d, of the protocol of June 12, 1935, speaks of "lines of separation" and of an "intermediate line" between them (the line of *hitos*). The conference maintained that military officers assigned by the conference exercised supreme authority in a neutral zone on either side of the line of *hitos* between the "lines of separation" (Map 5-A). Paraguayans, citing Article II, clauses a and c, asserted that there existed but one "line of separation"—the line of *hitos*. They maintained that they possessed unlimited authority right up to their side of this line (Map 5-B).

the suggestion, but the Paraguayans had balked. The Paraguayan decision was apparently prompted by a report from Paraguay's delegation in Buenos Aires,which argued that a sufficient number of police could not be recruited to prevent possible provocations by the Bolivians, that conflicts between the Paraguayan army and the special police force might occur, and that Paraguay and Bolivia would have to pay maintenance costs of the police force.[39] Citing the June 12 protocol, Paraguayan representatives informed the conference on November 2 that no zone of separation existed or could be created and that Paraguay would patrol all territory it held up to the one line of *hitos*. Uruguay replied by withdrawing on November 4 Colonel José Trabal, the one representative of the Neutral Military Commission still in the Chaco. Finally, as a result of Braden's direct negotiations with President Eusebio Ayala in December 1935, the Paraguayans grudgingly admitted the right of the conference to create a Chaco security system and police a neutral zone. After the protocol of January 21, 1936, was signed, two military observers again were dispatched to the area.[40]

A second aspect of Chaco military security then caused the conference unexpected and exasperating deadlock. Entrance to or exit from the Bolivian Oriente was primarily obtained by means of an international highway, built by Standard Oil, that linked Yacuiba, Argentina, with Santa Cruz, Bolivia. During the last days of Chaco hostilities, the section of this road between Villa Montes and Boyuibé had been interdicted by Paraguayan forces. The Neutral Commission had regulated traffic on the interdicted section, and following the departure of the commission, a mixed group of Bolivians and Paraguayans under Colonel José Trabal had continued this service.

[39] *Ibid.*, p. 308; United States, Department of State, *Papers Relating to the Foreign Relations of the United States, 1935*, V, 177. Gibson, United States plenipotentiary, declares that the Paraguayans agreed to the continuation of the zone of separation but then abruptly changed their position. However, in a special report to Asunción (Paraguay, Archivo, File 3, no. 50, Oct. 4, 1935, pp. 192–194), the Paraguayan delegation had concluded that "the protocol of June 12 does not create some neutral zone . . . [and] it [the zone] would be highly dangerous for our own rights" (*ibid.*, p. 197). See Map 5 for a graphic presentation of the conflicting interpretation of the neutral zone.

[40] U.S., Archives, RG 59, Decimal File 724.34119/424, no. 136, Braden (Buenos Aires) to Dept. State, Mar. 4, 1936, p. 1.

Unfortunately, after Trabal's departure on November 4, all conference security services in the Chaco lapsed, and both sides regained their original positions behind the line of *hitos*.[41] In effect, control of the international highway between Boyuibé and Villa Montes again reverted directly to Paraguay.

With the advent of the Franco government in February 1936, Paraguayan direction of traffic in the interdicted section became exceedingly irksome to the Bolivians; presumably, Asunción intended to use the road as a means of forcing Bolivian concessions in Buenos Aires. The condition of the road between Villa Montes and Boyuibé was allowed to deteriorate; meanwhile, Paraguayan harassment of truck convoys and passenger vehicles increased markedly between March and June 1936.[42] So incensed was the Bolivian army command that Major John Weeks, United States military observer in the Chaco, reported: "The present road control system molests the Bolivians so that it appears more important to most of them than the boundary question."[43] The conference intended to deal promptly with the question of Chaco security, but the February and May revolutions in Paraguay and Bolivia initially stalled matters. The outbreak of more provocative incidents along the Villa Montes–Boyuibé road spurred the mediators to action, and on August 5, 1936, they completed the "General Regimen of Rules for Military Observers Stationed in the Chaco Boreal."[44] This

[41] Argentina, Min. de Rel. Ext. y Culto, *Conferencia de paz*, pp. 118, 498–499. See Map 4 for a visual presentation of the Villa Montes–Boyuibé road situation.

[42] U.S., Archives, RG 59, Decimal File 724.34119/432, no. 143, Report 3 of Chaco Military Observers, Major Alves Bastos (Brazil), Braden (Buenos Aires) to Dept. State, Mar. 20, 1936, pp. 1–2. Bastos reported that "it [the road] has become almost impassable because of the lack of repairs. . . . The Paraguayans do not wish to keep it up because they say that the Bolivian trucks damage it." On May 21, 1936, the Paraguayans agreed to permit the Bolivians to repair the road (*ibid.*, Decimal File 724.34119/482, no. 184, Braden [Buenos Aires] to Dept. State, June 1, 1936, Enclosure 1, p. 1). On July 10, however, this permission was unexplainably withdrawn (*ibid.*, Decimal File 724.34119/539, no. 225, Braden [Buenos Aires] to Dept. State, July 27, 1936, Enclosure 1, p. 1).

[43] *Ibid.*, Decimal File 724.34119/508, no. 198, Braden (Buenos Aires) to Dept. State, June 23, 1936, Enclosure 1, p. 2.

[44] For a copy of the instructions, see United States, Department of State, *The Chaco Peace Conference*, Publication 1466, Conference Series 46, pp. 99–101.

security scheme recognized the existence of a neutral zone; since the Villa Montes–Boyuibé road passed through said zone, control of this artery therefore would revert to the conference. Revelation of these new rules to Juan Isidro Ramírez, Zubizarreta's replacement as president of the delegation under the Febrerista regime, kindled his immediate opposition. The Paraguayan diplomat feared that the mediators might attempt to tie payment for repatriated prisoners to Paraguayan acceptance of the new security scheme. On August 12 Ramírez reported to Foreign Minister Juan Stefanich that he was unalterably opposed to the August 5 regimen: "Neither personally nor as President of the delegation have I accepted even in principle, the plan by which it [the conference] reassumes the vigilance, control and execution of duties in the Neutral Zone."[45] The following day Ramírez sought out Saavedra Lamas and told the Argentine foreign minister it was not possible for the Paraguayan government to abandon the Villa Montes–Boyuibé road. Saavedra Lamas apparently found Ramírez's arguments convincing, for two days later the Paraguayan cabled Asunción that the payment of 2,400,000 Argentine pesos for prisoner maintenance would not be made dependent upon Paraguayan acceptance of the August 5 rules.

On August 20 the conference voted "to reassume the police and supervisory functions which pertain to it within the lines of separation of the armies drawn by the Neutral Military Commission, and which are accorded it by the protocol."[46] The same day Ramírez affirmed his recognition of the neutral zone. Later he told the mediators:

Paraguay once again, manifests its complete adherence to the peace formulas, and promises to collaborate effectively with the Conference of Peace in all matters having to do with the administration and control of the lines of separation of the armies. . . . There is on our part . . . absolutely no intransigency, nor any act that is even remotely able to indicate hostility or a hindrance to the beneficial action of the Conference of Peace for maintaining the lines of separation of both armies. We ourselves understand that

---

[45] Paraguay, Archivo, File 35, no. 27, delegation (Buenos Aires) to ministry, Aug. 12, 1936, p. 380.

[46] U.S., Dept. of State, *Chaco Peace Conference*, p. 105.

the Conference of Peace not only has the right of guarding and controlling, but also it is an obligation which it ought to execute.[47]

Did the Febreristas intend to respect the August 20 resolution or did they merely wish to forestall the mediators' wrath until they had collected the prisoner repatriation payment on August 25? It is certain only that Asunción's acquiescence would have meant surrender of the Villa Montes–Boyuibé road, a step that could easily have had serious internal repercussions.[48] The memorandum, presented to the mediators by Juan Isidro Ramírez on September 11, 1936, should be viewed in this light.

The Paraguayan Delegation does not admit under any circumstances, the existence of a neutral zone between the positions of the two armies. . . .

The Paraguayan Delegation does not accept nor give its consent to the "General Instructions for the Military Observers Stationed in the Chaco Boreal," which the Conference of Peace communicated to the Delegation with the date of August 5. . . .

The Paraguayan Delegation does not admit any necessity of a system of police and the control of the line of separation between the two armies. . . .

The Paraguayan Delegation does not accept even in principle that the Conference of Peace can itself assume the power of control of the road called International in the section occupied by the Paraguayan Army.[49]

[47] Paraguay, Archivo, File 22, Acta no. 72, Sesión Ejecutiva Comisión, Aug. 20, 1935, pp. 146–147. It is to be noted that on two occasions in this speech Ramírez recognizes the existence of "lines of separation." On August 19, 1936, Eugenio Martínez Thédy of Uruguay asked Ramírez whether Paraguay recognized the lines of separation; Ramírez replied in the affirmative (U.S., Archives, RG 59, Decimal File 724.34119/1021, no. 486, Minutes of Conference Meeting 69, Aug. 17, 1936, pp. 21–22). The Argentine-controlled secretariat did not release these minutes until September 15, 1937—twelve days before Ramírez was replaced.

[48] In his book Juan Isidro Ramírez (*La paz del Chaco: En defensa de la línea de hitos*, p. 50–58) states that rather than surrender the Villa Montes–Boyuibé road, the Franco government was prepared to refuse prisoner payment.

[49] Argentina, Min. de Rel. Ext. y Culto, *Conferencia de paz*, pp. 318–320. This memorandum was not made public until the conference ended in January 1939. In a special letter dated November 25, 1965, Dr. Juan Isidro Ramírez answered a series of questions presented to him by this author on October 15, 1965, in Asunción, Paraguay. Dr. Ramírez maintained that Paraguay was disposed to relinquish its control of the Villa Montes–Boyuibé road, but only if it received equitable compen-

This defiant statement, which reverted to the earlier Paraguayan stand, was followed by assurances from the president of the Paraguayan delegation that henceforth the conference could expect to receive Asunción's "loyal collaboration."[50]

Had the mediators accepted the Paraguayan challenge, the conference might have collapsed immediately. The mediators expeditiously moved to keep the Paraguayan reply confidential, but information about it somehow was leaked to the press. The full shock of the Paraguayan rejection was felt not only in Buenos Aires but also in La Paz. The Bolivian government never had been happy about either the number of prisoners repatriated or the emaciated condition of many of them. However, the Toro government had tempered its protests because it expected the conference to assume control of the Villa Montes–Boyuibé sector of the international road. Since Asunción decided otherwise and the 2,400,000 pesos had been turned over on August 25, Bolivia obviously had been duped again. A scapegoat was necessary, and on October 1, 1936, Tomás Elío resigned his position.[51]

The mediators made strenuous efforts to sway the Paraguayans, but Ramírez and his assistants could not be moved. When several conferees stated that Ramírez had verbally agreed to conference control of the neutral zone, the Paraguayan blandly retorted that he had whispered his objection to Isidoro Ruiz Moreno, a statement the Ar-

---

sation. Ramírez insisted that the August 5 regimen offered advantages only to Bolivia. The position taken by Ramírez in November 1965 contradicts much of the material listed in the Paraguayan archives, File 35, and in the United States State Department account of the conference (*Chaco Peace Conference*). The contradictory narratives make it clear that the Villa Montes–Boyuibé road had become an issue of internal political and psychological significance.

[50] Argentina, Min. de Rel. Ext. y Culto, *Conferencia de paz*, p. 320.

[51] Bolivian historians, Roberto Querejazu Calvo (*Masamaclay*, p. 464) and Miguel Mercado Moreira (*Historia diplomática de la guerra del Chaco*, p. 249) insist that Tomás Elío agreed to the release of the 2,400,000 pesos payment to Paraguay only because the conference mediators had informed him that if he did so, the August 5, 1936, regimen would go into effect. Calvo (p. 464) further insists that Elío had definite orders not to release the funds until he had received assurances that the August 5, 1936, plan had been accepted by Paraguay. The new Bolivian foreign minister, Enrique Finot, was an old rival of Elío's, and thus had no qualms about sacking him.

gentine delegate would neither affirm nor deny.[52] In a desperate effort to regain both prestige and room for diplomatic maneuver, the conference took two steps: on October 15 a stiff note was dispatched to Asunción reiterating conference prerogatives, and a joint Paraguayan-Bolivian military commission was proposed to draft a new regimen of Chaco security. Febrerista success in defying the conference gave rise to new insolence. On October 26 Asunción rejected the October 15 note and lectured the mediators on what matters the proposed commission might consider. The conferees passed over this new Paraguayan missive and warned that unless Asunción named representatives to the proposed commission by November 2 that body would be constituted without them. Paraguayan disinclination to reply forced the mediators' hand. On November 3 the Special Military Commission, to be presided over by Argentine General Martínez Pita, was established and charged with "the drafting of regulations of [for] the functions of vigilance and control referred to in the protocol of June 12, 1935 and January 21, 1936."[53]

The mediators had chosen to make a stand, but Asunción still held the leverage. No Chaco security scheme could be effected without Paraguayan consent, and the mediators were unprepared to force the issue. On November 25 Saavedra Lamas returned from his European vacation. With the Inter-American Conference for the Maintenance of Peace scheduled to open on December 1, the Argentine foreign minister decided that further security negotiations should be temporarily postponed. Exhausted and frustrated, the mediators did as they were bid and strove to regain their composure.

The struggle over the organization of a Chaco security system seemed destined to deadlock the conference. Wishing to avoid a collapse of negotiations, the mediators feverishly sought a means to

[52] U.S., Archives, RG 59, Decimal File 724.34119/627, no. 266, Braden (Buenos Aires) to Dept. State, Sept. 18, 1936, p. 2.

[53] *Ibid.*, Decimal File 724.34119/700, no. 315, Braden (Buenos Aires) to Dept. State, Nov. 3, 1936, Enclosure 2, p. 4. For Special Military Commission membership, see Appendix III.

Unknown to the mediators, Stefanich had ordered Ramírez (October 31, 1936) to take no part in the formulation of commission activities (Paraguay, Archivo, File 28, no. 87, ministry to delegation [Buenos Aires], Oct. 31, 1936, p. 116).

recover room for diplomatic maneuver. As early as October 3, 1936, Ramírez had informed Braden that if the September 11 memorandum did not become a paramount issue, the international road question might be "worked out satisfactorily."[54] On October 9 Ramírez stated Paraguay's intention of establishing, in cooperation with the conference, a system of control on the Villa Montes–Boyuibé road, as long as the system created "would not injure her [Paraguay's] rights."[55] As Asunción seemed disposed to adopt a more conciliatory attitude, the mediators regained maneuvering room by gradually acceding to Paraguayan wishes. On November 8 José de Paula Rodrigues Alves, acting conference president, privately informed Ramírez that the Paraguayan thesis regarding the neutral zone would be accepted.[56] When the commission was named on November 9, neither Paraguayan nor Bolivian officers were placed on its roster. It was from an unexpected source, however, that Asunción received additional satisfaction. On November 14 General Martínez Pita informed Ramírez that Paraguay possessed an excellent watchdog. Ramírez informed his capital that "he [Martínez Pita] told me that we could be sure of his pro-Paraguayan sympathies, and that he, as a soldier, will not consent that the favored position reached by the Paraguayan Army be abandoned."[57] With an ally heading the Special Military Commission, Asunción had nothing to fear.

Chaco conference business was delayed while meetings of the Inter-American Conference for the Maintenance of Peace were in progress, but by December 25, the Chaco mediators had resumed discussions. A resolution calling for a deadline on future territorial negotiations was passed. The foreign ministers of Paraguay and Bolivia had remained in Buenos Aires after the Inter-American Conference for the Maintenance of Peace ended, and their presence made possible rapid

[54] U.S., Archives, RG 59, Decimal File 724.34119/641, no. 206, Braden (Buenos Aires) to Dept. State, Nov. 3, 1936, p. 3.
[55] *Ibid.*, Decimal File 724.34119/673, no. 298, Braden (Buenos Aires) to Dept. State, Oct. 15, 1936, p. 13.
[56] Paraguay, Archivo, File 25, no. 124, delegation (Buenos Aires) to ministry, Nov. 9, 1936, p. 490.
[57] *Ibid.*, File 28, no. 199, delegation (Buenos Aires) to ministry, Nov. 14, 1936, p. 182.

progress on the security issue. When at a December 28 conference meeting Juan Stefanich commented that the road question would be settled and that he could not understand the conferees' lack of faith in Paraguayan promises, Brazilian and Peruvian delegates immediately took up the challenge. Rodrigues Alves suggested that Paraguay might allay the mediators' suspicions by agreeing to transit rules for the international road and remarked: "The Foreign Minister of Paraguay knows the Conference does not control . . . that road. I am unable to share the optimism of the Foreign Minister of Paraguay because I believe that the situation concerning the road causes the conference a great deal of uneasiness."[58] Stefanich replied that he was prepared to consider a regimen of transit rules, and on December 31 Martínez Pita produced a commission report on Chaco security. The general assured the mediators that "the Conference need no longer be concerned with the road question or the other security measures provided for in the protocols."[59] Commission proposals for Chaco security called for a mixed force of Paraguayan and Bolivian police to ensure security, prohibition of military instruction or discharge of weapons near the line of *hitos*, mutual recognition of the line of *hitos* as the boundary between Paraguay and Bolivia until the signature of a definitive peace treaty, and reciprocal use of the international road between Casa Alta, Boyuibé, Villa Montes, and Tartagal.[60] Juan Isidro Ramírez announced himself favorably disposed toward these recommendations and Martínez Pita appeared confident that the proposals would be accepted, but the pro-Paraguayan nature of the report raised demands for further revisions. Not until January 4, 1937, did the mediators declare themselves satisfied with the formula covering transit on the international road. Stefanich approved it, but the Bolivian representatives now manifested the conviction that intransigency paid dividends. When Saavedra Lamas demanded Bolivian submission, only rapid maneuvering by Spruille Braden and Rodrigues Alves prevented an open break. Finally, on January 9 Bolivia and Paraguay

---

[58] *Ibid.*, File 23, Acta no. 108, Dec. 28, 1936, p. 84.
[59] *Ibid.*, File 33, no. 111-98, delegation (Buenos Aires) to ministry, Dec. 31, 1936, pp. 519–520.
[60] *Ibid.*, p. 520.

accepted the conference formula. The agreement was to be kept secret, but unquestionably it was intended to bring a halt to Paraguayan harassment on the section of the international road controlled by Paraguay.[61]

The major points of the January 9, 1937, formula called for: (1) free commercial transit on the road that unites Boyuibé with Villa Montes "in such a way as to eliminate delays in the inspection of vehicles and persons where deemed necessary"; (2) absolute prohibition of the transit of troops and war materials except unarmed relieving troops; (3) slight withdrawal of Bolivian and Paraguayan troops in the immediate vicinity of the road "to be the subject of a later study by the commands and the governments"; (4) expense for the maintenance of the Villa Montes–Boyuibé road to be paid by Bolivia; and (5) supervision of the road traffic by conference military observers, who would be responsible for providing road travel permits.[62] Their efforts a success, the mediators now were overwhelmingly convinced of the necessity for rest and recuperation. On January 14, 1937, Braden informed Washington that "such alterations as the Bolivian Government desires may be taken care of in the detailed regulations which are in the process of drafting by the Special Military Commission."[63]

But Braden had not bargained for the unexpected. On January 4

[61] Ramírez of Paraguay refused to sign either the January 4 or January 9 agreement, but he apparently was overruled by Stefanich (U.S., Archives, RG 59, Decimal File 724.34119/747, no. 352, Braden [Buenos Aires] to Dept. State, Jan. 14, 1937, p. 3). No information regarding the January 9, 1937, agreement was made public until April 30, 1937 (*ibid.*, Decimal File 724.34119/954, no. 415, Braden [Buenos Aires] to Dept. State, April 30, 1937, p. 2).

[62] For the full text of the agreement of January 9, 1937, see U.S., Dept. of State, *Chaco Peace Conference*, pp. 106–107. "The bases" are admittedly vague, but any attempt to make them more explicit might have meant no agreement whatsoever.

[63] As written, Article I did not guarantee exclusive free transit to the Bolivians. On January 14, Alvéstegui of Bolivia received assurances from the mediators that "transit" (passage through the occupied zone from one Bolivian point to another), and not "traffic" (passage from a Paraguayan point into Bolivian areas with a return to a starting point in Paraguayan-held territory) was permitted by the agreement of January 9, 1937 (U.S., Archives, RG 59, Decimal File 724.34119/755, no. 358, Jan. 22, 1937, "Chaco Mediation: Bolivian Attitude toward Bases for Regulation of January 9," p. 4).

Martínez Pita told him that the commission would confer with both field commanders and work out all difficulties in one month's time.[64] On January 16 Pita informed Braden that constructing a system of regulations would take five to six weeks.[65] Between February 4 and March 1, however, the commission held no meetings and at a March 2 meeting, Braden hinted that the commission was guilty of unwarranted procrastination and flatly declared that Washington had instructed him to complete the drafting of regulations as soon as possible. Martínez Pita interpreted Braden's remarks as an accusation of negligence and immediately resigned as head of the commission. Later Braden announced that he had intended no insult but that perhaps his poor Spanish had resulted in some misunderstanding.[66]

On April 19 a draft of rules proposed by the commission was laid before the mediators. Saavedra Lamas curtly announced that said regulations would have to be accepted without change. Braden, Rodrigues Alves, and Nieto del Río remained unconvinced. Working with David Alvéstegui throughout the night of April 22, they virtually rewrote the draft of April 19. A collision followed on April 23. Saavedra Lamas was furious and challenged the new draft, but Braden, Rodrigues Alves, and Nieto del Río stood firm.[67] When the final vote was taken only the Uruguayans sided with Argentina, and Braden noted that "Lamas became purple with rage and emphatically declared the Paraguayans would pre-emptorily reject the regulations."[68]

Earlier, in Asunción, and as recently as April 19,[69] at the conference, Paraguay had sought the inclusion of a statement to guarantee both reciprocity of transit rights on the international road and recognition of its unilateral right to terminate Bolivian transit privileges in

[64] *Ibid.*, Decimal File 724.34119/830, no. 400, Braden (Buenos Aires) to Dept. State, Jan. 13, 1937, p. 7.

[65] *Ibid.*, Decimal File 724.34119/743, no. 9, Braden (Buenos Aires) to Dept. State, Jan. 16, 1937, pp. 2–3.

[66] *Ibid.*, Decimal File 724.34119/842, no. 407, minutes of March 2, 115, Braden (Buenos Aires) to Dept. State, April 20, 1937, pp. 16–22.

[67] *Ibid.*, Decimal File 724.34119/850, no. 412, Braden (Buenos Aires) to Dept. State, April 26, 1937, pp. 2–6.

[68] *Ibid.*, p. 9.

[69] Paraguay, Archivo, File 29, no. 128, delegation (Buenos Aires) to ministry, April 30, 1937, p. 42.

case of emergency.[70] The regulations of April 23 fulfilled neither of these goals and Ramírez reported, "in general, it cannot be denied that the resolution [April 23, 1937] is in keeping with the January 9, 1937, agreement."[71] Despite this admission Ramírez was adamantly opposed to the April 23 regulations because they did not guarantee Paraguayan territorial control up to the line of *hitos*. When Paraguay did consent to the new rules on May 7, Ramírez deposited a note with the conference secretariat stating that "in case of eventualities which endanger its security or its internal and external peace, the right is granted to denounce or to bring to an end the facilities granted for free transit."[72] Stefanich had informed the delegation that he considered this right to close the road in case of danger a "reserva" (reservation), and in his note of May 7, Ramírez described this right as irrevocable.[73] On May 15 the mediators unconditionally rejected this Paraguayan reservation. Asunción appeared to concede by sanctioning the April 23 regimen on May 18—or so the mediators thought.[74]

Three days later, an article by Enrique Finot appeared in *La Nación*, a prominent Argentine newspaper; Finot asserted that the January 9 accord and the April 23 rules established a neutral zone in the Chaco.[75] Whatever concessions Paraguay may have made on May 18

[70] U.S., Archives, RG 59, Decimal File 724.34119/835, no. 405, Braden (Buenos Aires) to Dept. State, April 18, 1937, p. 3.

[71] Paraguay, Archivo, File 29, no. 128, delegation (Buenos Aires) to ministry, April 30, 1937, p. 42.

[72] *Ibid.*, File 28, no. 62, ministry to delegation (Buenos Aires), May 1, 1937, p. 325.

[73] *Ibid.*, File 21, C-11, Ramírez to Saavedra Lamas, May 7, 1937, p. 127.

[74] Braden reports that Paraguay "unqualifiedly" accepted the regulation (U.S., Archives, RG 59, Decimal File 724.34119/766, no. 69, Braden [Buenos Aires] to Dept. State, May 22, 1937, p. 1). This does not seem to be the case (Argentina, Min. de Rel. Ext. y Culto, *Conferencia de la paz*, p. 582). Paraguay accepted the April 23 plan but with "the understanding that it [plan] does not alter the provisions of the existing protocols and the assurance that it will be strictly applied in accordance with same, as this Delegation has invariably advocated." Such an acceptance could hardly be unqualified.

[75] Paraguay, Archivo, File 34, NR-13, 2PR-6172, 589/587, May 23, 1937, pp. 288–289. Finot's claims were vehemently denied by the shaky Febrerista government. On May 30 Finot claimed in *La Prensa*, another Buenos Aires paper, that statements attributed to him concerning a neutral zone in the Chaco were "inexact"

were swiftly subjected to reconsideration. Stefanich was angry in his denunciations of Finot; speaking in Asunción on June 6, the foreign minister presented an extremely controversial interpretation of the April 23 regimen. The conference replied indirectly by starting negotiations of the territorial question and reasserting its Chaco security prerogatives. Nonplussed, Stefanich forwarded a blistering retort: the April 23, 1937, regulations established "reciprocal" commercial transit regulations; the January 9 agreement was unilaterally revocable; and negotiation of the territorial question could not begin until diplomatic relations had been reestablished between the former belligerents.[76] Although received on June 8, this document was not submitted to the mediators until June 10.

Asunción's mood plainly indicated that a test of strength was in the offing. By mysterious means Ramírez learned that Colonel Trabal of Uruguay and Captain Vacca of Argentina were headed for the Chaco to put the April 23 regulations into operation.[77] On June 18 Saavedra Lamas informed both La Paz and Asunción of the conference's intentions. Stefanich's denunciation was prompt and vigorous: Paraguay could not allow the regulations to become effective until certain "necessary explanations"[78] had been received. On June 19

(*ibid.*, File 34, no. 36, delegation [Buenos Aires] to ministry, May 31, 1937, p. 113).

[76] *Ibid.*, File 34, "Comunicado de la Delegación Paraguaya publicada el 8 junio de 1937," pp. 9–13.

[77] *Ibid.*, File 34, no. 46, delegation (Buenos Aires) to ministry, June 14, 1937, p. 46. Ramírez telegraphed Stefanich that "extra-legally, I am informed that Wednesday, the 16th, Colonel Trabal and Captain Vacca are embarking for Villa Montes for the purpose of putting into operation the April 23 regulations." Ramírez quizzed Raúl Araya, secretary of the Argentine delegation, about the Trabal-Vacca trip. He was informed that the two officers were going to the Chaco only to deliver items urgently needed by the military observers then on duty. On June 16 Ramírez quizzed Trabal and received the same answer. The same day Ramírez departed from Buenos Aires for Asunción (*ibid.*, File 30, R-188, 189, 190, delegation [Buenos Aires] to ministry, June 15 and 16, 1937, pp. 101–106).

In a letter to this writer dated April 4, 1966, Spruille Braden made the following comment about Ramírez's means of obtaining information: "I do not know how Ramírez got his information, but his getting it was par for the course when all delegates and secretaries were pledged to secrecy."

[78] Paraguay, Archivo, File 34, 45/49/40—484, Stefanich to Saavedra Lamas, June 19, 1937, p. 275.

Stefanich followed this telegram with another demanding that the justice of the Paraguayan position on the road question be accepted by the conference.[79] When, on June 21, Colonel Trabal tried to find the Paraguayan regional commander to inform him of his mission, he encountered not only Colonel Ramón Paredes but also Juan Isidro Ramírez. In a heated discussion the Paraguayan diplomat rejected any attempt to enforce the April 23 regimen until the conference provided Paraguay with reciprocity of transit.[80] On July 10, 1937, Ramírez presented a fifty-page brief to the conference. In it he denied that the January 9, 1937, agreement had ever granted free transit on the Villa Montes–Boyuibé Road exclusively to Bolivia.[81] The conference reacted on July 12 by passing a new resolution that reaffirmed its right to create and enforce a Chaco security system. On August 2 Spruille Braden formally replied to the contentions of Ramírez. The North American delegate argued that in the discussions of April 17, 1937, Ramírez had admitted that the transit rules were originated to cover the Paraguayan-held sector of the road; furthermore, reciprocity had not been intended because Bolivia was being charged with exclusive maintenance of the road; finally, transit rights were useless to the Paraguayans because they were prohibited from remaining overnight at either Villa Montes or Boyuibé.[82] Neither the July 12 resolution nor Braden's rebuttal caused much alarm in Asunción; as long as the conference made no new attempt to execute the April 23 rules, Paraguay could withstand the mediators' castigation.

The Liberal Party's return to power in Paraguay in August 1937 caused the conference to mark time with busy work, but a new incident brought the security problem back into prominence. On September

---

[79] *Ibid.*, no. 75, ministry to delegation (Buenos Aires), June 21, 1937, p. 330.

[80] In a letter to this writer, November 25, 1965, Juan Isidro Ramírez related his recollection of the event: "The Neutral Military Commission [Trabal and Vacca], without informing my delegation, wanted to surprise the Paraguayan command in the Chaco. . . . Happily, I was in the Chaco at the time, but the Neutral Military Commission was ignoring my presence in the Chaco. Then they confronted me, and I showed them that they had no right to proceed as they had done, and that I would bring up the question in the Conference."

[81] Argentina, Min. de Rel. Ext. y Culto, *Conferencia de paz*, pp. 594–655.

[82] *Ibid.*, pp. 651–655.

10 two Chaco military observers were arrested near Puesto Casal by a Paraguayan patrol.[83] Prompt apologies were forthcoming, but the mediators' wrath was not so easily appeased. On September 16 the conference passed still another resolution in an attempt to put the April 23 regulations into effect. Eleven days later the Paraguayan delegation sought a temporary stay in the execution of the September 16 resolution.[84] The final confrontation came on October 5. Chaco military observers, on orders from the conference, visited the regional Paraguayan commander and sought his consent to begin operations under the April 23, 1937, regimen. They received a curt refusal, and the April rules joined their August 5, 1936, counterpart in the limbo of discarded regulations.

On September 27, 1937, the old Paraguayan delegation headed by Juan Isidro Ramírez and including Juan José Soler and Marco Laconich resigned. A Liberal delegation under the direction of Gerónimo Zubizarreta arrived in Buenos Aires on October 11, 1937.[85] Nine days later they introduced a new intransigency into the proceedings: the January 9, 1937, agreement had not been ratified by the national Congress and therefore was unconstitutional. In effect, even had the Febreristas accepted the April 23 regulations, the Liberal regime could not be bound by them. However, Gerónimo Zubizarreta did not come to Buenos Aires empty-handed. On November 10 he unveiled a new

---

[83] U.S., Archives, RG 59, Decimal File 724.34119/1009, no. 173, Braden (Buenos Aires) to Dept. State, Sept. 11, 1937, pp. 1–2. The military observers, Major Vedia (Uruguay) and Colonel Lisboa (Chile), were taken into custody despite the fact they had documents proving their identity. Paraguayan military forces held them nearly five hours. Further difficulties subsequently developed. Martínez Pita announced that the two military observers were arrested east of the line of *hitos*, therefore in Paraguayan territory. Major Weeks (U.S.A.) and Colonel Lisboa both insisted that Puesto Casal was west of the line of *hitos* and in Bolivian territory (*ibid.*, Decimal File 724.34119/1127, no. 567, Braden [Buenos Aires] to Dept. State, Nov. 19, 1937, p. 3).

[84] The Paraguayan delegation previously had telegraphed Asunción and advised the government "to close transit" on the Villa Montes–Boyuibé road (Paraguay, Archivo, File 34, no. 87, delegation [Buenos Aires] to ministry, Sept. 17, 1937, p. 152).

[85] *Ibid.*, File 32, C-45, Ramírez to Saavedra Lamas, Oct. 1, 1937, p. 1. The old delegation eventually passed into exile. Higinio Arbo and Efraím Cardozo were the other replacements.

proposal establishing a *modus vivendi* in the Chaco. His document of ten articles provided for mutual disarmament and the continuation of the status quo in the Chaco; inexplicably, it said nothing about transit on the Villa Montes–Boyuibé road.[86] The Paraguayan diplomat originally held high hopes for his security scheme, but two weeks ensued before the mediators passed it on to La Paz. As Paraguay had twice rejected security formulas accepted by Bolivia, the Bolivian reaction was predictable. On January 24, 1938, the Busch government's rejection of the plan was received in Buenos Aires. Bolivian displeasure had not been unforeseen, and by the time La Paz indicated its dissent the mediators were entirely engrossed in the territorial question. Rather belatedly, it had been tacitly admitted that further discussion of the security question could not possibly yield favorable results.

In a special memorandum dated September 14, 1936, United States Assistant Secretary of State George Butler commented, "it is difficult to understand on what possible basis Paraguay can claim that it does not recognize a neutral zone."[87] Mr. Butler's puzzlement is hard to understand. As Juan Isidro Ramírez later admitted to Saavedra Lamas, the conference possessed the right to create a Chaco security system; what the Paraguayans wished to avoid was "the effect of the execution of that right."[88] Paraguay had just received 2,400,000 pesos; acceptance of either the August 5, 1936, or April 23, 1937, regimen would produce accusations from Liberal Party partisans that the Febreristas were peddling national territory for pecuniary advantages. The interdiction of the international road was seen in Asunción as a means of prying concessions from Bolivia. Under these circumstances the Franco

---

[86] For a copy of the proposal see U.S., Dept. of State, *Chaco Peace Conference*, pp. 123–124.

[87] U.S., Archives, RG 59, Decimal File 724.34119/612, Memorandum, G. Butler (Division of Latin American Affairs) to Beaulac, Sept. 14, 1936, p. 3.

[88] Paraguay, Archivo, File 28, no. 227, Ramírez to Carlos Saavedra Lamas, Dec. 8, 1936, pp. 257–258. Ramírez stated that "Paraguay had never denied that the conference had the right to maintain and control the lines of separation of the armies." Compare this statement made in private to Saavedra Lamas with the Paraguayan declaration of September 11, 1936.

government could fabricate the bases necessary to ignore a neutral zone until the Bolivians produced the necessary *quid pro quo*.

But why, if Paraguay viewed its Villa Montes–Boyuibé road position as a lever, did that nation accept the January 9, 1937, pact? Only months later did the mediators discover the truth: General Martínez Pita had promised the Paraguayans reciprocity on the international road and other advantages.[89] But Martínez Pita did not meet his commitment, and thus the Febrerista government was forced to demand reciprocity. Asunción's insistent demand made little economic sense; yet it was an excellent ploy for internal consumption and a guaranteed means of bedeviling Bolivians. The ultimate acceptance of conference security measures by the Franco government thus was unlikely from the start.

The Bolivian role in destroying any possibility of a workable security plan is less obvious. Until September 1936 La Paz counted upon the conference's terminating Paraguayan interdiction of the international road. After the disaster of September 11, 1936, the Bolivians instituted a new policy designed to solve the problem independently. When in November 1937 Zubizarreta presented his Chaco security plan, conditions had changed perceptibly. Two months before Bolivia had completed a cutoff route that nullified the importance of the Paraguayan-held section between Villa Montes and Boyuibé.[90] Realizing that the stranglehold had been broken, Zubizarreta was prepared to make a concession. His November 10 plan was vague, but privately he informed the mediators that "every liberty of transit will be given [to the Bolivians] over the Villa Montes–Boyuibé road."[91] When

---

[89] U.S., Archives, RG 59, Decimal File 724.34119/1075, no. 531, Attached Memorandum, Braden (Buenos Aires) to Dept. State, Oct. 13, 1937, p. 1. Braden's denunciations of Martínez Pita knew no bounds: "General Martínez Pita's inexcusable remissness thus is responsible for the months which have been wasted on this question." The unanswered question is whether Martínez Pita made the promises on his own or whether his actions had the sanction of Saavedra Lamas. In a letter dated April 9, 1966, this writer asked Mr. Braden's opinion. On April 14, 1966, Braden replied, "undoubtedly the General acted in collusion with Saavedra Lamas."

[90] U.S., Archives, RG 59, Decimal File 724.34119/1014, no. 493, Braden (Buenos Aires) to Dept. State, Sept. 9, 1937, p. 3.

[91] U.S., Dept. of State, *Foreign Relations, 1937*, V, 43. Zubizarreta did not dis-

these factors are considered, La Paz's reaction to the Paraguayan plan provides crucial insight into Bolivia's overall policy. In its January 24, 1938, message of rejection La Paz demanded that the April 23, 1937, rules be put into effect: "The Government of Bolivia believes that the means of security established by the Conference of Peace are based on the power which has been given it by the protocol making its execution [April 23 rules] imperative . . . the means of security established by the protocol cannot be literally thrown aside, fellow delegates."[92] Bolivia, in short, refused to sanction any security plan of Paraguayan origin.

Mr. Butler was unable to understand that victory and vindication, not peace and security, were the goals of the former belligerents. The weapons were no longer bullets and bombs, but the ends remained the same. Unless the mediators could conceive a plan to make both Paraguay and Bolivia appear triumphant, agreement on the question of Chaco security was attainable only by coercion.

The failure of the conference to establish a system of security in the Chaco was a serious defeat because some kind of arrangement was sorely needed. As early as September 1935 the Bolivians and Paraguayans had begun to send military patrols across the line of *hitos*. On October 3 and 9, 1936, the sound of gunfire again reverberated across the Chaco; only through the timely intervention of the military observers was an uneasy cease-fire reimposed. In July 1937 a member of an infiltrating Paraguayan patrol was captured, and the prisoner readily admitted Paraguayan probing of Bolivian defenses.[93] In the ensuing five months the number of patrols, fire fights, and captured prisoners increased alarmingly. The Chaco tragedy of 1932 seemed ready for re-enactment in 1938.

At this point the conference began its long climb from the slough of defeat. Admittedly, the conference was vacillating and ineffective,

---

close whether Paraguay would cede the unilateral right to close the road in case of internal or external danger.

[92] Argentina, Min. de Rel. Ext. y Culto, *Conferencia de paz*, p. 728.

[93] Uruguay, Ministerio de Relaciones Exteriores y Culto, Archivo de Relaciones Exteriores, Montevideo, File 1980/29, 88/937, Periz-Coeho (La Paz) to Montevideo, July 27, 1934, pp. 1–2.

but by 1938 it was the sole alternative to renewed hostilities. Better to negotiate at length than to resume a combat that might draw in the mediating states! Since continuation of negotiation had become almost an end in itself, the conferees could take up the territorial question, assured that if the latter were solved the security issue would take care of itself.

7. THE TERRITORIAL QUESTION

SPRUILLE BRADEN: *There will be a gentlemen's agreement.*

ENRIQUE FINOT: *A gentlemen's agreement implies that there are men, and the conference is made up of women. It has no word.*

Conversation, July 1, 1938

By a secret exchange of notes between the Conference and the parties it will be agreed with Bolivia that the western line awarded will go no further west than Esmeraldas to 27 of November. . . . Paragraph (b) above must never (repeat never) be known.

Spruille Braden to Department of State, July 6, 1938

ꙄꙄ

POSSIBLY THE MOST propitious event paving the way for final Chaco settlement was Carlos Saavedra Lamas' departure as conference chairman on February 21, 1938.[1] His farewell opened the

---

[1] Consensus concerning the character of Saavedra Lamas is unlikely. In a letter to the author dated November 15, 1965, Pablo Santos-Muños, former secretary-general of the conference and Argentine delegate after May 1937, depicted Saavedra Lamas as a capable and efficient foreign minister "who was always optimistic regarding the success of the negotiations." In an interview, October 21, 1965, Asunción, Paraguay, Juan Isidro Ramírez characterized Saavedra Lamas as a great man. Writing to Spruille Braden, former delegate Nieto del Río of Chile expressed a unique description of the Argentine foreign minister: "He has a capacity for both good and evil,

way for increased cooperation among the mediator states, for the new Argentine chancellors were more interested in finding a solution than in garnering glory. The breakthrough came between April 16 and 18, 1938, after Spruille Braden had led a contingent of negotiators to La Paz. During his sojourn in the Bolivian capital the United States plenipotentiary received a definite bid that became the basis for proposals later tendered to Paraguay. The signing of the Treaty of Peace, Friendship, and Limits on July 21, 1938, capped with success three years of laborious negotiation.

Succeeding events proved anticlimactic. On September 2, 1938, the Chaco Arbitral College opened its sessions. It had taken three years to concert the definitive treaty, but the arbitral award was handed down in five weeks. On November 28, 1938, the Mixed Commission for the Demarcation of the Boundaries between Paraguay and Bolivia was established to determine the boundary.[2] This commission is still at work.[3] Its labors admittedly have been slow, but no angry protests

---

but even when he does good, it is with evil intent" (United States, National Archives, Washington, D.C., Department of State, RG 59, Decimal File 724.34119/ 1007, no. 482, Braden [Buenos Aires] to Dept. State, Aug. 27, 1937, p. 3).

[2] The membership of the commission was confirmed on January 27, 1939. Actual field work began on May 1, 1939. In his first report, dated March 28, 1940, Argentine Colonel Baldomero J. de Biedma admitted that the marker-laying program was behind schedule, but he blamed bad roads and astronomical and mathematical errors made by other commissions. Colonel de Biedma's second report on May 15, 1941, noted that four of the eleven intended markers had been correctly plotted and laid. In his January 16, 1943, report, de Biedma again complained of rains, bad roads, and lack of transport. In general the commission worked only from May to September, and all money had to be appropriated by Paraguay and Bolivia. See Uruguay, Ministerio de las Relaciones Exteriores y Culto, Archivo de Relaciones, Exteriores, Montevideo, File 1980/29: *Paraguay y Bolivia: La cuestión de limites*, no. 445/941, Martínez Thédy (Buenos Aires) to Montevideo, June 2, 1941, pp. 1–2; 198hg, no. 113/943, Martínez Thédy (Buenos Aires) to Montevideo, Feb. 1, 1943, p. 1.

[3] Paraguay, Ministerio de Relaciones Exteriores, Archivo de Relaciones Exteriores, Asunción, Folio 32-2-E, *Tratado de paz, amistad y limites, Paraguay y Bolivia: Suscrito en Buenos Aires el 21 de julio, 1938. (1) Copias de documentos relativos a los tratados de paz, amistad y limites del julio-1938. (2) Recortes periodísticos correspondientes al año 1938*, D.O.T.A.I., #0209, Foreign office to Agusto Fuster (La Paz), March 15, 1963, p. 1. In 1963 General Otto Hebling became the new head of the Mixed Commission. Great progress was made under Hebling, but he was replaced by General Gonzalo Gomez of Argentina in 1967. Although the com-

have emanated from Bolivia or Paraguay. The Chaco boundary dispute had dragged on for eighty-six years (1852–1938) and thus far the commissioners have passed only thirty-two (1938–1970) in demarcating the frontier.

The June 12, 1935, protocol provided for the termination of direct negotiations when, in the mediators' opinion, concertation of a definitive agreement proved impossible. The parties then were to draft an arbitral *compromis* for submission to the International Court of Justice at the Hague. Until the *compromis* was agreed upon, the conference could not adjourn. This provision invited disaster. Direct negotiation fails if no accord is reached and the disputants have made their ultimate concessions, but in formulating a mutual agreement to accept arbitration, each party usually insists in full on its particular rights, real or imagined. If, then, Bolivia and Paraguay could not reach agreement through direct negotiation, how was agreement on an arbitral *compromis* to be expected? If efforts to contract said arbitral agreement foundered, was the conference bound to continue? At times it is impolitic to ask probing questions. June 1935 appears to have been one of these moments: "Had it not been for this *compromis*, Bolivia would not have signed the protocol, and the war would have gone on."[4]

It was the Paraguayans who unceremoniously jolted the conferees back to reality. At the eighth plenary session on July 31, 1935, their delegation blandly announced that sovereignty over its captured Chaco territory could not even be discussed.[5] Gerónimo Zubizarreta intimated

mission virtually finished its work in July 1969 when it demarcated a disputed area of the northeastern Chaco, on July 31 the Bolivian government protested, and final settlement has still not been made.

[4] Spruille Braden, "A Resumé of the Role Played by Arbitration in the Chaco Dispute," *Arbitration Journal*, 2, no. 4 (October 1938), 392. In addition Mr. Braden explored the possibility of constructing an arbitral *compromis*. He concludes that the extremely nationalistic outlook of both disputants nullified the possibility of accord on a *compromis*.

[5] U.S., Archives, RG 59, Decimal File 724.34119/103, no. 28, Gibson (Buenos Aires) to Dept. State, Aug. 1, 1935, p. 7. The president of the Paraguayan delegation was simply following his instructions (Paraguay, Archivo, *La conferencia de paz de Buenos Aires*, File 1, "Instrucciones para la delegación a la conferencia de Buenos Aires," July 1935, p. 15). On the necessity of holding the line of *hitos*, the instructions are explicit: "For us this frontier must be an intangible line." On the

that the conference must at all times accept the Paraguayan interpretation of what its rights and duties entailed. Further negotiation of the territorial question was judged premature, and the conference proceeded to consider other issues. Nevertheless, informal conversations on boundaries and territorial concessions continued. Despite the Paraguayans' seemingly intransigent stand, José de Paula Rodrigues Alves began to push for the fabrication of a comprehensive peace package. The Brazilian argued that even if the offer were rejected, the minimum territorial demands of both antagonists would be established. Rodrigues Alves' initiative gained support, and on October 15, 1935, a comprehensive peace plan was handed to Bolivian and Paraguayan representatives. The Brazilian delegate's scheme called for a Chaco frontier established along a line from Fortín d'Orbigny to Bahía Negra, a demilitarized zone thirty kilometers wide on each side of the frontier, a free zone for Bolivia at Puerto Casado, total repatriation of prisoners, and reestablishment of diplomatic relations.[6] Both nations replied officially on November 5. The Bolivian memorandum was etched in sarcasm and indicated a disbelief in the mediators' sense of equity; Asunción's reply suggested that the mediators had taken leave of their senses.[7] The reaction to the proposals of October 15 convincingly demonstrated that, psychologically, Bolivia and Paraguay were still at war; frank and fruitful discussions concerning Chaco frontiers were not yet possible.

The conferees avoided territorial discussions throughout most of 1936. On December 8 of that year, while the Inter-American Conference for the Maintenance of Peace was in session, the mediators agreed to appoint a special subcommittee to discuss the boundary question with representatives of the former belligerents. Chilean Foreign Minister Miguel Cruchaga Tocornal, Brazilian Foreign Minister

---

question of a port, Paraguay was prepared to offer Bolivia free port facilities, but any attempt by the conference to provide Bolivia with a littoral on the Paraguay River must cause "the immediate collapse of direct negotiations" (*ibid.*, p. 15).

6 Argentina, Ministerio de Relaciones Exteriores y Culto, *La conferencia de paz de Buenos Aires*, pp. 768–773. See Map 6 for the boundary proposed on October 15, 1935.

7 United States, Department of State, *The Chaco Peace Conference*, pp. 125–134.

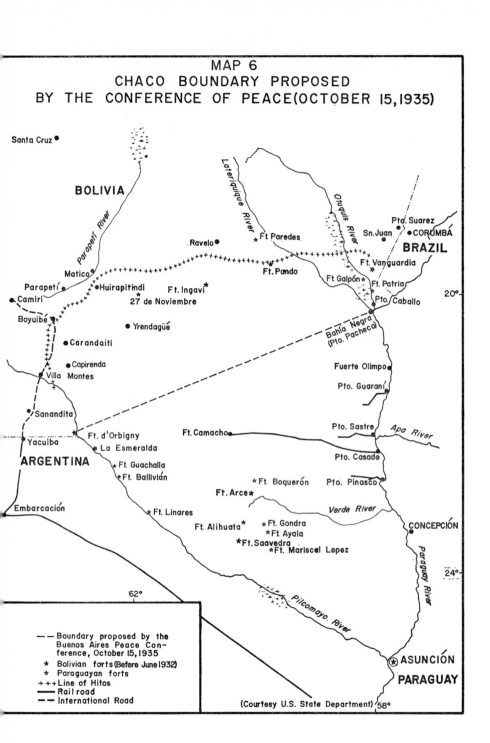

MAP 6
CHACO BOUNDARY PROPOSED
BY THE CONFERENCE OF PEACE(OCTOBER 15,1935)

Santa Cruz ●

BOLIVIA

Parapeti River

Lateriquique River

Otuquis River

.Ravelo ●

★ Ft. Paredes.

Pto. Suarez

Sn. Juan ● CORUMBÁ

BRAZIL

Matica ●

Ft. Pando

Ft. Vanguardia

Parapeti ●

● Huirapitindi

Ft. Ingavi ★

Ft. Galpón ★

Ft. Patria

20°

● Camiri

27 de Noviembre

Pto. Caballo

Boyuibé ★

● Yrendagüe

Bahía Negra
(Pto. Pacheco)

● Carandaiti

● Capirenda

Fuerte Olimpo ●

Villa Montes

Pto. Guaraní

● Sanandita

Pto. Sastre

Apa River

Ft. d'Orbigny

Ft. Camacho ●

Yacuiba

● La Esmeralda

Pto. Casado

ARGENTINA

★ Ft. Guachalla

★ Ft. Ballivián

★ Ft. Boquerón

Pto. Pinasco

Ft. Arce ★

Embarcación

★ Ft. Linares

Verde River

CONCEPCIÓN

Ft. Alihuata ★

★ Ft. Gondra

★ Ft. Ayala

★ Ft. Saavedra

★ Ft. Mariscal Lopez

Paraguay River

24°

62°

Pilcomayo River

ASUNCIÓN

PARAGUAY

— — Boundary proposed by the
Buenos Aires Peace Con-
ference, October 15,1935
★ Bolivian forts (Before June 1932)
★ Paraguayan forts
+++ Line of Hitos
—— Rail road
— — International Road

(Courtesy U.S. State Department) 58°

José Carlos de Macedo Soares, and Spruille Braden, representing Cordell Hull, were selected. On December 10 this "Committee of Three," as it was dubbed, began to hold separate sessions with Bolivian and Paraguayan delegations. Progress was infinitesimal, since both parties adopted diametrically opposed positions.[8] On December 10 Macedo Soares proposed a peace formula calling for Paraguayan withdrawal from the Villa Montes–Boyuibé road and a free rather than a sovereign port for Bolivia on the Paraguay River.[9] The Altiplano diplomats stated that the Toro government was adamant regarding the necessity of a sovereign port. On December 11 and 12, the same proposals were rejected by the Paraguayans because Ramírez refused to consider any kind of river port for Bolivia.[10]

Despite these differences, the committee presented tentative boundary proposals to both delegations on December 15. The suggested border ran along the route from Fortín d'Orbigny to Capirenda to Carandaiti to the Parapetí River near Santa Fe to Fortín Galpón. The Bolivians' remonstrance was firm but civil; they announced they would resume hostilities rather than allow Paraguay to reach the Parapetí River.[11] Paraguayan diplomats, however, seized the opportunity to press their own proposals upon the committee. Juan Isidro Ramírez angered the subcommittee by repeatedly insisting that the line of *hitos* had to be accepted as the basis for any future territorial settlement. On December 16 he finally rejected all the formulas proposed by the committee. The three negotiators then produced a new offer; the Villa Montes–Boyuibé road would go to Bolivia and all territory east of a line drawn between Bahía Negra and Linares to Paraguay. Ramírez replied that he did not reject the proposal; he simply "refused to consider it."[12]

---

[8] Argentina, Min. de Rel. Ext. y Culto, *Conferencia de paz*, pp. 776–778, 794–795.
[9] *Ibid.*, p. 776.
[10] *Ibid.*, p. 778. According to Juan Isidro Ramírez (*La paz del Chaco: En defensa de la línea de hitos*, p. 77), Cruchaga Tocornal proposed a cash settlement of $10,000,000 if the Paraguayans would grant Bolivia a sovereign port.
[11] Uruguay, Archivo, File 1980/29, Appendix 869/937, "Estado actual del problema del Chaco en lo concerniente al diferendo fundamental; método de negociación-fórmulas posibles," Nov. 10, 1937, p. 5.
[12] Argentina, Min. de Rel. Ext. y Culto, *Conferencia de paz*, p. 782.

Following a series of violent exchanges with the Paraguayan delegation's president on December 19, Macedo Soares, Braden, and Cruchaga Tocornal attempted to bypass Ramírez by firmly requesting Foreign Minister Juan Stefanich's presence in Buenos Aires. On December 24 the Paraguayan chancellor appeared, and the next day the committee submitted two proposals to Stefanich. The first suggested a frontier from Fortín d'Orbigny to Fortín Galpón by way of Carandaiti, Capirenda, and Santa Fe (on the Parapetí River); the second called for a Chaco boundary running from Ballivián through Fortín 27 de Noviembre to Bahía Negra and stipulated that Paraguay would receive a sum of money from Bolivia.[13] On December 26 Stefanich rejected the second plan but allowed that the first might serve as the basis for further discussions and insisted that this information be withheld from the Bolivians.[14] Since the committee members had not told Stefanich that the frontier he favored was the one that the Bolivians had declared they would fight rather than accept (December 15, 1936), the Committee of Three could easily honor the Paraguayan's demand. Under these circumstances, further progress appeared unlikely. The Committee of Three therefore terminated its mediatory activities on December 26 when Enrique Finot of Bolivia and Juan Stefanich signed a joint declaration expressing their belief in the possibility of ultimate settlement.

After December 26 the Committee of Three met several times to draw up five concluding recommendations: (1) Bolivia should receive a free, but not a sovereign, port on the Paraguay River; (2) the Paraguayan frontier should not reach the Parapetí River; (3) a line south and east of the line of *hitos* should form the permanent frontier between Paraguay and Bolivia; (4) the Villa Montes–Boyuibé road problems should be adjusted; and (5) both parties should be disposed to consider a cash settlement. In his commentary the United States repre-

[13] Uruguay, Archivo, File 1980/29, Appendix A 869/937, "Estado Actual," Nov. 10, 1937, p. 5.

[14] *Ibid.*, p. 5. "Estado Actual" says Stefanich categorically rejected the second proposal. A slightly different version is found in Juan Stefanich, *La diplomacia de la revolución*, pp. 23–24. Stefanich claims that the proposals were not acceptable because they did not guarantee Paraguay a portion of the petroleum zone.

sentative concluded that although no agreement was presently attainable, a Paraguayan retreat of fifty to one hundred kilometers eventually would be forced by mounting financial and transportation difficulties.[15]

The only tangible gain from these exploratory conversations was the acquisition of concrete information about the needs and aspirations of both parties. More might have been accomplished had the committee been fully cognizant of events transpiring on December 11, 1936. Following their first session with the Committee of Three, Ramírez and Juan José Soler sought a meeting with Saavedra Lamas. The Argentine foreign minister had not desired the Chilean and Brazilian foreign ministers' appointment to the subcommittee's activities.[16] After some preliminary fencing, Saavedra Lamas demanded Paraguayan terms for the settlement of the territorial question. Ramírez replied that Paraguay must have all the territory it presently occupied; the rest of the Chaco could be submitted to arbitration. The president of the Paraguayan delegation provides the only narrative of what followed: "We added that now was the time to discover if Paraguay and Argentina are truly friends. Dr. Lamas . . . showed himself decidedly partial to adopting the line of *hitos* as a base of solution."[17] Pressing their advantage, Ramírez and Soler then broached the subject of

15 U.S., Archives, RG 59, Decimal File 724.34119/748, no. 853, "Conclusion of the Committee of Three on the Territorial Question," Braden (Buenos Aires) to Dept. State, Jan. 14, 1937, p. 10. As early as December 28, Braden reported to his superiors that "both Foreign Ministers contemplate a cash settlement" (United States, Department of State, *Papers Relating to the Foreign Relations of the United States, 1936*, V, 105). The basis for this conclusion is not found in either of the sources noted above.

16 Paraguay, Archivo, File 28, no. 241, delegation (Buenos Aires) to ministry, Dec. 19, 1936, p. 272. Ramírez reported that the presence of Macedo Soares and Cruchaga Tocornal on the committee was extremely vexing for Saavedra Lamas.

Spruille Braden's commentary on his committee colleagues provides a penetrating insight into the personal vendettas being waged. "Macedo Soares is determined, alone or through the Committee of Three, to conclude a final Chaco peace treaty within the next few weeks. Saavedra Lamas resents the intervention of the Brazilian and Chilean Chancellors and . . . will keep his hand in the negotiations. Cruchaga [Tocornal] is confused on the whole situation but prefers any leadership other than that of Saavedra Lamas" (U.S., Dept. of State, *Foreign Relations, 1936*, V, 90).

17 Paraguay, Archivo, File 28, no. 231, delegation (Buenos Aires) to ministry, Dec. 12, 1936, p. 273.

petroleum. Following another meeting that evening, Saavedra Lamas ordered an anonymous Argentine petroleum engineer to construct a boundary proposal, based on the line of *hitos*, that would assure Paraguay a portion of the petroleum zone.[18] Elated by Saavedra Lamas' espousal of Paraguayan aims, Ramírez promptly telegraphed Asunción and outlined his strategy for dealing with the Committee of Three: "The thing most beneficial for us presently is to gain time, blocking the efforts of the subcommittee, discouraging them so that it will be impossible [for them] to obtain any advantages."[19]

Saavedra Lamas must have known that neither Bolivia nor the mediators could have agreed to the terms Ramírez envisaged. In view of the fact that the Argentine foreign minister already was plotting a petroleum and railway agreement with Bolivia, the assurances given Ramírez seem antithetical to Argentine national interests. The answer appears to be that the wily Argentine was playing both ends against the middle. Encouraged by Argentine support, Ramírez and Soler could be counted on to check the subcommittee. Saavedra Lamas was prepared to sustain the unpleasantness of Paraguayan enmity in return for an exclusive rail and petroleum pact with Bolivia.[20] In December 1936 there was, however, no certainty that such an agreement would be reached. If Argentine persuasion proved unavailing, Saavedra Lamas then could keep faith with Asunción. Since Argentine economic interests were predominant in Paraguay,[21] acquisition of petroleum

[18] *Ibid.*, p. 273. On the night of December 11, a conference was held at which Saavedra Lamas, Soler, Ramírez, and the unnamed engineer were the sole participants. The engineer advised Ramírez that "the zone adjacent to the international road" was rich in oil, but so was the area along the Parapetí River. The technician suggested that if the final solution hinged on Paraguayan withdrawal from the road, Paraguay could do so, and as *quid pro quo* demand territorial compensation along the Parapetí. Ramírez concurred but pointed out that Paraguayan retreat from the Villa Montes–Boyuibé road would have to be the "object of financial negotiation."

[19] *Ibid.*, no. 234, Dec. 12, 1936, pp. 279–280.

[20] Refer to the previous chapter; see also U.S., Archives, RG 59, Decimal File 724.34119/720, no. 331, Enclosure 5, Memorandum, Braden, Dec. 17, 1936, p. 98. Bolivian Foreign Minister Finot informed the Committee of Three that Argentina intended to build a railroad from Yacuiba to Santa Cruz through Villa Montes. Finot reported that Saavedra Lamas had promised him that if the conference did not do so, Argentina would cause the removal of Paraguayan troops from the Villa Montes–Boyuibé road.

[21] The nature of Argentine economic domination in Paraguay is discussed in

territory by Asunción could hardly be viewed as an unfortunate event. The virtually stillborn endeavors of the Committee of Three conclusively demonstrated that as long as the mediators were working against each other, the former belligerents had no reason to reduce their demands.

With renewed energy and purpose, the Chaco Peace Conference reopened talks on December 25, 1936, and unanimously endorsed a resolution to establish a time limit of four months for negotiations; if no agreement was reached, the conference would declare direct negotiation over and initiate work on the arbitral *compromis*, reserving for itself the right to fix the bases for the *compromis* if the former belligerents could not agree.[22] On April 21, 1937, the mediators, again unanimously, endorsed Spruille Braden's call for territorial negotiations irrespective of difficulties over Chaco security regulations. Disregarding the thorny paths of protocol, delegates of the United States, Brazil, and Chile held a dinner for Argentine President Agustín P. Justo on April 29 and severely castigated Saavedra Lamas' handling of the conference.[23] On June 8 the mediators resolved that negotiations on the territorial question had begun; two weeks later they decided to put a five-month deadline on direct negotiations. On July 12 the conference reaffirmed the June 8 resolution. Spruille Braden lamented the lack of progress one month later, saying "little useful

---

Chapter 1. Further evidence is provided in U.S., Archives, RG 59, Decimal File 724.34119/311 1/2, "Summary of Chaco Mediation Efforts and the Work of the Buenos Aires Peace Conference: April to November 1935," G. H. Butler, Dec. 10, 1935, p. 165.

[22] Paraguay, Archivo, File 23, Acta 107, Dec. 25, 1936, p. 106. In a letter to the author dated April 14, 1966, Spruille Braden noted that the resolution was "not taken too seriously," and its essential aim was to pressure the former belligerents.

[23] See U.S., Archives, RG 59, Decimal File 724.34119/844, no. 63, Braden (Buenos Aires) to Dept. State, April 30, 1937, p. 2; and U.S., Dept. of State, *Foreign Relations, 1937*, V, 10–18. The dinner was arranged with Argentine Vice-President Julio Roca acting as intermediary. Nieto del Río (Chile), Spruille Braden (U.S.A.), and Rodrigues Alves (Brazil) realized that in appealing for the intervention of President Justo they were engaged in daring diplomacy. The three mediators felt that they would have "no reason for regret . . . in view of the attitude of the Argentine Foreign Minister which was evaluated as being fatal for the peace of America."

discussion on the territorial question has been had in the Conference since last December."[24]

The immobilization of the Chaco peacemakers can be partially attributed to the uncertain disposition of Oriente petroleum and the political instability of Bolivia and Paraguay. Much of the remaining inaction can be traced to the conflict of United States, Chilean, and Brazilian representatives with Saavedra Lamas. Although all parties supported the December 25, 1936, resolve, friction over the sector of the international road between Villa Montes and Boyuibé again had split the conference into openly contentious factions. By March 1937 Saavedra Lamas was convinced that Braden and Rodrigues Alves were plotting to move the conference to Rio de Janeiro.[25] The Argentine foreign minister became further incensed when the United States, Brazilian, and Chilean representatives forced the adoption of the April 23, 1937, security regimen over his fierce objections. Finally Spruille Braden's continued demand for discussion of the territorial issue reached a climax on April 28 in a heated argument between the United States diplomat and the Argentine chancellor.[26] Saavedra Lamas, who had maintained that heavy pressure on the Paraguayans might force them to abandon the conference, immediately conferred with Ramírez. The Argentine charged that since the United States, Chile, and Brazil had formed a bloc, he would need assistance in thwarting their designs. Ramírez pledged his cooperation and wired Asunción: "I told him that he could be completely certain that Paraguay was not to be the plaything of the mediators' politics, and that we are in the conference to defend our rights, nothing more."[27]

The April 29 dinner for President Justo was interpreted by Saavedra Lamas as a brazen attempt to wrest control of negotiable prerogatives from his grasp. On May 8 he and Ramírez again conferred. The

[24] U.S., Dept. of State, *Foreign Relations, 1937*, V, 19.

[25] Paraguay, Archivo, File 29, no. 63, delegation (Buenos Aires) to ministry, March 4, 1937, p. 130.

[26] U.S., Archives, RG 59, Decimal File 724.34119/837, no. 39, Braden (Buenos Aires) to Dept. State, April 28, 1937, pp. 1–2.

[27] Paraguay, Archivo, File 28, no. 123, delegation (Buenos Aires) to ministry, April 28, 1937, p. 52.

former denounced the agitation of the "triumvirate,"[28] while the Paraguayan expressed concern, since Asunción was not interested in territorial negotiations under conditions it deemed unfavorable. On May 13 strategy was decided. To forestall territorial discussions by the conference Paraguay would push for the reestablishment of diplomatic relations between Paraguay and Bolivia. Once relations had been restored, "necessarily the conference would have to agree to an opportunity for both Paraguayan and Bolivian Ministers . . . to contemplate the methods and forms of direct agreement. Meanwhile, the conference would be able to suspend its activities."[29]

On May 25 Bolivia and Paraguay agreed to reestablish relations; unfortunately intemperate statements by Finot and Stefanich and Paraguayan disavowal of the April 23, 1937, transit rules vitiated execution of the agreement. On June 8 the conference, spurred on by the implacable "triumvirate," resolved that territorial negotiations be inaugurated. Three days later an outraged Ramírez confronted Saavedra Lamas and demanded to know why the mediators were being allowed "to throw stones at Paraguay."[30] Saavedra Lamas retorted that the conference had gotten out of hand but that Paraguay could ease the situation by appearing more conciliatory. To prevent Braden, Rodrigues Alves, and Nieto del Río from attaining their ends, the Argentine diplomat first called on Colonel Abraham Schweitzer, the special agent sent by Saavedra Lamas to determine whether the new Franco government intended to obey the protocols of June 1935 and January 1936. Schweitzer warned the mediators against precipitate attempts at frontier settlement. He stated flatly that the Paraguayan army considered the line of *hitos* a permanent frontier and, therefore, that any concessions on the part of the Franco government would bring it down. He did concede, however, that Paraguay still desired the naming

28 *Ibid.*, File 29, no. 141, delegation (Buenos Aires) to ministry, May 15, 1937, p. 17. "La Trilogía" is the derisive title given by Saavedra Lamas to the working alliance of Nieto del Río, Braden, and Rodrigues Alves. Ramírez's communique expressed concern, for the three men were trying to force a new deadline on the period of direct negotiations.
29 *Ibid.*, p. 18.
30 Paraguay, Archivo, File 30, R-180, delegation (Buenos Aires) to ministry, June 11, 1937, pp. 126–127.

of a committee to investigate war responsibilities.[31] The "triumvirate" remained unconvinced, so the Argentine foreign minister dropped his mask of discretion and resorted to obstruction and intrigue in an effort to halt territorial discussions.[32]

The departure of Colonels Toro and Franco from La Paz and Asunción in July and August 1937 ended further progress. Initially, at least, the succeeding governments were hardly paragons of stability, and their serious consideration of boundary proposals was, therefore, hardly feasible. From mid-August until the end of November, discussion of the territorial question was suspended, and doubts about the possibility of a settlement of this problem could no longer be ignored. Braden was convinced that juridical arbitration for the Chaco was a chimera, but Sumner Welles continued to consider the idea because he doubted that the territorial dispute would ever be settled by direct negotiation.[33] Indeed, Welles's pessimism seemed justifiable when in October 1937 the new Paraguayan delegation reached Buenos Aires without instructions to consider any territorial withdrawal. Meanwhile, the Busch government was waiting to see if its petroleum

---

[31] U.S., Archives, RG 59, Decimal File 724.119/3441, no. 456, "Chaco Mediation: A Report Submitted by Colonel Abraham Schweitzer," Braden (Buenos Aires) to Dept. State, July 31, 1937, pp. 2–3.

[32] *Ibid.*, Decimal File 724.34119/894, no. 434, Braden (Buenos Aires) to Dept. State, June 9, 1937, p. 3. Saavedra Lamas canceled the meeting of May 29. When Braden called for one on May 30 Saavedra Lamas declared himself "too tired" to attend (*ibid.*). Meetings for May 31 and June 2 also were postponed. The Argentine foreign minister continued this policy through July, canceling seven of thirteen scheduled meetings. He even sought to have Braden replaced by hinting to Sumner Welles that the United States plenipotentiary was involved in a plot to move the conference to Rio de Janeiro (*ibid.*, Decimal File 711.00.76, Memorandum to State Department, Conversation with Argentine Ambassador Espil, July 16, 1937, p. 1).

[33] Disturbed by Paraguay's second rejection of the April 23, 1937, rules and the internal instability of both states, Sumner Welles telegraphed Braden (Oct. 28, 1937) that "it would seem to be becoming more than evident that direct negotiations cannot be successfully undertaken at least for a considerable time to come. . . . If my judgment on this point is correct, the only course left would appear to be resort to the Hague Court" (U.S., Dept. of State, *Foreign Relations, 1937*, V, 29). Braden took sharp issue with Welles, declaring that "even granting jurisdiction were accepted and award made by the Court, Paraguay would not accept the ruling, Bolivia would try to enforce it, and Paraguayan resistance would probably lead to a renewal of war."

politics would improve its prospects at the peace table, and Saavedra Lamas was plotting to outflank the other mediators and gain a free hand as Chaco peacemaker.[34] Most of October and November were committed to fruitless discussion of security regulations, but on December 2, 1937, Braden, Rodrigues Alves, and Barreda Laos pressed a new peace formula on Zubizarreta. The proffered frontier was to run from "some point on the Pilcomayo between d'Orbigny and Ballivián, north to approximately latitude 20° south, then eastward to the inner bay of Bahía Negra." In addition, Bolivia was to receive limited free port facilities at Puerto Casado and pay Paraguay a sum that would be used to construct a trans-Chaco railway. Mutual renunciation of war responsibilities and a "well-implemented" nonaggression pact were also stipulated.[35] The confidential presentation of peace plans had been forbidden by Saavedra Lamas, but the Brazilian and North American delegates had become increasingly selective in complying with the Argentine chancellor's directives. Zubizarreta produced his counteroffer on December 6. As had all previous Paraguayan representatives, he demanded recognition of the line of *hitos* as the permanent frontier, and territorial compensation in exchange for withdrawal from the Villa Montes–Boyuibé road. The Braden–Rodrigues Alves–Barreda Laos trio found it "totally unacceptable."[36] Since intensive proceedings were impossible without Saavedra Lamas' consent, the "rebel" mediators marked time until the Argentine diplomat completed his tenure of office. On February 21, 1938, the long-awaited event occurred.

Although Zubizarreta had no doubts about his ability to handle unfriendly mediators, he did fear an attempt to subvert his truculent defense of Paraguayan prerogatives. The day Saavedra Lamas stepped down, Zubizarreta wired Asunción: "The delegation of my Presidency believes that it is its duty to suggest to the Government the idea

[34] U.S., Archives, RG 59, Decimal File 724.34119/1167, no. 603, Braden (Buenos Aires) to Dept. State, Dec. 31, 1937, pp. 2–3. On December 31 Saavedra Lamas sent a personal letter to Germán Busch via Dr. Araoz, Argentine ambassador to La Paz, stating that the conference could not possibly succeed. The communication urged that Argentina be made the sole mediator in the Chaco dispute.
[35] U.S., Dept. of State, *Foreign Relations, 1937*, V, 39.
[36] *Ibid.*, p. 44.

of renouncing the adhesion of our country to the jurisdiction of the Permanent Court of International Justice."[37] Zubizarreta argued that with Saavedra Lamas gone, conference negotiations might easily take an unfavorable turn; for this possibility, the nation had to be ready.[38] The Paraguayan government, therefore, promptly and secretly enacted his suggestion into law.[39] The efficacy of this artifice lay in its simplicity. Now neither arbitral *compromis* nor unilateral appeal for juridical intervention could drive Paraguay from the line of *hitos*. Direct negotiations became the sole route to settlement, and Zubizarreta barred that road.

The other mediators would not discover the secret activities of the Paraguayan government for some months, but they too were readying a few surprises. As far back as October 12, 1937, Barreda Laos of Peru had postulated the kind of strategy the mediators soon would employ to force settlement of this complicated issue: "If we are to arrive at a negotiated boundary through the direct mediation of the Conference of Peace, the method most advisable will be to begin negotiations, holding to the lowest possible minimum the aspirations of the two parties, then to proceed by ceding territory inch by inch."[40]

The first hint that Barreda Laos' strategy would be pressed into service came on February 26, 1938, when Manuel Ramón Alvarado, interim Argentine foreign minister, brusquely dismissed Zubizarreta's request for a three-month recess. On March 8 the president of the Paraguayan delegation repeated his petition and received another rebuff. The same day the conference resolved "forthwith to establish a committee of the Whole, which, to the exclusion of all secondary and collateral problems, shall dedicate itself with energy and determination by means of continuous sessions until all its resources have been ex-

---

[37] Paraguay, Archivo, File 39, no. 64, delegation (Buenos Aires) to ministry, Feb. 21, 1938, p. 311.

[38] *Ibid.*, p. 311.

[39] *Ibid.*, File 40, Decreto 6172 (Reservado), law 1298, April 26, 1938, p. 88. On May 11, 1933, Paraguay had signed the optional clause of the statute for the Permanent Court of International Justice. This clause provided that in case of a dispute between two states that had signed it, the court might establish immediate jurisdiction. By law 1298, Paraguay withdrew its adherence to the optional clause.

[40] Ramírez, *La paz del Chaco*, p. 239.

hausted, to reach a solution of the territorial and frontier question by direct agreement as previously stipulated in the protocols."[41] To no one's surprise, the new committee's chairmanship passed to the man who had consistently pressed for continuous talks—Spruille Braden. The North American plenipotentiary wasted no time; he quickly pushed new proposals on both Paraguayan and Bolivian delegations and demanded acceptance or concessions. Convinced that a conspiracy had been formed against them, the Paraguayans stood firm and stalled for time. Altiplano delegates proved more malleable but adamantly insisted on a Paraguay River littoral.

The mediators now deemed the time ripe for confrontation. Two committees were formed: Chilean, Peruvian, and Argentine representatives departed for Asunción, while Brazilian, Uruguayan, and United States diplomats left for La Paz.[42] The committee led by Isidoro Ruiz Moreno of Argentina encountered obstinant opposition to its efforts in the Paraguayan capital and returned to Buenos Aires, completely unsuccessful. The Braden-led contingent enjoyed similar treatment in La Paz until the night before its departure. Bidden to come unaccompanied to the home of Miguel Tcheniqueas, Braden found himself closeted with Colonel Germán Busch and a Señor Etchenique, who represented the Patiño mining interests. As head of the ruling junta, Busch stated that he was prepared to accept the boundary that Foreign Minister Eduardo Diez de Medina had sketched on April 15 (Guachalla to Fortín 27 de Noviembre to Ingavi to Puerto Pacheco [Bahía Negra]); as an ultimate concession, the Bolivian chief announced that he would also countenance a frontier running from Fortín d'Orbigny to Fortín 27 de Noviembre to Ravelo to Puerto Pacheco.[43] In either case, Bolivia would pay Paraguay £200,000 for ceding a littoral at Puerto Pacheco (Bahía Negra).

41 U.S., Archives, RG 59, Decimal File 724.34119/1261, no. 656, Braden (Buenos Aires) to Dept. State, May 10, 1938, Enclosure 1, p. 1. Braden reported that "for the first time in over two years, an intelligent, incisive effort can now be made to reach a final solution" (U.S., Dept. of State, *Foreign Relations, 1938*, V, 92).

42 U.S., Dept. of State, *Foreign Relations, 1938*, V, 102–105.

43 In an interview conducted on June 8, 1965, in New York City, Mr. Braden stated that his night ride to meet Colonel Germán Busch was a harrowing experience. See Map 7 for a graphic presentation of the Busch proposal.

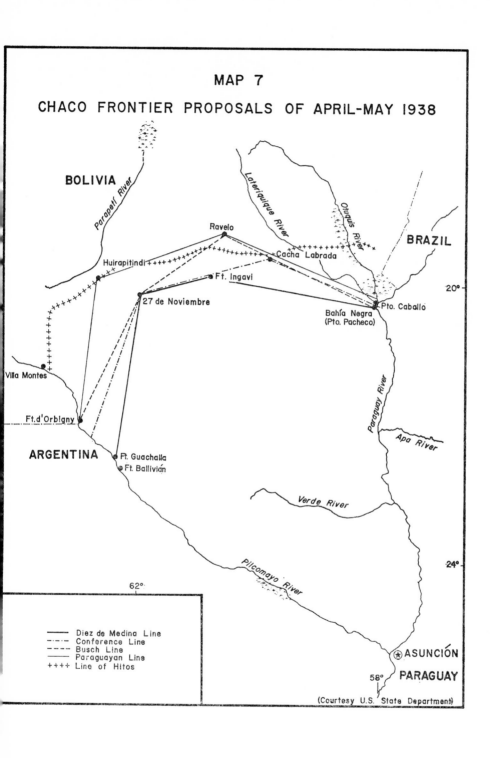

MAP 7

CHACO FRONTIER PROPOSALS OF APRIL-MAY 1938

BOLIVIA

Parapeti River

Lateriquique River

Otuquis River

BRAZIL

Ravelo

Huirapitindi

Cacha Labrada

Ft. Ingavi

27 de Noviembre

Pto. Caballo

Bahía Negra
(Pto. Pacheco)

·20°·

Villa Montes

Paraguay River

Ft. d'Orbigny

Apa River

ARGENTINA

Ft. Guachalla

Ft. Ballivián

Verde River

62°

Pilcomayo River

·24°·

——— Diez de Medina Line
—·—·— Conference Line
— — — Busch Line
——— Paraguayan Line
++++ Line of Hitos

⊛ ASUNCIÓN

58° PARAGUAY

(Courtesy U.S. State Department)

Busch's offer was to be kept confidential, at least insofar as the other
mediators were concerned, but Braden quickly informed Washington
that a "gentlemen's agreement" existed between himself and the Bolivian president.[44] Returning to Buenos Aires, the North American
diplomat took as a basis the two proposals acceptable to Busch and
then urged upon the conferees his own Chaco boundary. He claimed
that a line from a point midway between Fortín Guachalla and Fortín
d'Orbigny to Fortín 27 de Noviembre to a point between Fortín Ingavi and Fortín Ravelo, through Cocha Labrada to a point on the Paraguay River between Puerto Caballo and Bahía Negra would bring
about a definitive territorial settlement (see Map 7). Since the Ruiz
Moreno mission had failed and since no alternatives seemed feasible,
the other mediators acquiesced and on April 20 formally accepted
Braden's compromise boundary plan. The first real breakthrough on
the territorial question had been achieved.

Two days later José María Cantilo, the new Argentine foreign
minister, took office as conference president. However, administrative
changes apparently had no effect on the redoubtable Gerónimo Zubizarreta. Pressed by the mediators to make a new boundary offer, the
chief of Asunción's delegation outlined a tentative proposal on April
24, and then on May 3 formally offered this plan to the conference.
The Paraguayan-sanctioned frontier would run from Fortín d'Orbigny
to Huirapitíndi to Ravelo and thence to the Otuquis River, the understanding being that Bolivia would not receive a littoral on the Paraguay River (see Map 7). Zubizarreta's solution to the Chaco territorial question generated no enthusiasm among the mediators, who
accepted a new negotiational strategy on May 5. Argentine President
Roberto Ortiz also announced his support of the forthcoming efforts.[45]

[44] The source for the boundary details is given in U.S., Archives, RG 59, Decimal
File 724.34119/1305, no. 18, Braden (Buenos Aires) to Dept. State, April 14,
1938, p. 1. Evidence that Braden did not tell his colleagues of his nocturnal adventure is found in Uruguay, Archivo, File 1980/29 (unnumbered), Manini Ríos
(Buenos Aires) to Montevideo, May 9, 1938, pp. 1–3. In his official report to
Foreign Minister José Espalter, Manini Ríos described the trip to La Paz as unsuccessful.
[45] U.S., Dept. of State, *Foreign Relations, 1938*, V, 118. In a meeting between the
mediators and President Ortiz of Argentina, the latter argued that the greatest re-

Hoping to repeat the May 1935 success, on May 16 the conference addressed invitations to the Paraguayan and Bolivian foreign ministers, soliciting their presence in Buenos Aires for the presentation of a new peace package. By May 24 Cecilio Báez of Paraguay and Eduardo Diez de Medina of Bolivia had reached the Argentine capital. The events that followed were to try men's souls and tempers to the utmost.

When on May 5, 1938, the mediators adopted a plan of action, it marked the first time since October 1935 that all parties were operating in concert for territorial settlement.[46] The aforesaid unity over plans did not always extend to their execution. Chaco mediators had decided on May 13 that a commission of military officers would draft a justification for the proposed boundary. Conflict erupted over the military commission's right to change the conference's suggested frontier in case of geographical difficulties. Uruguay and Argentina supported full power for the commission, but representatives of the other four mediatory states insisted that the commissioners do only as they were bid. There were still other unresolved problems. Braden, Rodrigues Alves, and the new Chilean delegate, Manuel Bianchi, were convinced that only Argentina could make Paraguay yield. Despite the May 5 assurances of President Ortiz, there was considerable anxiety as to what were ultimate Argentine intentions.[47] Finally, while the new Argentine foreign minister, Cantilo, was inclined to be more cooperative

---

sponsibility for peace was Argentina's. Ortiz further stated that if the conference failed, war would be renewed and "conceivably some of us might be pulled in" (*ibid.*).

[46] Uruguay, Archivo, File 1980/29 (unnumbered), Manini Ríos (Buenos Aires) to Montevideo, May 9, 1938, pp. 2–3. For example, the mediators had agreed that if one of the two disputant states rejected the final offer, after twenty days the conference would begin work on the arbitral *compromis*. If after seventy days there was no agreement, "the Conference will immediately convene in order to be briefed on the state of negotiations . . . in order to secure the fulfillment of its high commission."

[47] U.S., Archives, RG 59, Decimal File 724.34119/1360, no. 684, Braden (Buenos Aires) to Dept. State, May 24, 1938, p. 2. The North American delegate suspected that the Argentine's basic intention was to end the conference gracefully, whether a peace were achieved or not.

than Saavedra Lamas, both his knowledge of conference problems and his prowess as a negotiator were suspect in certain quarters.[48]

Following the arrival of the Bolivian and Paraguayan foreign ministers on May 24, the mediators initiated their grand offensive. Presidents of six American nations dispatched strong telegrams to their counterparts in Bolivia and Paraguay, urging acceptance of the terms about to be presented. Public reaction to these dispatches was hardly auspicious.[49] Typical was the commentary of *Patria*, a leading Asunción newspaper: "This strong urging is an insolence by the Yankee government, an impermissible insolence."[50] Then on May 26 Cecilio Báez, Paraguayan foreign minister, broke his arm. The presentation of proposals, scheduled for that afternoon, was set back twenty-four hours. Having displayed the proper solicitude for Báez's health, the mediators braced themselves for the crucial battle.

The presentation of the conference's "final" proposals came in secret session on May 27. The new frontier between Bolivia and Paraguay would run along a line from Esmeralda to Fortín 27 de Noviembre, east to Cerro Christian, and from there to a nameless lake (19°40' south latitude and 59°5' west longitude); it would terminate on the Paraguay River at kilometer 1257 (a few miles below Puerto Caballo).[51] The boundary provided Bolivia with a token littoral on the Paraguay River north of Bahía Negra, and the Paraguayans were to receive £200,000, ostensibly for installations constructed in territory that would be ceded to Bolivia. Before either of the former belligerents had replied, Bolivian intelligence on May 30, 1938, handed Braden and Rodrigues Alves a copy of a telegram from Zubizarreta to his capital. The intercepted message provided the two mediators with good

---

[48] See U.S., Dept. of State, *Foreign Relations, 1938*, V, 112–116, 123, 130, 141, 144, 146. Braden characterized Cantilo as irresolute, pessimistic, and seriously deficient as a negotiator.

[49] See U.S., Archives, RG 59, Decimal File 724.34119/1362, Welles to Braden (Buenos Aires), May 23, 1938, p. 1. The texts forwarded to Bolivia and Paraguay were submitted to Roosevelt by Sumner Welles.

[50] *Ibid.*, Decimal File 724.34119/1399, no. 620, Howard (Asunción) to Dept. State, June 2, 1938, Enclosure 1, p. 1.

[51] Argentina, Min. de Rel. Ext. y Culto, *Conferencia de paz*, pp. 823–827. See Map 8 for a presentation of conference terms.

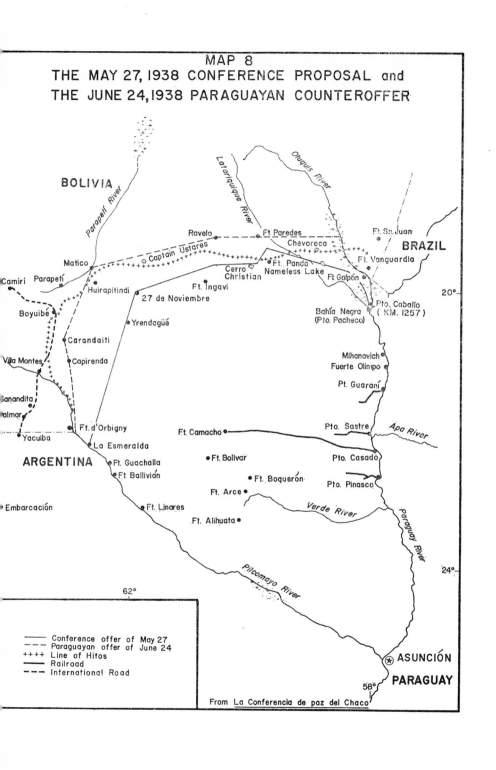

MAP 8
THE MAY 27, 1938 CONFERENCE PROPOSAL and
THE JUNE 24, 1938 PARAGUAYAN COUNTEROFFER

BOLIVIA

Parapetí River
Lateriquique River
Otuquis River

Ravelo
Ft. Paredes
Chevoreca
Ft. Sn. Juan

BRAZIL

Captain Ustares
Matico
Cerro Christian
Ft. Pando
Ft. Vanguardia
Nameless Lake
Ft. Galpón

Camiri Parapetí
Huirapitindi
Ft. Ingavi
27 de Noviembre

20°

Pto. Caballo
(KM. 1257)

Boyuibé
Yrendagüá
Bahía Negra
(Pto. Pacheco)

Carandaiti

Villa Montes
Capirenda
Mihanovich
Fuerte Olimpo

Pt. Guaraní

Sanandita
Palmar

Ft. d'Orbigny
Ft. Camacho
Pto. Sastre
Apa River

Yacuiba
La Esmeralda

ARGENTINA
Ft. Guachalla
Ft. Bolivar
Pto. Casado

Ft. Ballivián
Ft. Boquerón
Pto. Pinasco

Ft. Arce
Embarcación
Ft. Linares
Verde River

Paraguay River

Ft. Alihuata

Pilcomayo River

24°

62°

Conference offer of May 27
Paraguayan offer of June 24
++++ Line of Hitos
Railroad
International Road

ASUNCIÓN

58°   PARAGUAY

From La Conferencia de paz del Chaco

reason to doubt Asunción's acceptance, for it read in part: "We [Paraguayan delegation] will reject the proposal in accordance with written instructions from the Government."[52] Bolivian acceptance of the terms was received on May 31. Paraguay's rejection was announced on June 1 and was followed the next day by an unexplained leak to the press of the May 27 boundary proposals. Renewed exhortation to Zubizarreta proved fruitless. Attempts to circumvent him through appeals to Báez only demonstrated that the Paraguayan foreign minister would not overrule the president of the delegation.[53] Realizing that new moves would necessitate a *de facto* recess in the bargaining sessions, the Paraguayans agreed on June 10 to produce a counterproposal. Their earlier enthusiasm dissipated, the mediators were now content to mark time until Asunción presented some offer that might provide the basis for further bargaining.

Conference stalemate did not mean that the Paraguayans were oblivious to mounting pressures. President Ortiz had informed Asunción that no Argentine assistance could be expected in case of a renewed conflict. On May 19 the Ortiz government reinforced its admonition by refusing to let Paraguay purchase replacement aviation parts. On June 9 Argentine Minister José Alcalá delivered an ultimatum in Asunción: unless Paraguay displayed a more conciliatory attitude, the conference would terminate negotiations and name Paraguay the responsible party.[54] The next day the Paraguayan consul in Chile telegraphed that the Bolivian army had been increased to thirty-five or forty thousand troops.[55] Steadily growing diplomatic pressure and the

---

[52] U.S., Archives, RG 59, Decimal File 724.34119/1370, no. 129, Braden (Buenos Aires) to Dept. State, May 31, 1938, p. 2.

[53] *Ibid.*, Decimal File 724.34119/1425, no. 167, Braden (Buenos Aires) to Dept. State, June 26, 1938, p. 2. Zubizarreta intimated to Braden that Báez was a political appointee, not highly regarded by the Paiva Government (*ibid.*, Decimal File 724.34119/1370, no. 129, Braden [Buenos Aires] to Dept. State, May 27, 1938, p. 3). Braden had already concluded before the terms were presented on May 27 that Zubizarreta, not Báez, would make the final decision to accept or reject the proposals. However, in a letter dated May 22, 1966, Dr. Efraím Cardozo stated that "Dr. Báez was not an official named for political reasons."

[54] Paraguay, Archivo, File 40, Memorándum Reservado (unnumbered), ministry to delegation (Buenos Aires), June 9, 1938, p. 5.

[55] *Ibid.*, File 44, ministry to delegation (Buenos Aires), June 11, 1938, p. 66. The

unrelieved succession of disturbing reports and events eventually affected even the previously imperturbable Paraguayans. Báez privately informed Uruguayan and Argentine negotiators on June 15 that Paraguay would accept the May 27 frontier minus the Paraguay River frontage for Bolivia. Twenty-four hours later the acting foreign minister in Asunción, Luis Argaña, told the Uruguayan legate he was optimistic about conference success. Returning to Buenos Aires from Asunción, Paraguayan delegate Efraím Cardozo allegedly informed Braden of the Paiva government's concern with Zubizarreta's intransigence and the army's insistence that another offer be made prior to any capitulation.[56]

All talk of Paraguayan capitulation, however, was relatively premature. On June 24 the Paraguayans made their counterproposal calling for a frontier from Fortín d'Orbigny to the Otuquis River, through Capirenda, Carandaiti, Matico (on the Parapetí River), and Ravelo.[57] This offer closely resembled the first proposal of the Committee of Three made to Juan Stefanich on December 25, 1936, and represented explicit formulation of Asunción's continuing demand: any withdrawal from the international road necessitated territorial concessions north of the line of *hitos*. Within twenty-four hours, the negotiators had emphatically rejected this proposal, a result Zubizarreta had accurately predicted.[58] At this point Cantilo lost patience; on the afternoon of June 25 he confronted Báez and Zubizarreta with another ultimatum: Paraguay must make another offer, and if Bolivia rejected it direct negotiations would be terminated. The Argentine foreign minister

Uruguayan legate reported that Paraguay estimated sixteen thousand Bolivian troops were on the line of *hitos* (Uruguay, Archivo, File 1980/29, 43/938–7, Areco [Asunción] to Montevideo, June 13, 1938, p. 1).

56 U.S., Archives, RG 59, Decimal File 724.34119/1570, no. 735, Memorandum of Conference Activities, June–July 1938, Braden (Buenos Aires) to Dept. State, Aug. 11, 1938, p. 2 (hereafter this report will be referred to by MOCA and page number); Decimal File 724.34119/1379, no. 614, Howard (Asunción) to Dept. State, May 26, 1938, p. 3.

57 Argentina, Min. de Rel. Ext. y Culto, *Conferencia de paz*, pp. 845–846. See Map. 8.

58 Zubizarreta commented caustically that "those gentlemen are in love with their own formula" (Paraguay, Archivo, File 40, no. 117, delegation [Buenos Aires] to ministry, June 24, 1938, p. 203).

had acted unilaterally in presenting his demand, and Braden and Rod-rigues Alves had to make haste to block his venture.[59] That evening a confidential revelation of the June 24 Paraguayan proposals violently angered the Bolivian delegates. Straightaway Eduardo Diez de Medina produced a memorandum condemning Asunción's intransigence as having destroyed the possibility of negotiated settlement; only with difficulty was he induced to withhold this missive from the press.[60]

On June 26 the conference directed a new offer to Zubizarreta: the May 27 frontier minus a littoral for Bolivia and no financial payment. At last convinced that collapse of negotiations meant war, Zubizarreta authorized Cardozo to work out a settlement with the mediators. Since the junior Paraguayan delegate was willing to consider the June 26 frontier as a basis for negotiation, Braden sensed that "peace depends on our discovering the right procedure to follow."[61] Cardozo, Braden, and Manuel Bianchi hastily constructed a plan that stressed arbitration and popular plebiscite. The new formula called for the conference to take as minimum and maximum positions the May 27 offer and the June 24 counterproposal and create a new boundary, not by juridi-cal arbitration, but by arbitration *ex aequo et bono*.[62] The president of any mediator state could act on behalf of the other chief executives

[59] MOCA, p. 3. Braden did not relate how Cantilo's plans were thwarted. He simply wrote, "It was essential that the ultimatum given the Paraguayans by the Argentine Minister of Foreign Affairs be side-tracked and negotiations be kept alive" (*ibid.*).

[60] U.S., Dept. of State, *Foreign Relations, 1938*, V, 148. Following violent pro-tests from the mediators, Finot and Diez de Medina announced that they would withhold the document until June 29. The memorandum was never released. Wash-ington pressure and a stiff note from Aranha, Brazilian foreign minister, to Diez de Medina, helped to force the suppression of the document (MOCA, p. 4).

[61] U.S., Dept. of State, *Foreign Relations, 1938*, V, 146.

[62] *Ibid.*, p. 154. The origin of this so-called *ex aequo et bono* formula, unofficially called the "Roosevelt formula" by Braden, is by no means clear. In a letter dated May 22, 1966, Dr. Efraím Cardozo declared that "I passed on the ideas of the [*ex aequo et bono* formula] in order to prevent a Bolivian move [of threats to retire from the conference] in an unofficial manner, and Mr. Braden decided to adopt them as his own, bring the proposals into the open without my consent." In a letter dated May 9, 1966, Spruille Braden wrote on the same subject that "I would say that it grew pretty much like Topsy out of discussions by all the Delegates and that no one is entitled to take credit for it."

In a third communication dated December 1, 1967, Manuel Bianchi of Chile

and was to make the award following the signature of a *compromis* by Asunción and La Paz. The *compromis* would be ratified by the Bolivian Constitutional Convention and by plebiscite in Paraguay.[63] In this fashion, Paraguayan acquiescence to conference pressure would be effectively masked. On the evening of June 29 Braden obtained the approval of both President Ortiz of Argentina and Diez de Medina of Bolivia for the plebiscite and arbitration scheme.[64] The following day Busch of Bolivia ordered Diez de Medina to accept the May 27 frontier minus littoral and payment. Prospects of settlement rose perceptibly, but Gerónimo Zubizarreta had come to regret his conciliatory mood of the previous forty-eight hours. Officially presented with the *ex aequo et bono* procedural plan (the title Braden, Cardozo, and Bianchi had given their plebiscite and arbitration scheme) on June 30, he categorically rejected it.[65] On July 1 the Paraguayan government formally rejected the June 26 boundary offer, a despairing Cantilo again prepared to end direct negotiations,[66] and Spruille Braden severed personal relations with the Bolivian delegation because of a

---

called the *ex aequo et bono* formula "a united effort" on the part of the mediators plus the representatives of the ex-belligerents."

[63] U.S., Dept. of State, *Foreign Relations, 1938*, V, 154.

[64] MOCA, p. 5. Diez de Medina gave only provisional approval to the arbitration and plebiscite scheme on June 29. In a letter dated May 9, 1966, Spruille Braden relates how he also obtained the approval of the Argentine president: "It was at that time [June 29] that I got Zubizarreta's memorandum which that same afternoon I showed to President Ortiz telling him that it would bring the peace treaty. As you may recall, he very much doubted that it would, but because of my insistence that this was the solution, he made me his ambassador with full authorization to accept anything for his government that I accepted for my own."

[65] Efraím Cardozo, interview, Asunción, Paraguay, October 15, 1965. Cardozo suggested that Zubizarreta, who apparently had given provisional consent to the arbitration and plebiscite plan, changed his mind chiefly because Saavedra Lamas had informed him that the Bolivians were tired of bargaining and would soon make significant concessions. Spruille Braden took the same position (U.S., Dept. of State, *Foreign Relations, 1938*, V, 157).

[66] *Ibid.*, p. 160; and MOCA, p. 8. Braden later charged that the abridged conference minutes, which were subsequently constructed to cover the period from June 24 to July 9, had been rewritten to protect Cantilo (U.S., Archives, RG 59, Decimal File 724.34119/1566, no. 733, Braden [Buenos Aires] to Dept. State, Aug. 17, 1938, p. 3).

spat with Enrique Finot.[67] Reason and bullion had been tried and found wanting; secrecy and coercion now would be pressed into service.

Since United States, Brazilian, Peruvian, and Chilean representatives had agreed to the plebiscite and arbitration scheme, work on a draft treaty began on July 2 under Braden's overall direction.[68] The same day General Estigarribia, now Paraguayan minister to Washington, landed in Buenos Aires; after discussions with members of his national delegation he accepted the terms Zubizarreta had rejected. Meanwhile, unaware that Braden had already begun drafting a treaty, the still forlorn Cantilo first presented another alternative to the former belligerents and then on July 4 sought from the mediators forty-eight hours "in which, if possible, to bring the parties into agreement."[69] *De facto* direction of negotiations had passed to Braden, who considered time to be an essential factor, but Cantilo was still conference president, and refusal of his petition might have created serious difficulty. The Argentine foreign minister was, therefore, granted his request.

Meanwhile in Asunción resistance was buckling. On June 27 Ernesto Vidal, Chilean consul, demanded Paraguayan acceptance of the June 26 offer before June 29.[70] Zubizarreta held fast, but on July 1 Captain José Bozzano, minister of war and marine, informed the delegation that he accepted the June 26 boundary and the *ex aequo et bono* procedural plan.[71] On July 3 and 4 large Bolivian army units

---

[67] MOCA, p. 9. In the heat of the discussion Finot was quoted as saying, "I laugh at the United States." Braden engaged in no social conversation and few direct dealings with either Bolivian diplomat until they extended an apology on July 5.

[68] U.S., Archives, RG 59, Decimal File 724.34119/1448, no. 184, Braden (Buenos Aires) to Dept. State, July 6, 1938, p. 9. Cardozo announced his acceptance of the arbitration and plebiscite scheme on July 2 even though Zubizarreta was still opposed to it. However, following Finot's argument with Braden, Rodrigues Alves had to persuade the Bolivian delegation to accept the scheme all over again.

[69] U.S., Dept. of State, *Foreign Relations, 1938*, V, 159–160.

[70] Paraguay, Archivo, File 20 (*confidencial y reservado*), Memorandum of Ministro Argana, June 27, 1930, p. 38.

[71] In his letter of May 22, 1966, Cardozo wrote of Captain Bozzano's action: "Captain Bozzano was Minister of War and the Navy. His support of the formula was the equivalent of the Army and the Navy."

began to deploy along the line of *hitos*. Almost simultaneously a power struggle between Estigarribia and Zubizarreta ended with the latter's resignation from the delegation.[72] On July 5 President Paiva telegraphed his acceptance in principle of the arbitration and plebiscite plan.[73] Both former belligerents were now provisionally in agreement on terms, but they trusted neither each other nor the mediators.[74] Furthermore, revelation of the accepted boundary might initiate drastic action by nationalistic elements in either country. On the afternoon of July 5, Braden, Rodrigues Alves, Bianchi, and Barreda Laos met in Braden's office and "agreed that it would be unwise for Dr. Cantilo to continue the negotiations alone."[75] Cantilo then was properly briefed, and on the evening of July 5 both former belligerents verbally agreed to conference arrangements.[76] On July 6 a committee comprising Braden, Ruiz Moreno, and Barreda Laos began to draft a secret treaty that would provide Paraguay and Bolivia with the desired guaranties.[77] Work on both this document and an explanatory map was speedily completed the next day. On the other hand, dickering and maneuvering over wording of a second treaty to be made public (calling for *ex aequo et bono* arbitration) continued until the afternoon of July 8.

[72] U.S., Dept. of State, *Foreign Relations, 1938*, V, 161–162; and Uruguay, Archivo, File 1980/29, no. 26 L.1498, and no. 61 L. 1492, Martínez Thédy (Buenos Aires) to Montevideo, July 4, 1938, July 7, 1938, p. 1. In particular the Uruguayan report notes that Zubizarreta's deposition was not brought without a sharp struggle.

[73] Paraguay, Archivo, File 40, no. 107, Paiva to Báez (Buenos Aires), July 5, 1938, p. 263.

[74] U.S., Dept. of State, *Foreign Relations, 1938*, V, 160. "The Paraguayan position is that logically the whole zone between their counter proposal [June 24] line and the Conference line [May 27] minus the littoral must be submitted to arbitration. The Bolivian position is that the Western line of the award must be written into the arbitral compromise as being Esmeralda, 27 of November, Captain Ustares, because . . . they [the Bolivians] did not trust the arbitrators to award it. . . . Therefore, on discovering a procedure satisfactory to both parties depends the peace."

[75] MOCA, p. 12.

[76] U.S., Archives, RG 59, Decimal File 724.34119/1448, no. 184, Braden (Buenos Aires) to Dept. State, July 6, 1938, pp. 1–4.

[77] MOCA, p. 13; and U.S., Archives, RG 59, Decimal File 724.34119/1454, no. 186, Braden (Buenos Aires) to Dept. State, July 8, 1938, pp. 1–2. See Appendix VII.

On that evening both secret agreements (map and protocol) and the draft arbitration treaty (the public document) were ready for signature when a distraught Cantilo announced that "the whole program is off";[78] he had talked to Zubizarreta, who was opposed to the entire project and procedure. Braden and Bianchi immediately forced the necessity of reconsideration upon the Argentine foreign minister, pointing out that Zubizarreta could not be considered spokesman for the delegation.[79] By 11:30 that evening Cantilo again was prepared to proceed with the ceremonies. The final corrections and verbal adjustments were made in the Argentine Foreign Office between midnight and 2:00 A.M. with the Bolivians and Paraguayans in different rooms. The most serious problem developed when shortly after 2:00 A.M., Diez de Medina announced that he would retire and return to sign the documents on the morrow. After years of inconclusive discussion, the mediators were too close to success to allow the Bolivian an opportunity to change his mind. After hearing some frantic entreaties, Diez de Medina consented to remain, and by 2:40 A.M. all documents had been signed.[80] Later that morning the agreement on a treaty of arbitration was announced to the world.

Having drawn up an arbitral treaty and another treaty that, in effect, nullified the proposed arbitration, the mediators were faced with keeping the second document secret. The vanquished Zubizarreta reached Asunción on July 13. He had promised to remain silent concerning various secret arrangements, but he chose to act otherwise. Fortunately Estigarribia and Cardozo had been flown to Asunción on July 11, and, aided by Luis A. Riart, they managed to silence Zubizarreta.[81]

[78] MOCA, p. 15.

[79] *Ibid.*, pp. 15–16. Bianchi, the Chilean delegate, "buttonholed Cantilo forcibly," and shouted at him that Zubizarreta was "talking through his wounds." In a letter dated December 1, 1967, Bianchi affirmed the accuracy of Braden's report.

[80] MOCA, pp. 15–16.

[81] *Ibid.*, pp. 16-17. Braden reported that "Zubizarreta had indicated he would not openly oppose the treaty" (U.S., Dept. of State, *Foreign Relations, 1938*, V, 166). The North American suspected that this promise would not be kept. Zubizarreta made a determined effort, but the Directorio of the Liberal Party decided to support the treaty (U.S., Archives, RG 59, Decimal File 724.34119/1496, no. 635, Howard [Asunción] to Dept. State, July 14, 1938, p. 2).

It was the ineffectual Cantilo who launched a detailed discussion of the confidential agreement in a July 17 morning plenary session. Before the Argentine foreign minister had completed his speech, Estigarribia rose and announced that his nation would not be part of any secret arrangements, such compacts being "repugnant to the public sentiment of Paraguay."[82] The tactful Barreda Laos promptly suggested a temporary adjournment. The minutes of the evening session of the same day contain the following narrative: "Ambassador Braden says that his government has a firm policy in the sense of not signing any treaty that has a secret section, and since the United States intends to sign the treaty, this one is not able to have any secret clauses."[83] In this fashion another pitfall was circumvented.

The date for the official signing of the public treaty was set for July 21 because President Ortiz of Argentina wished to declare a national holiday. On July 19, however, the mediators assembled to affirm the confidential arrangements. Paraguayan representatives appeared satisfied, but the Bolivians did not. Elío's June 1935 and August 1936 misadventures apparently had inculcated paranoiac fears of betrayal; Diez de Medina demanded new assurances that the conference would honor the secret arrangements of July 9. Argentine and Bolivian chancellors soon were making angry threats, the former calling negotiations off, the latter demanding that his special train be prepared for departure. Once again Rodrigues Alves and Braden came to the rescue. A special sketch approximating what the boundary would look like was drawn for Diez de Medina and another confidential note hastily fabricated. It stated that Bolivia considered the secret arrangements "an integral part of the [arbitration] treaty, and therefore, if the award is not in accordance with the document, Bolivia will be free to protect her rights appropriately."[84] Paraguayan representatives could not allow themselves to be considered remiss in the defense of the na-

[82] MOCA, p. 18; and U.S., Archives, RG 59, Decimal File 724.34119/1602, no. 749, Braden (Buenos Aires) to Dept. State, Aug. 26, 1938, p. 3.
[83] U.S., Archives, RG 59, Decimal File 724.34119/1602, no. 749, Braden (Buenos Aires) to Dept. State, Aug. 26, 1938, p. 2, of evening session.
[84] *Ibid.*, Decimal File 724.34119/1489, no. 206, Braden (Buenos Aires) to Dept. State, July 20, 1938, pp. 1–2.

tional patrimony. They now demanded and received written assurances from Cantilo concerning the western Chaco boundary and possession of *fortines* Patria and Galpón.[85]

On July 21, 1938, at 3:00 P.M., the Treaty of Peace, Friendship, and Limits between the Republics of Bolivia and Paraguay was handed down for posterity. Heart of the covenant was the *ex aequo et bono* formula providing equity arbitration for supposedly disputed Chaco territories. Even a careful reading of the treaty leaves a confused idea of what territory actually was subject to arbitration. Again, Spruille Braden provided adequate enlightenment. To a State Department official who had difficulty interpreting the treaty he wrote, "You will recall from my reports at the time, Article 2, Paragraph C, [July 21, 1938 treaty] was purposely so phrased as to make it impossible for anyone to define the western zone."[86]

Both Brazil and Argentina now took steps to prevent a successful coup against the Paiva government.[87] Even before the July 21 treaty was signed, Findlay Howard, United States minister in Asunción, pre-

---

[85] Paraguay, Archivo, Folio 30-2-E, *Tratado de paz, amistad y límites, Paraguay y Bolivia: Suscrito en Buenos Aires el 21 de julio, 1938. (1) Copias de documentos relativos a los tratados de paz, amistad y límites del julio-1938. (2) Recortes periodísticos correspondientes al año 1938.* In this folio, unmarked except for the number "7," was a note from Cantilo to Báez dated July 21, 1938, that says, "In my capacity as President of the Conference of Peace, and representing it, with the full powers which the arbitrators have delegated to it, in agreement with all the things contained in your worthy note, the boundary line in the North and East of the Chaco will leave forts Galpón and Patria under Paraguayan control."

The Paraguayans also received another note marked "4°" and dated July 21, 1938, which fixed the eastern limit of the western zone to be awarded: "The line of the award of the western region of the Chaco never will be able to go more to the east of whatever point of the line than that which goes from [Fortín] 27 of November to Pozo Hondo on the Pilcomayo River with the inflexion necessary so that in any case, Yrendagüé remains under its jurisdiction."

[86] U.S., Archives, RG 59, Decimal File 724.34119/1779, Braden (Bogotá) to Butler, Feb. 18, 1939, p. 1. See Appendix VIII, Article II, clause c of July 21, 1938, treaty.

[87] U.S., Archives, RG 59, Decimal File 724.34119/1510, no. 213, Braden (Buenos Aires) to Dept. State, July 26, 1938, p. 2. The Paraguayans were deathly afraid that details of the secret agreement would somehow be made public in Bolivia and that the revelation would prevent approval of the July 21, 1938, treaty by plebiscite.

dicted that the stipulated plebiscite would overwhelmingly sanction the treaty; the following month he was proven correct.[88] Meanwhile in Bolivia "three long, secret sessions"[89] were necessary, but the Busch junta ruthlessly silenced rabid nationalists and ratified the treaty. On September 2, 1938, the Chaco Arbitral College initiated its proceedings. Its meetings were secret, but its membership consisted of the same diplomats who had signed the treaties of July 1938. While Bolivian and Paraguayan representatives went through the motions of presenting legal and historical arguments for the college's consideration, a new military commission labored in the Chaco to report on the geographical characteristics of the zones allegedly to be awarded.[90] Perhaps the most significant problems brought before the Arbitral College were the Paraguayan request for the town of Cururenda and the Bolivian desire for a favorable frontier readjustment in the vicinity of Esmeralda.[91] The college did serve a valuable purpose, however. Its existence and ostensible arbitral activity signified to the Bolivian and Paraguayan peoples that neither side had dictated the peace.

[88] *Ibid.*, Decimal File 724.34119/1496, no. 635, Howard (Asunción) to Dept. State, July 14, 1938, p. 4. The final vote, certified by the Paraguayan Supreme Court on August 24, 1938, was 135,835 in favor, 13,207 opposed, and 559 blank votes.

[89] Eduardo Diez de Medina, *De un siglo al otro*, p. 375; MOCA, p. 17. Former presidents Hernán Siles, Bautista Saavedra, and Colonel David Toro all opposed the treaty of July 21, 1938.

[90] For a list of the members of the Advisory Military Commission see Appendix III. Even before it was officially established on August 28, 1938, Colonel Ernesto Florit, commission commander, protested that months, rather than five weeks, would be needed to make an accurate geographical survey. His protest was rejected. The pragmatic Mr. Braden again provides the explanation: "When dealing with two nations subject to sudden changes in the government, it is best to get such matters [as arbitration] definitely concluded as soon as possible" (U.S., Archives, RG 59, Decimal File 724.34119/1603, no. 750, Braden [Buenos Aires] to Dept. State, Aug. 26, 1938, p. 2).

[91] Paraguay, Archivo, File 39, no. 159 (*muy confidencial y reservado*), delegation (Buenos Aires) to ministry, Oct. 6, 1938, p. 103. Neither side was prepared to make sufficient concessions, and the matter was finally dropped. In reply to a question on this matter, Spruille Braden wrote on June 13, 1966, "We did not have any real furor over Cururenda or any of the other details. We had buttoned up everything so securely, particularly with the map which we had made the parties initial, showing exactly where the line was to run."

MAP 9
ARBITRAL AWARD OF OCTOBER 10, 1938

BOLIVIA

Parapetí River

Lateriquique River

Otuquis River

Ravelo ●
●Ft. Paredes
Chevoreca
●Ft. Sn. Juan

BRAZIL

Captain Ustares
●Ft. Pando
Palmar de las Islas
Nameless Lake
●Ft. Galpóri
●Ft. Vanguardia

Parapetí ●
●Camiri
●Huirapitindi
27 de Noviembre
●Ft. Ingavi

20°

●Boyuibé
●Yrendagüé
Bahía Negra
(Pto. Pacheco)

●Carandaiti

●Capirenda
●Villa Montes
Mihanovich ●
Fuerte Olimpo ●
Pto. Guaraní

Sanandita ●
●Palmar
Ft. d'Orbigny
Ft. Cururenda
Yacuiba;
●La Esmeralda
ARGENTINA
●Ft. Guachalla
●Ft. Ballivián

Pto. Sastre ●
Apa River
Pto. Casado ●

●Ft. Boquerón
Pto. Pinasco ●

●Embarcación

Verde River

Pilcomayo River

Paraguay River

24°

⊛ ASUNCIÓN
PARAGUAY

62°

58°

From La Conferencia de paz del Chaco

On October 10 the Chaco Arbitral College handed down a frontier that matched the line determined on July 9. Bolivians were able to take heart because the enemy had been driven back from the Oriente oil fields; Asunción's spokesmen could point with pride to their exclusive retention of the Paraguay River littoral and some extensive territorial acquisitions. Admittedly, the populace of neither nation was ecstatic about the settlement, but too much had been gained to gamble it all in another military venture. The result might be termed peace through frustration of aggressive instincts. The Chaco Arbitral College liquidated itself on October 14, its mission accomplished.[92]

After almost eight years and several false starts, Paraguay and Bolivia officially renewed diplomatic relations on November 26, 1938. The advance of Bolivian forces to the new frontier was accomplished without incident, and on December 28, 1938, both sides verified that the arbitral award had been carried out—but not before Bolivia had secretly agreed to pay Paraguay for allegedly valuable installations left in the evacuated area.[93]

The Chaco dispute seemed on the verge of liquidating itself, but as usual, the orthodox norms of diplomatic endeavor could not be applied. Efraím Cardozo, Paraguayan delegate had been readying a long-neglected responsibility for immediate conference consideration. More than three years earlier Saavedra Lamas had given sweeping assurances that a Chaco economic conference would be called. Clauses

[92] See Map 9 for a graphic presentation of the arbitral award of October 10, 1938.

[93] Paraguay, Archivo, File 38, nos. 213 and 200, delegation (Buenos Aires) to ministry, Dec. 18 and 22, 1938, pp. 31, 40. The Bolivians refused to pay for any roads or buildings built by the Paraguayans in the region between the old line of *hitos* and the frontier of October 10, 1938, until Paraguayan troops retired from the area. On December 22 Bolivia agreed to pay 100,000 Argentine pesos for the installations, but payment would be made only with the occupation of the zone by Bolivian troops.

In Paraguay, Archivo, Folio 79-2-E (*Planillas y notas sobre la liquidación general según resúmenes de las planillas de 1933–34, 36; Rendición de cuentas comprobantes de la delegación del Paraguay*) there is an unnumbered receipt for a check of 100,000 pesos. The number of the check is 143504, drawn on the First National Bank of Boston in Buenos Aires. Also with the check receipt was a letter of acknowledgment from Cantilo to the Paraguayan foreign minister, Captain Elías Ayala. The letter was dated February 10, 1939.

5 and 6 of the June 12, 1935, protocol bound the mediators to take steps to remedy Bolivian and Paraguayan commercial and transit problems. In mid-December the Paraguayan delegate broached the subject to Allen Haden, United States assistant delegate. Haden reported that he could support the plan if Peru and Chile did likewise. The Peruvians replied by vetoing the project.

Undeterred, Cardozo continued his efforts. Buoyed by Brazilian and Uruguayan support for a Chaco economic conference, Cardozo forwarded a strong memorandum to Cantilo on January 11, 1939. The Paraguayan threatened that unless some attempt were made to remedy the transit and commercial problems of his nation as well as those of Bolivia, he would oppose conference closure. The United States had on the previous day already indicated its profound disinterest in a Chaco economic conference, but it was Cantilo who provided the final blow. Replying on January 13, 1939, the Argentine foreign minister announced that agitation for an economic conference "would hinder"[94] future consideration of Paraguayan-Bolivian economic difficulties. Thus when the peace conference closed on January 23, 1939, the mediators resolved that they had fulfilled their mission despite having done nothing about commercial and transit problems between Paraguay and Bolivia.[95]

The mediators departed from Buenos Aires, but Washington was distrustful of Latin American diplomatic security. In answer to an earlier query, Allen Haden replied on January 28, "with regards to the destruction of the secret agreement which you will recall was agreed upon, Cardozo informs us that he is leaving for Asunción next Saturday; that he is returning here [Buenos Aires] thereafter on private business; that he will bring with him the Paraguayan copy; Finot is requesting transmission of the Bolivian copy; Finot, Cardozo and Cantilo will meet in a room and simultaneously toss their copies into

94 Paraguay, Archivo, Folio 32-3-E, document 228, Cantilo to Cardozo, Jan. 13, 1939, p. 1.
95 U.S., Archives, RG 59, Decimal File 724.34119/1755, no. 21, Haden (Buenos Aires) to Dept. State, Jan. 23, 1939, p. 1. Because of the transportation problems noted, both Paraguay and Bolivia refused initially to sign the final resolution. Not until the morning of January 23 did Paraguay agree to sign the final act.

an open fire."[96] The United States assistant delegate apparently had forgotten that the unexpected was always the *modus operandi* in Chaco negotiation. Seven months later, through an intermediary, Haden informed State Department officials that "so far as he [Haden] is aware, none of the copies of this agreement have been destroyed."[97] The Chaco feud is officially settled, but a nation-state has neither permanent friends nor immutable enemies. The original documents probably remain where knowledgeable diplomats can lay hands on them—just in case.

[96] *Ibid.*, Decimal File 724.34119/177 1/2, Haden (Buenos Aires) to Dept. State, Jan. 28, 1939, p. 1. In May 1966 the author forwarded the quoted material from Haden's letter to Spruille Braden. Braden, in a letter of June 2, 1966, replied, "the secret document to be destroyed was the one in which the arbitral award really was covered in full together with a map before the actual arbitration proceedings were entered into." Refer again to Appendix VII.

[97] *Ibid.*, Decimal File 724.34119/1777 1/2, Haden (Buenos Aires) to Butler, Feb. 7, 1939, p. 1. Written on this communiqué and dated August 1939 was the information quoted. Said information was passed on to Butler from Haden by "A.S.C. [unable to identify]."

8. THE PEACE CONFERENCE AND INTER-AMERICAN DIPLOMACY

> ... it [Chaco dispute] has been solved because of the determination of the parties to the controversy to find an equitable and peaceful settlement, and because of the efficacy of the inter-American system of consultation and cooperation.
> I cannot too strongly emphasize ... that the peaceful solution of this old dispute has served to strengthen greatly the peace machinery which we have set up in this hemisphere.
> Sumner Welles, July 27, 1938

> The actors in this scandalous episode [the Chaco peace settlement] ... which is called the treaty of July 21, will never be forgiven by the generations of the future.
> Marco Antonio Laconich, La paz del Chaco

IN JULY 1938 Spruille Braden forwarded a special communiqué from a Chaco military observer to Washington and appended his own comments: "The report demonstrated fairly conclusively that hostilities would have been renewed in the Chaco had the Conference failed to bring about agreement through direct negotiations."[1] On June 24, 1938, The Bolivian Constitutional Convention had authorized the Busch government to raise $4,000,000 for arms because the Chaco peace conference was expected to fail.[2] The Bolivian president's national mobilization order of July 2 and the subsequent concentration of Bolivian forces along the line of *hitos* were probably acts intended to intimidate the Paraguayans, but informed judgment supports the linkage of mediation failure and the reappearance of gunsmoke in Chaco skies.[3] In light of these circumstances, General Estigarribia's intervention in Chaco negotiation must be considered decisive. The hero of the Chaco War was perhaps the only person with sufficient prestige to make concessions and still escape denunciation as a traitor. Estigarribia as Paraguayan ambassador to the United States, had no authority over the delegation at Buenos Aires, but nevertheless he accepted conference terms for Paraguay and deposed Zubizarreta as delegation president.[4] The general took a calculated risk, but the prospective dangers were sufficient for him to waive convention. Continued intransigence meant war or, at the very least, new military purchases and increased tension along the line of *hitos*. Peace became preferable to renewed cataclysm over a few thousand kilometers of dubious value.

[1] United States, National Archives, Washington, D.C., Department of State, RG 59, Decimal File 724.34119/1550, no. 722, Braden (Buenos Aires) to Dept. State, Aug. 4, 1938, pp. 1–2.

[2] *Ibid.*, Decimal File 724.34119/1426, no. 31, Prendergast (La Paz) to Dept. State, June 27, 1938, p. 1.

[3] Eduardo Diez de Medina, *De un siglo al otro*, p. 367. The former foreign minister of Bolivia stated that failure of the Chaco conference would have led to renewed war. See also Justo Pastor Benítez, *Estigarribia: El soldado del Chaco*, p. 152. The former Paraguayan minister held that Estigarribia believed the June and July 1938 conference effort to be the final hope for Chaco peace. Spruille Braden reiterated this conviction in a special letter dated November 2, 1965. He declared that if the July 1938 negotiations had failed "the two ex-belligerents would have gone back to fighting, [and] unquestionably Argentina, Brazil and Chile would have become involved in the war."

[4] In his letter of May 22, 1966, Dr. Efraím Cardozo confirms the fact that Estigarribia had no legal or diplomatic authority to intervene in Chaco conference negotiations: "General Estigarribia had only his great moral authority. When he arrived in Buenos Aires from Washington, he had no official power over the Paraguayan delegation."

In September 1937 and February 1938 Estigarribia had told United States and Brazilian diplomats that a frontier similar to the one offered on May 27 or June 26 could be acceptable to him.[5] Thus, the latter's timely arrival was hardly accidental. Spruille Braden wrote in a special report that he was "satisfied that the constructive stand taken by General Estigarribia in supporting Dr. Cardozo and which played so important a part in our success was largely a result of his conversations in Washington with the Department."[6] Paraguay's hero came to Buenos Aires ready for battle; with Hull, Welles, and Spruille Braden among his collaborators, the odds were against the opposition.

United States reaction to Estigarribia's successful sally was prompt. Even before the August 1938 plebiscite took place, Washington had sanctioned preliminary studies of Paraguayan financial and economic problems.[7] Officially, discussions on a proposed loan did not begin until March 1939. Following a June 13, 1939, exchange of notes, the United States agreed to extend credits "not exceeding $500,000 at any one time to assist the Government of Paraguay in expanding foreign commerce and economic relations with the United States through a policy of meeting promptly commercial obligations to United States

[5] U.S., Archives, RG 59, Decimal File 724.34119/1013, no. 176, Braden (Buenos Aires) to Dept. State, Sept. 15, 1937; Decimal File 724.34119/1218, no. 633, Braden (Buenos Aires) to Dept. State, Feb. 7, 1938, Enclosure 1, p. 1. Braden, with Rodrigues Alves in agreement, worked out a Chaco frontier "from some point on the Pilcomayo River between Fortines D'Orbigny and Ballivián running north to approximately Lat. 20° south, then eastward to the inner bay of Bahía Negra." Bolivia was to pay a cash indemnity to Paraguay and the latter would provide free port facilities for Bolivia on the Paraguay River (*ibid.*, Decimal File 724.34119/1007, no. 482, Braden [Buenos Aires] to Dept. State, Aug. 31, 1937, p. 7).

[6] *Ibid.*, Decimal File 724.34119/1570, no. 735, Memorandum of conference activities, June–July 1938, Braden (Buenos Aires) to Dept. State, Aug. 11, 1938, p. 11. In an interview, June 8, 1965, New York City, Spruille Braden said, "I threw out Zubizarreta." It would appear that Mr. Braden was quite responsible for Estigarribia's trip to Buenos Aires.

[7] U.S., Archives, RG 59, Decimal File 724.34119/1510, no. 213, Braden (Buenos Aires) to Dept. State, July 26, 1938, p. 1; and Decimal File 724.34119, no. 719, Braden (Buenos Aires) to Dept. State, p. 1. On Paraguayan request, William Dana, commercial attaché in Argentina, was sent to Asunción to carry out an economic, financial, and agricultural survey. A report later was forwarded from Dana to the Department of State.

Nationals and Concerns, and reducing seasonal and unusual [exchange rate] fluctuations."[8] The Department of State had long been aware that Paraguay wished to escape Argentine economic domination.[9] Through financial assistance, Washington could simultaneously help a nation in need and increase its own influence in a part of the Americas where that influence had been distinctly limited.

The policy of still another military figure, Colonel Germán Busch, had a marked effect upon the crucial negotiations of 1938. Previously, the Tejada Sorzano and Toro governments had insisted upon the necessity of a useful Paraguay River littoral for Bolivia. The instability of these regimes meant that major concessions might have caused their demise. Evidence that Busch was in a somewhat stronger position is seen in his secret offer to Spruille Braden in April 1938. By merely accepting a littoral in the Bahía Negra area and by offering to pay for it, the Bolivian president demonstrated his realization that an outlet of essentially psychological value was all his nation could expect to obtain on the lower Paraguay River. This admission was crucial, for had the acquisition of a port been a *sine qua non*, the negotiations would have collapsed.

A series of fortuitous events also helped Busch face the realities of his situation. In June 1935 Tomás Elío had warned the more uncompromising members of the delegation that Bolivia had lost the Chaco; all the nation could hope to achieve was the preservation of its control of the petroleum areas.[10] When Colonel Busch seized power in May 1937, Standard Oil's wells had become nationalized property, and Argentina was helping YPFB operate them. The burgeoning Argentine-Brazilian struggle for dominance in the Oriente gave Busch the

---

[8] United States, Department of State, *Papers relating to the Foreign Relations of the United States, 1939*, V, 758–765. Estigarribia had also sought credits to build a road from Asunción to the Brazilian border at Yguazú. Such a road would help to break Paraguayan dependence upon the Rio de la Plata–Paraná–Paraguay River system. The loan later was provided through the Export-Import Bank.

[9] For a study of Argentine economic predominance in Paraguay, see U.S., Archives, RG 59, Decimal File 724.34119/311/1/2, "Summary of Chaco Mediation Efforts and the Work of the Buenos Aires Peace Conference; April to November, 1935," G. H. Butler, p. 165.

[10] Roberto Querazu Calvo, *Masamaclay*, pp. 431–432.

advantage, and the resulting Gutiérrez-Brandão Treaty provided a potentially useful outlet for Oriente products at terms that La Paz considered satisfactory. Psychological needs could at last be relegated to a secondary consideration and the realities as outlined by Elío given priority. Security for the national petroleum wealth demanded a Paraguayan retreat in the western Chaco, and the conference proposals of May 27 and June 26 (both accepted by Bolivia) met these requirements. Altiplano diplomats skillfully concealed from the conferees the knowledge that the Busch government would have paid up to £400,000 simply to force the Paraguayans to retreat a reasonable distance from the petroleum fields.[11] As this goal was achieved without renewed hostilities or the expenditure of the capital, Busch may be said to have shrewdly determined the national destiny.

Finally, Sumner Welles and others of the State Department hierarchy wasted no time asserting that the Chaco peace settlement strengthened inter-American peace machinery. Actually the gentlemen in question maintained a discreet silence concerning the special benefits that the United States derived from the peace. As early as 1936 Washington had become concerned over the possibility of Fascist penetration of the Americas and the absence of safeguards in dealing with this eventuality.[12] The probability of new war in Europe loomed larger and larger, and the prospect of United States involvement could not be overlooked. The Washington government believed that it could not afford the continued irresolution of the Chaco question—a problem that the Fascist powers might manipulate for their own purposes.

When the Chaco settlement is compared with the stated ideals of the conferees, the usual chasm between principles and performance

[11] Diez de Medina, *De un siglo al otro*, p. 374.

[12] In an interview (October 16, 1965, Asunción, Paraguay) Juan Isidro Ramírez stated that Franklin D. Roosevelt (who was in Buenos Aires for the first days of the Inter-American Peace Conference of December 1936) told him that the Chaco dispute must be settled promptly because he (Roosevelt) feared a war would break out in Europe. Roosevelt believed that the United States would probably become party to the conflict; consequently, Chaco peace was necessary so that the United States would not be involved simultaneously in a war in Europe and in one in South America.

becomes a formidable abyss. For example, the declaration of August 3, 1932, had proclaimed the nonrecognition of territories obtained by military conquest. Although written into the June 1935 and January 1936 protocols, the doctrine was surreptitiously buried in 1938. No *de jure* ruling was sought, and the October 1938 award recognized Paraguayan sovereignty over practically all the territory conquered prior to June 14, 1935. In addition, both Braden and the State Department had declared their opposition to secret understandings.[13] Circumstances forced a rapid reappraisal of the situation; guarantees were clandestinely given, and millions in both Americas were led to believe that the Chaco settlement had been a case of "open Covenant(s) openly arrived at." Furthermore, conference closure without action on the transit and commercial problems of Bolivia and Paraguay violated the June 12, 1935, protocol.[14] The latter's binding force must be considered in effect, since the July 1938 treaty does not address itself to these issues. Such utter disregard for solemn pledges again demonstrates that nations, American or otherwise, do not feel bound to honor promises that clash with their vested interests. To this repetitious tale of expedient action, the mediators might state in self-defense that action or nonaction in the specific instances cited jeopardized the possibility of concluding a permanent peace. While the moralist might insist that alternative means to settlement were plausible, he could do so only by ignoring certain critical factors.

First, the August 3, 1932, declaration was made before Paraguayan victories indicated which side would possess *de facto* control of most of the Chaco. Inclusion of this declaration into the protocol of June 1935 was feasible chiefly because the conference was supposed to establish responsibility for the war. The question of war responsibilities

---

[13] U.S., Dept. of State, *Foreign Relations, 1938*, V, 137–139. Rodrigues Alves had remarked to Braden as early as June 7, 1938, that some kind of secret agreement might be necessary to break the negotiational deadlock. Braden reported to the Department of State, "I have stated that I do not like the latter idea" (*ibid.*, p. 137). On June 9, 1938, the Department of State replied, "the Department concurs in your opinion that no agreement should be made to keep secret the terms of any agreement accepted by the two parties" (*ibid.*, p. 139).

[14] See the protocol of June 12, 1935, Article I, clause 5, in Appendix II.

soon degenerated into a sham battle mired in technicalities. The mediators tacitly acknowledged that naming the war's instigator and a peace settlement were nonconcomitant goals. As late as June 1938 the Paraguayan leadership demanded recognition of the line of *hitos* as the legal frontier. Recognizing that Paraguay held the territory and that the conference possessed no other means than military intervention to force juridical determination of ownership, a Paraguayan stepback of 50 to 150 kilometers was really a major victory.

Secondly, the aversion of Braden and the State Department to secret agreements can be understood, but it was hardly realistic. Considering the instability of the governments in Paraguay and Bolivia, the lack of mutual trust, and the limited time available to the mediators in June and July 1938, the choice was narrowed to confidential notes and documents or no peace at all.

Thirdly, since Bolivia and Paraguay were landlocked, any attempt to remedy the economic or transit problems of either state must seriously affect the interests of at least one mediator nation. The proposed means of handling the problems, a Chaco economic conference, was in itself a dangerous undertaking.[15] The United States, for example, was prepared to aid Paraguay independently, but relations with Bolivia had entered a critical period due to La Paz's nationalization of Standard Oil properties. Peru and probably Chile feared any Bolivian move that might modify the 1929 Tacna-Arica settlement. Argentine opposition was engendered in part by the Oriente railway issue and the prospect of fresh conflict with Brazil and/or Chile if that question were immediately reopened. Any action that tended to divide the limitrophe states conceivably jeopardized the permanency of a Chaco settlement.

Because the antagonists conceived of justice as the triumph of national interest, the definitive Chaco settlement was neither moral, impartial, nor faithful to previously stated goals; instead it was an agreement that all interested parties could accept. Fortified by more than

---

[15] Paraguay, Congreso Nacional, *La paz con Bolivia ante el poder legislativo*, pp. 90, 95–96. Particularly in the Paraguayan Senate, representatives lamented the fact that the Chaco Conference of Peace had closed without taking any action with regard to solving Paraguayan-Bolivian economic difficulties.

thirty years of peace in the Chaco, it is reasonable to assume that the mediators made an optimum settlement and thereby performed a commendable service to humanity. Such a naked sanction of power politics and secret diplomacy will no doubt disturb some advocates of increased inter-American cooperation and understanding. In fact, this writer does not unequivocally condone the employment of such principles in international politics. Yet where the alternatives are peace and war, no method that might solve a dispute as bloody as the Chaco affair should be arbitrarily discarded.

Bolivia and the Origins of the Chaco Combat of June 1932

Eduardo Arze Quiroga relates that Salamanca and General Filiberto Osorio, Bolivian chief of staff, knew of the presence of various buildings on the western shore of Pitiantuta (Chuquisaca to the Bolivians) Lagoon.[1] Osorio desired a reconnaissance mission but, in the words of Salamanca, "a hundred times we agreed that under no circumstances was a conflict to be provoked, not even a skirmish with the Paraguayan forces."

The aggressive nature of the Bolivian army command in the Chaco had long been a problem,[2] and excessive caution should have been exercised by all concerned. Rogelio Ayala Moreira criticizes Major Oscar Moscoso's commander, Colonel Francisco Peña, for he declares that Moscoso received "incomplete instructions."[3] Aquiles Vergara Vicuña blames Osorio for failing to "fully comprehend the precise sense of the presidential suggestion," and Peña, for failing to instruct Moscoso on the delicacy of his mission.[4] Arze Quiroga joins Vergara Vicuña claiming that Moscoso did not proceed with the caution his orders specified.[5]

Moscoso, in his own defense (a letter dated October 5, 1932), charges that Colonel Peña on orders from Osorio, commanded him "simply and plainly to occupy the lagoon, knowing that a Paraguayan fort existed there."[6]

[1] Eduardo Arze Quiroga, *Documentos para una historia de la guerra de Chaco: Seleccionados del archivo de Daniel Salamanca*, I, 235–236.

[2] United States, National Archives, Washington, D.C., Department of State, RG 59, Decimal File 724.3415/1172, no. 70, Feely (La Paz) to Dept. State, Feb. 4, 1931.

[3] Rogelio Ayala Moreira, *Por qué no ganamos la guerra del Chaco*, pp. 114–115.

[4] Aquiles Vergara Vicuña, *La guerra del Chaco*, I, 6–7.

[5] Arze Quiroga, *Documentos*, I, 244.

[6] *Ibid.*, p. 327.

The official Bolivian account of the June 15, 1932, incident and the Paraguayan counterattack of July 15, 1932, concluded that no Paraguayan *fortín* was to be found on the west shore of Pitiantuta Lagoon and only "abandoned huts" were located on the eastern shore.[7] The account insists that the Paraguayan recapture of Fortín Carlos Antonio López on July 15, 1932, was an act of unprovoked aggression.

The most recent Bolivian authors have helped to clarify some of the mysteries surrounding the Fortín Antonio Carlos López incident.[8] Reconnaissance airplanes had spotted huts on the eastern shore of the lagoon in April 1932; whether they were occupied was not ascertained. However, on May 21, 1932, Lieutenant Colonel Salinas of the general staff ordered that the lagoon be occupied.[9] The Bolivian army believed that the nonaggression pact being negotiated in Washington would soon be signed and a positional status quo declared. Furthermore, a road network between *fortines* was under construction, and the occupation of a water point like Pitiantuta Lagoon was deemed essential.

Once Moscoso reported his attack, it became known that the Paraguayans had occupied the huts spotted on the lagoon's eastern shore. President Salamanca drafted a withdrawal order, but by secret telegram Osorio ordered Colonel Francisco Peñaranda (Colonel Peña's replacement as commander of the Fourth Division) to send a telegram protesting any withdrawal and stressing the distance Major Moscoso would have to travel with only a limited supply of water.[10] Faced with the opposition of the general staff as well as the majority of his cabinet, Salamanca dropped the withdrawal issue.[11] Peñaranda ordered Moscoso to move to the western shore of the lagoon; it was here the Paraguayans attacked on July 15, 1932.

Mercado Moreira holds that President Salamanca was merely the victim of officer corps duplicity.[12] Calvo argues that Salamanca was victim of a trap he had inadvertently fashioned for himself.[13] Salamanca had long supported a maximum expansion policy in the Chaco; now that he was presi-

[7] Uruguay, Ministerio de Relaciones Exteriores y Culto, Archivo de Relaciones Exteriores, Montevideo, File 1980/29: *Paraguay y Bolivia: La cuestión de límites,* "Comunicado oficial de la legación de Bolivia," July 28, 1932, pp. 1–2.

[8] Robert Querejazu Calvo, *Masamaclay,* pp. 36–43; Miguel Mercado Moreira, *Historia diplomática de la guerra del Chaco,* pp. 88–96.

[9] Mercado Moreira, *Historia diplomática,* p. 89.

[10] *Ibid.,* p. 93; Calvo, *Masamaclay,* p. 41.

[11] Mercado Moreira, *Historia diplomática,* p. 95.

[12] *Ibid.,* pp. 92–93.

[13] Calvo, *Masamaclay,* pp. 31–32.

dent, it was only natural for the army to display a mood of open bellicosity. The problem was that the Fortín Antonio Carlos López incident led to general war. Salamanca believed that the officer corps had tricked him and publicly denounced General Osorio on September 21, 1932. The result was a growing chasm between the president and the officer corps.

In summary, Salamanca opposed any war with Paraguay in 1932 and wanted no conflict over control of the lagoon. The Bolivian army wanted the lagoon; however, once it obtained control and despite its recapture by the Paraguayans in July 1932, no military mobilization was declared. Mercado Moreira demonstrates that few reinforcements were sent to the Chaco until September 1932.[14] The Bolivians were unprepared for war and simply did not believe the Paraguayans would react effectively. Unfortunately for them, Moscoso's action proved to be the needed impetus; hence the conclusion stated in the body of this study.

[14] Mercado Moreira, *Historia diplomática,* pp. 95–96.

APPENDIX II

Protocol of June 12, 1935[1]

Their Excellencies Dr. Luis A. Riart, Minister of Foreign Affairs of the Republic of Paraguay, and Dr. Tomás Manuel Elío, Minister of Foreign Affairs of the Republic of Bolivia, having met at the Ministry of Foreign Affairs and Worship of the Argentine Republic at Buenos Aires on the twelfth day of the month of June of the year one thousand nine hundred and thirty-five in the presence of the members of the Mediation Commission set up for the purpose of promoting the solution of the conflict existing between the Republic of Paraguay and the Republic of Bolivia, namely: His Excellency Dr. Carlos Saavedra Lamas, Minister of Foreign Affairs and Worship of the Argentine Republic; His Excellency Dr. José Carlos de Macedo Soares, Minister of Foreign Affairs of the Republic of the United

[1] United States, Department of State, *The Chaco Peace Conference,* pp. 49–52.

States of Brazil, and His Excellency Dr. José Bonifacio de Andrada e Silva, Ambassador of the United States of Brazil; His Excellency Dr. Luis Alberto Cariola, Ambassador of the Republic of Chile, and His Excellency Dr. Félix Nieto del Río, Special Delegate Plenipotentiary of the Republic of Chile; His Excellency Alexander Wilbourne Weddell, Ambassador of the United States of America, and His Excellency Hugh Gibson, Special Ambassador Plenipotentiary of the United States of America; His Excellency Dr. Felipe Barreda Laos, Ambassador of the Republic of Peru; and His Excellency Dr. Eugenio Martínez Thédy, Ambassador of the Republic of Uruguay;

Their Excellencies the Ministers of Foreign Affairs of the Republic of Paraguay and of the Republic of Bolivia, having exhibited their full powers, which were found to be in good and due form, decided, under the auspices of the said Mediation Commission, to conclude an agreement, *ad referendum* to their respective Governments, on the following bases:

I

To request the mediatory group kindly to ask His Excellency the President of the Argentine Nation immediately to convene the Peace Conference for the following purposes:

1. To ratify formally the present agreement.
2. To settle any practical questions which may arise in the execution of the measures of security adopted for the cessation of hostilities.
3. To promote the solution of the matters in dispute between Bolivia and Paraguay by direct agreement between the parties, it being understood that, should the direct negotiations fail, Bolivia and Paraguay undertake, by this agreement, to settle the Chaco matters in dispute by means of juridical arbitration (*arbitraje de derecho*) herewith designating the Permanent Court of International Justice of The Hague as arbiter.

   The Peace Conference shall terminate the direct negotiations when, in its opinion, the time has arrived to declare that no possibility exists of reaching thereby a definitive solution; in this event, the parties shall proceed to draw up the arbitral *compromis*; the Peace Conference cannot relinquish its functions as long as the arbitral *compromis* is not definitively agreed upon.
4. To promote, when it is deemed opportune, agreement between the parties with regard to the exchange and repatriation of prisoners, bearing in mind the practices and principles of international law.

5. To establish a system of transit, trade, and navigation which will take into account the geographical position of the parties.

6. To promote facilities and agreements, of a different kind, intended to encourage the development of the two belligerent countries.

7. The Peace Conference shall set up an international commission which shall render an opinion on the responsibilities of every order and of every kind arising from the war; if the conclusions of this opinion are not accepted by one of the parties, the Permanent Court of International Justice of The Hague shall definitively settle the question. The Governments of the Republics of Bolivia and Paraguay undertake to obtain legislative approval of the present agreement within a period of ten days from the date of its signature.

II

The definitive cessation of hostilities on the basis of the present positions of the belligerent armies.

The positions of the armies in conflict shall be determined as follows:

a) A twelve days' truce is agreed upon in order that a neutral military commission, composed of representatives of the mediating nations, may fix intermediate lines between the positions of the belligerent armies. The truce shall begin at midnight, meridian of Córdoba, on the day on which the Neutral Military Commission, having already arrived at the field of action, considers itself ready to begin its mission.

The Neutral Military Commission shall hear the belligerent military commanders in order to determine the line of separation between the armies, and it shall decide cases of discrepancies. When its mission has been fufilled it shall so inform the Peace Conference.

b) On the expiration of the period of truce established under clause a, it shall be extended by the Peace Conference until the measures of security provided for in article III have been put fully into effect.

c) After hearing the military commanders of the belligerents, the Neutral Military Commission shall decide as to the modifications in the line of separation between the armies which experience may show to be advisable.

d) During the truce and its extension the lines of separation between the armies shall be maintained under the guaranties of the Peace Conference, for which purpose the Neutral Military Commission shall watch over and supervise them.

III

The adoption of the following measures of security:

1. Demobilization of the belligerent armies, within a period of ninety days from the date of the fixing of the line of separation between the armies referred to in article II, in the manner to be established by the Neutral Military Commission, after hearing the belligerent military commanders, and up to the limit fixed in the following clause.
2. Reduction of military effectives to the maximum figure of 5,000 men.
3. An engagement not to make new purchases of war material, other than that indispensable for replacement, until the conclusion of the treaty of peace.
4. In signing the present agreement in the presence of the mediators, the parties undertake the obligation of "non-aggression."

The Neutral Military Commission shall be charged with the supervision of the execution of the measures of security until they are carried out in their entirety. When these have been carried out, the Peace Conference shall declare the war to be terminated.

As soon as the execution of the foregoing military securities and guaranties is initiated in the field of operations, which measures must be completely carried out within the maximum time-limit of ninety consecutive days, the study of the matters in dispute shall be initiated at the same time, and the Peace Conference shall exercise the functions specified in article I.

IV

The declaration of the third of August 1932, regarding territorial acquisitions, is recognized by the belligerents.

V

In deference to the humane sentiments of the belligerents and mediators, firing will be suspended from twelve o'clock noon, June 14 (meridian of Córdoba).

In virtue whereof they, by common accord, and together with the representatives of the mediatory states, subscribe this protocol, in duplicate, and sign and seal it on the date and at the place indicated above.

(Signed)

> *Luis A. Riart*
> *Tomás M. Elío*
> *Carlos Saavedra Lamas*
> *José Carlos de Macedo Soares*

José Bonifacio de Andrada e Silva
Luis Alberto Cariola
F. Nieto del Río
Alexander W. Weddell
Hugh Gibson
Felipe Barreda Laos
Eugenio Martínez Thédy

(Seal: Ministry of Foreign Affairs and Worship of Argentina)

L. A. Podestá Costa
DIRECTOR GENERAL

APPENDIX III

Diplomatic and Military Personnel

DIPLOMATIC PERSONNEL

Argentine Delegation (from July 1, 1935)

Chairman of the Delegation and President of the Conference
　Dr. Carlos Saavedra Lamas, Argentine Minister of Foreign Affairs (until February 1938)
　Dr. José María Cantilo, Argentine Minister of Foreign Affairs (from March 1938)

Delegates
　Dr. Isidoro Ruiz Moreno
　Dr. Luis A. Podestá Costa (until March 1936)
　Dr. Roberto Levillier (March–August 1936)
　Dr. Ricardo Bunge (August 1936–May 1937)
　Dr. Pablo Santos-Muñoz (from May 1937)
Secretary General of the Conference
　Dr. Luis Podestá Costa (July 1935–March 1936)
　Dr. Roberto Levillier (March–August 1936)

Dr. Ricardo Bunge (August 1936–May 1937)
Dr. Pablo Santos-Muñoz (from May 1937)

Secretaries
Dr. Héctor Ghiraldo (July 1935–August 1936)
Dr. Pablo Santos-Muñoz (July 1935)
Dr. Ricardo Bunge (July 1935–August 1936)
Dr. Raúl Rodrígues Araya (August 1936–May 1938)
Dr. Alejandro Guillermo Ronde (also secretary of the conference; from March 1938)

Military Adviser
Colonel Ernesto Florit (July 1, 1935–February 1938)

Bolivian Delegation

Chairmen of the Delegation
Dr. Tomás Manuel Elío, Minister of Foreign Affairs (June 1935–January 1936; August–October 1936)
Dr. Carlos Calvo (January–August 1936)
Dr. David Alvéstegui (October 1936–May 1938)
Dr. Enrique Finot (from May 1938)

Plenipotentiary Delegates
Dr. Bautista Saavedra
Dr. Juan María Zalles
Dr. Carlos Calvo
Dr. Carlos Víctor Aramayo
Dr. Carlos Romero (appointed August 1936)

General Adviser
Dr. Eduardo Diez de Medina

Brazilian Delegation

First Delegates
Dr. José Bonifacio de Andrada e Silva, Ambassador to Argentina (to July 15, 1935)
Ambassador José de Paula Rodrigues Alves

Second Delegate
Sr. Edmundo da Luz Pinto (after July 15)

Third Delegate
  Sr. José Carlos de Macedo Soares (until March 11, 1937)

Alternate Delegate
  Sr. Orlando Leite Ribeiro (after July 15)

Chilean Delegation

Delegates
  Ambassador Luis Alberto Cariola (June 1935–October 1936)
  Ambassador Félix Nieto del Río (June 1935–March 1938)
  Ambassador Luis Barros Borgoño (October 1936–January 1939)
  Ambassador Manuel Bianchi (April–December 1938)

Paraguayan Delegation

Chairmen of the Delegation
  Dr. Gerónimo Zubizarreta (July 1935–March 1936; October 1937–July 1938)
  General José Félix Estigarribia (from July 1938)

Delegates
  Dr. Vicente Rivarola
  Dr. Venancio B. Galeano
  Dr. Higinio Arbo
  Sr. César A. Vasconsellos
  Dr. J. Isidro Ramírez (April 1936–September 1938)
  Dr. Miguel Angel Soler (April 1936–September 1937)
  Sr. Marco Antonio Laconich (March–September 1937)
  Dr. Efraím Cardozo (from October 1937)
  Dr. Luis A. Riart (from July 1938)

Adviser and Secretary General
  Dr. Efraím Cardozo

Peruvian Delegation (from June 1935)

Chairman of the Delegation
  Dr. Felipe Barreda Laos, Ambassador to Argentina

Delegate
  Sr. Luis Fernán Cisneros, Minister to Uruguay

Uruguayan Delegation

Delegates
  Dr. José Espalter
  Dr. Pedro Manini Ríos
  Dr. Eugenio Martínez Thédy

Delegation of the United States of America[1]

Delegates
  The Honorable Hugh Gibson, Ambassador to Brazil (July–November 1935)
  The Honorable Spruille Braden (November 13, 1935–October 15, 1938)
  The Honorable Alexander W. Weddell (October 1938–January 1939)

Assistants to the Delegate
  Allan Dawson, Foreign Service Officer (July 1935–June 1936; named alternate delegate)
  Allen Haden (October 1938–January 1939)

Secretaries to the Delegation
  Hayward G. Hill, Foreign Service Officer (July 1935–August 1936)
  Allen Haden (from August 1936)

MILITARY PERSONNEL[2]

Neutral Military Commission

Argentina
  General of Brigade Rodolfo Martínez Pita
  Lieutenant Colonel Jorge J. Manni
  Captain Juan E. A. Vacca

Brazil
  Colonel Estevão Leite de Carvalho
  Major Aníbal Gomes Ribeiro
  Captain João Saraiva

  Assistants
    Major Pery Constant Bevilacqua
    Major Jeitor de Fontoura Rangel
    First Lieutenant Hortencio Pereira de Britto

---

[1] United States, Department of State, *The Chaco Peace Conference*, pp. 31–36.
[2] *Ibid.*, pp. 36–39.

Chile
  General of Brigade Carlos Fuentes Rabé
  Colonel Jorge Tagle Montt
  Lieutenant Colonel Guillermo Pimentel Feliú
  Lieutenant Colonel José María Santa Cruz
  Captain Mardoqueo Múñoz Moraga

Peru
  Colonel Germán Yáñez
  Commander Carlos Morla
  Major José del C. Marín
  Major Enrique Barreta Díaz

Uruguay
  General Alfredo R. Campos
  Colonel José E. Trabal
  Captain Raúl Barlocco
  Captain José F. Baptista Vedia

United States of America
  Major John A. Weeks
  Captain Frederick Dent Sharp

Special Repatriation Commission

Argentina
  Colonel Ernesto Florit
  Captain Robert J. Baldassare

Bolivia
  Lieutenant Colonel José Rivera L.
  Captain Noel Manje
  Captain Germán Parada

Brazil
  Captain Armando Villa Nova Pereira de Vasconcellos
  Major Pery Constant Bevilacqua
  Major Aníbal Gomes Ribeiro

Chile
  Lieutenant Colonel Guillermo Pimentel Feliú

Paraguay
    Colonel Eduardo Torreani Viera
    Major Joel Estigarribia

Peru
    Lieutenant Colonel Ricardo Alayaza T.

Uruguay
    Lieutenant Colonel Homero N. Toscano
    Captain Roberto R. Puig

Special Military Commission

Argentina
    General Division Rodolfo Martínez Pita, President
    Captain Juan Esteban A. Vacca

Brazil
    Major Aníbal Gomes Ribeiro
    Captain Armando Villa Nova Pereira de Vasconcellos

Chile
    General of Division Carlos Fuentes Rabé
    Lieutenant Colonel Guillermo Pimentel Feliú
    Lieutenant Colonel Alfonso Valenzuela

Peru
    Colonel Fernando Melgar
    Lieutenant Colonel Ricardo Alayaza T.

Uruguay
    General Alfredo R. Campos
    General José E. Trabal
    Major Raúl Barlocco

United States of America
    Colonel Lester Baker
    Major John A. Weeks

Advisory Military Commission

Argentina
    Colonel Ernesto Florit, President
    Captain Juan J. Polero

Brazil
    Major Djalma Polli Coelho
    Captain D. Pedro de Costa Leite
    Captain (aviation) Arnaldo Damara Canto

Chile
    Major Ernesto Würth Rojas

Peru
    Major Víctor Vallaneuva

Uruguay
    Captain Roberto R. Puig

United States of America
    Major Lawrence C. Mitchell

APPENDIX IV

Protocolized Act, January 21, 1936[1]

(TRANSLATION)

In Buenos Aires, on the Twenty-first day of January 1936, meeting in the residence of the President of the Republic, the Plenipotentiary Delegates of the Republic of Bolivia, Dr. Tomás M. Elío, Minister of Foreign Affairs, and Dr. Carlos Calvo, and the Plenipotentiary Delegates of the Republic of Paraguay, Dr. Gerónimo Zubizarreta and Dr. Vicente Rivarola, having in mind the conciliatory affirmations and suggestions received from the Peace Conference and under the auspices and the moral guaranty of said Conference, in a desire promptly to reach a definitive settlement of their differences, agree to the following:

Article I: The Contracting parties confirm the obligations deriving from the protocol of June 12, 1935, and, consequently, reiterate their willingness to continue to honor as they have hitherto honored:

[1] United States, Department of State, *The Chaco Peace Conference*, pp. 83–86.

(1) The stipulations relating to the Peace Conference convoked by His Excellency the President of the Argentine Republic, to the ends established in article I of the protocol of June 12, 1935 (clauses 2, 3, 5, 6, and 7), with the exception of clause 1, which has already been fulfilled by said Conference's resolution of July 1, 1935, and of clause 4, when article IV and the subsequent articles of the present convention have been executed;

(2) The stipulations relating to the definitive cessation of hostilities on the basis of the positions of the then belligerent armies, as has been determined by the Neutral Military Commission in the manner provided by clauses (a), (b), (c), and (d) in article II of the protocol of June 12, 1935;

(3) The stipulations relating to the measures of security adopted in clauses 2, 3, and 4 of article III of the protocol of June 12, 1935;

(4) The recognition of the declaration of August 3, 1932, on the acquisition of territory, as set forth in article IV of the protocol of June 12, 1935.

Article II: The measures of security appearing in clauses 2, 3, and 4 of article III of the protocol of June 12, 1935, as well as that deriving from clause 2 of article I of the present convention, shall be maintained until the provisions of article I, clause 3, of said agreement of June 12 are carried out in their entirety.

Article III: The Peace Conference shall decide the practical questions which may arise in putting the measurements of security into effect in accordance with the provisions of article I, clause 2, of the mentioned protocol, for which purpose the contracting parties hereby authorize the Conference to designate one or more special commissions to subordinate to it.

Article IV: The parties shall proceed to the reciprocal return of prisoners of war, beginning the return within thirty days of the date of the last legislative approval of the present document, undertaking to continue it without interruption until complete liberation of the prisoners, in accordance with the time limits and rules which may be fixed by the Peace Conference, or the Executive Committee set up by it in case it temporarily suspends its labors, bearing in mind the exigencies of the organization and effecting of transportation which it deems should be taken into consideration. Concentration of the prisoners and preparations for their return shall be begun as soon as this document has been signed.

Prisoners on the sick list who cannot be immediately transferred will nevertheless be freed, and their transfer will be accomplished as soon as possible.

Article V: Both parties hereby request the Peace Conference to depute a special Commission to deal with everything concerned with the return of the prisoners, in accord with the authorities of the respective countries. Such special commission shall be subject to the Peace Conference, or to the Executive Committee acting for it during any period of temporary suspension of its labors.

Article VI: In case it should be necessary or advisable to utilize means of communication in neighboring states to facilitate repatriation, the Governments of Bolivia and Paraguay (Paraguay and Bolivia) shall request, sufficiently in advance, the necessary authorization from the governments of those states.

Transportation shall be effected in accordance with the measures and conditions agreed upon by the mentioned states on the basis of traffic needs, local security, sanitary requirements, or other factors not foreseen.

Article VII: Expenses incurred in the transportation of prisoners through the territory of a third state shall be borne by the country of which they are nationals.

Article VIII: The contracting parties, taking into consideration the number of prisoners and considering the expenses incurred, hereby agree to compromise that matter, stipulating that the Government of Bolivia shall refund to the Government of Paraguay the equivalent of two million eight hundred thousand (2,800,000) pesos, Argentine legal tender, in pounds sterling at the closing rate on the twentieth day of January, one thousand nine hundred and thirty-six, that is, one hundred and fifty-four thousand two hundred and sixty-nine pounds, nineteen shillings, five pence (£154,-269/19/5), and the Government of Paraguay shall refund to the Government of Bolivia the equivalent of four hundred thousand (400,000) pesos, Argentine legal tender, in pounds sterling at the same rate, that is, the sum of twenty-two thousand and thirty-eight pounds, eleven shillings, four pence (£22,038/11/4), the resulting balance of one hundred and thirty-two thousand two hundred and thirty-one pounds, eight shillings, one pence (£132,231/8/1) in sight drafts on London, equivalent to two million four hundred thousand (2,400,000) pesos, Argentine legal tender, at the rate mentioned, to be paid thus terminating all present or future differences on the matter.

This balance shall be deposited in the Central Bank of the Argentine Republic, within thirty days from the date of the last legislative approval of this agreement, to the order of the Minister of Foreign Affairs of the Argentine Republic and the Chairman of the Peace Conference who will place it to the order and disposal of the Government to which it is due as soon as the special committee informs the said Minister that the stipulations of this document have been fully complied with as regards the reciprocal liberation of the prisoners of war.

Article IX: The parties agree to renew their diplomatic relations as soon as possible.

Article X: The present protocolized act shall be subject to the legislative approval of the respective Congresses in accordance with constitutional provisions in effect.

By virtue of which they subscribe in three copies and by mutual agreement, jointly with the representatives of mediatory states, to the present protocolized act, which they sign and seal on the date and in the place indicated above.

(Signed)

José de Paula Rodrigues Alves
Félix Nieto del Río
Spruille Braden
Felipe Barreda Laos
Eugenio Martínez Thédy
Tomás M. Elío
Carlos Calvo
Gerónimo Zubizarreta
Vicente Rivarola
Carlos Saavedra Lamas

APPENDIX V

Repatriation of Bolivian and Paraguayan Prisoners[1]

BOLIVIA

In accordance with the mathematical basis decided upon, a special commission required of the Bolivian representatives an accounting for 2,578 Paraguay prisoners shown on the lists of July 25, 1935, (photographic copies) given to the Conference of Peace by the delegation of their country, the following being the final accounting:

(a) Repatriated
    January 23–March 7, 1936 .... Officers......... 6
    May 13–June 12, 1936 .... Officers......... 94
    May 13–June 12, 1936 .... Troops......... 2,391
    August 15, 1936 .... Troops......... 7
                                                    ────────
                                                      2,498

(b) Freed in La Quiaca
    August 15, 1936 .... Troops......... 6[2]
    Repatriated and freed 2,504

(c) Died in captivity
    July 25, 1935–June 10, 1936 .... Troops......... 58

(d) Escaped
    Escaped from concentration camps ...... Troops......... 16
[Total]   ────────
                                                         2,578

The Bolivian authorities will continue to seek the 16 escaped men to repatriate or free them.

PARAGUAY

For the reasons stated in the report of August 3, 1936, to the Peace Conference, the special commission did not have any mathematical basis for its negotiations, but required of the Paraguayan authorities through its

1 Copied from United States, Department of State, *The Chaco Peace Conference*, pp. 91–94.
2 Returned to Bolivia.

executive subcommittee #5 the presentation or capture of all those prisoners known or believed to exist, the following being the final accounting:

(a) Repatriated

March 8, 1936 ....Officers.........   3
May 2–July 3, 1936 ....Officers......... 346
May 2–July 3, 1936 ....Troops.........16,589[3]
August 8–February 13, 1937 ....Troops.........   99
                                                        ———
                                                       17,037

(b) Freed in Formosa

July 4, 1936 ....Troops.........   4
August 8, 1936–February 13, 1937 ......Troops.........   71
                                                        ———
                                                       17,112

(c) Died in captivity

April 15–June 30, 1936 ....Officers.........   1
April 15–June 30, 1936 ....Troops.........   28[4]
April 24, 1936 ....Troops.........   2
                                                        ———
                                                       17,143

(d) Escaped

Escaped from concentration camp ....Troops.........   31
[Total]   ———
                                                       17,174

[3] Including two dying en route and one hospitalized in Formosa.
[4] According to Paraguayan lists.

APPENDIX VI

Petroleum Exploration in Paraguay and Bolivia, 1938–1970

PARAGUAY

Following the October 1938 territorial award, the Pure Oil and Union Oil companies contracted with Asunción for exploration rights in the Paraguayan Chaco. Both companies carried on extensive drilling between 1942 and 1949. Pure Oil then retired from the field, but Union Oil proceeded to raise five wells in the northeastern Chaco.[1] Near Picuiba #4 well temporarily produced petroleum, but its moderate flow soon turned to water. Late in 1955 spokesmen for Union Oil announced that $7,000,000 had been invested in Chaco petroleum explorations, and the prospect of making significant strikes did not justify further expenditure. All exploratory activities ceased at the end of the year.

In 1958 Petróleo Guaraní S.A. (PEGASA), a company of Brazilian origin, began drilling operations in the Chaco but achieved no positive results. In February 1963 the same company signed a new exploratory contract with the Paraguayan Ministry of Public Works and Communications. In 1966–1967 the Placid Oil Company dug two wells in the northwest Chaco near the Bolivian border. Neither this company nor the Brazilian organization has enjoyed any success. The explorations of the last thirty years would seem to have confirmed the earlier verdict that petroleum deposits of commercial value do not exist in that part of the Chaco held by Paraguay as of June 14, 1935, or in that part received on October 10, 1938.

BOLIVIA

On March 8, 1939 the Bolivian Supreme Court rejected the final appeal of the Standard Oil Company and that company's properties were legally expropriated. YPFB needed Argentine assistance to operate the confiscated wells and lacked the funds for further development and expansion. Production on the former Standard Oil properties had dropped to 950 barrels daily in 1945. Some improvement was made during the next decade, but by 1955 consumption had outstripped production. The Bolivian government passed new legislation tending to encourage petroleum exploitation in the Oriente by private investors. Production rose from roughly 3,000,000 barrels in 1955 to about 15,000,000 barrels in 1968. Accounting for about 75 per cent of this production was the Bolivian Gulf Oil Company which obtained a forty-year lease on property in the Department of Santa

[1] United States, Department of the Interior, *Geology and Mineral Resources in Paraguay: A Reconnaissance*, Geological Survey Paper 327, prepared by Edwin B. Eckel, Charles Milton, and Pedro Tirado Sulsona, pp. 82–83. The five wells were located at Santa Rosa, La Paz, Pirizal, Orihuela, and Picuiba. Only the Picuiba well produced any petroleum.

Cruz. This company subsequently made rich strikes near Caranda (1960), Calpa (1961), and Tatarenda (1964). With an eye toward future exploitation, Gulf loaned YPFB $5,000,000 to build a trans-Andean pipeline from Sica Sica on the Altiplano to Arica, Chile. This pipeline was completed in 1960. Four years later Gulf loaned YPFB another $2,000,000 allegedly to make the Sica Sica–Arica oleoduct functional. In return, the Bolivian national company granted Bolivian Gulf permission to build a connecting pipeline from Caranda to Sica Sica. This line was completed in July 1966; the following September the first tanker loaded with crude oil pumped from the Caranda field left Arica, bound for California. The outlet not technologically possible when Standard Oil dug the first wells in the Oriente, had become a reality.

Argentine interest in Oriente petroleum products has remained significant. In 1955 a pipeline was completed from Camiri to the railhead at Yacuiba. Argentine importation reached 800,000 barrels annually, and in 1960 Argentina completed a large pipeline from Buenos Aires to Campo Duran on the Argentine-Bolivian border. A further agreement was reached in July 1968. YPF, YPFB, and Bolivian Gulf signed a pact whereby up to 4.25 million cubic feet of natural gas would be supplied daily to Argentina through a new pipeline from southeastern Bolivia to Campo Duran.[2] These developments would seem to corroborate the views of those Argentines who had seen their nation as the natural consumer for Oriente petroleum products. Unfortunately for Argentina and Gulf Oil, history repeated itself. On October 19, 1969, the government of General Alfredo Ovando Candia nationalized the North American company's holdings without compensation. Work on the pipeline to Campo Duran ceased immediately, and no further construction efforts have been initiated. The similarity with past events does not end here; in February 1970 official discussions between Bolivia and Brazil concerning the construction of a pipeline from Santa Cruz to Corumbá were begun. Clearly, the disposition of Oriente petroleum remains an explosive issue in Latin American politics.

---

[2] "The News in Brief," *Petroleum Press Service*, 35, no. 8 (August 1968), 315. The pact was to run for a twenty-year period, the price paid by YPF to be fixed at $8(U.S.) per 1,000 cubic meters of gas. Deliveries were tentatively scheduled to begin in 1970.

APPENDIX VII

Confidential Agreement, July 9, 1938

(See following pages for translation)

Paraguay-Bolivia
Acta
Rubricada en la ciudad de Buenos Aires
9 de Julio de 1938

Teniendo en cuenta que los Gobiernos de Bolivia y Paraguay, han con-
venido entregar el laudo arbitral de los Presidentes de las seis Naciones
mediadoras representadas en la Conferencia de Paz, la determinación de la
línea divisoria en el Chaco entre Bolivia y Paraguay;

Que el Tratado de Paz, Amistad y Límites rubricado en esta ciudad el
día nueve de Julio de 1938 entre aquellos dos Gobiernos establece en su
Artículo 1°, las zonas del Chaco dentro de las cuales debe fijarse la men-
cionada línea divisoria:

Que el mismo Tratado faculta a los Presidentes designados Arbitros a
delegar sus Funciones de Delegados Plenipotenciarios;

Que los Presidentes de las Repúblicas Mediadoras han delegado sus
facultades de Arbitros en sus respectivos Representantes en la Conferencia
de Paz, con Poderes suficientes;

Que la Conferencia ha comprobado, debidamente asesorada por sus
técnicos militares y por las manifestaciones que separadamente le hicieron
las Delegaciones de Paraguay y Bolivia, cual sería dentro de dicha zona,
una delimitación transaccional basada en los puntos de coincidencia que
existen;

La Conferencia de Paz, con pleno conocimiento de estos antecedentes y
teniendo por única mira satisfacer las necesidades y aspiraciones de las
Partes, no tiene inconveniente en anticipar que la única línea divisoria que
significa la solución razonable y definitiva del diferendo entre Paraguay y
Bolivia, es la siguiente:

Partiendo del lugar denominado Esmeralda, en la orilla izquierda del
Rio Pilcomayo, irá directamente al punto conocido con el nombre de 27

de Noviembre, con la inflexión que fuera necesario hacer para que Irinda-
gué quede al Oriente de dicha línea; de 27 de Noviembre, al punto más
alto del Cerro Capitán Ustarez; de allí, en línea recta, hasta la intersección
del camino Ravelo-Ingavi con la Cañada del Palmar de las Islas; desde
dicho punto, también en línea recta, al Fortín Paredes; desde allí, hasta la
cumbre del Cerro Chevoreca; y descenderá al Río Negro u Otuquis para
terminar en el thalweg de su desembocadura en el Río Paraguay, quedando
expresamente excluído todo el litoral del Rio Paraguay, desde la desembocadura del Rio Otuquis o Negro al Sud.

Y al declararlo asi, los Delegados que la integran manifiestan que el
laudo respetará fiel y escrupulosamente dicha línea que, a su juicio, es la
única que interpreta la voluntad transaccional de las Partes y la opinión de
los técnicos militares.

En fe de lo cual, rubrican el presente documento los Ministros de Relaciones Exteriores de Paraguay y Bolivia y los Delegados de los Países Mediadores en la Conferencia de Paz, en Buenos Aires, a nueve días del mes
de Julio de mil novecientos treinta y ocho.

(Signed)

> *Cecilio Báez.*
> *Eduardo Diez de Medina.*
> *José María Cantilo.*
> *José de Paula Rodrigues Alves.*
> *Orlando Leite Ribeiro.*
> *Spruille Braden.*
> *Eugenio Martínez Thédy.*
> *Manuel Bianchi.*
> *Felipe Barreda Laos.*
> *Luis Fernán Cisneros.*
> *Isidoro Ruiz Moreno.*
> *Pablo Santos-Muñoz.*
> *Enrique Finot.*
> *Efraím Cardozo.*

TRANSLATION

Act Drawn Up in the City of
Buenos Aires, July 9, 1938

Considering that the Governments of Bolivia and Paraguay have agreed to accept the arbitral award to be made by the Presidents of the six mediator nations represented in the Conference concerning the delimitation of a Chaco boundary line between Bolivia and Paraguay;

[Considering] that the Treaty of Peace, Friendship, and Limits formulated in this city the ninth of July, 1938, between the two governments establishes in its first article, the zones of the Chaco in which the dividing line ought to be established;

[Considering] that the same treaty empowers the Presidents designated arbitrators to delegate their functions to Plenipotentiary Delegates:

[Considering] that the Conference has verified, perfectly aided by its military technical personnel and through statements which the Delegations of Paraguay and Bolivia made to it separately, that there will be within said Zone, a compromise boundary based on the points of agreement which exist.

The Conference of Peace, having studied the antecedents available, and having as its sole intention the satisfaction of the needs and aspirations of the parties, does not find it improper to anticipate that the only dividing line which means a reasonable and definite solution of the difference between Bolivia and Paraguay, is the following:

Starting at the place named Esmeralda on the left bank of the Pilcomayo River it [boundary] will go directly to the locality known by the name of 27 of November, deviating as may be necessary in order that Irindaqué [sic] remains to the East of said line; from 27 of November to the highest point of Cerro Captain Ustarez; from there in a straight line to the intersection of the Ravelo-Ingavi road with the Cañada [ravine] del Palmar de las Islas; from said point also in a straight line to Fortín Paredes; from there, up to the highest point of Cerro Chovoreca; and it will go down to the Río Negro or Otuquis [River] to end in the center of its mouth at the Río Paraguay, being expressly excluded the entire littoral of the Paraguay River, from the mouth of the Río Otuquis or Negro southwards.

And upon declaring it [boundary] thusly, the Delegates who take part in this transaction declare that the award will faithfully and scrupulously respect said line which, in their judgment, is the only one which interprets the transactional will of the parties and the opinions of the military and technical advisers.

In keeping with this situation, the Foreign Ministers of Paraguay and Bolivia and the Delegates of the Mediating Countries at the Conference of Peace in Buenos Aires, draw up the present document, on the ninth of July, 1938.

COMMENTARY

This document was found in the Paraguayan Foreign Office in October 1965. According to the Department of State files Braden had transmitted an earlier draft to the confidential agreement to be drawn up, but he reported that it was "discarded at the last moment."[1] The second draft "while not changing the sense matter, lays more emphasis on the parties having arrived at a coincidence of opinion on the frontier line."[2]

This writer sought to verify whether the draft reported in No. 191 was the same as the document found in the Paraguayan Foreign Office. In a letter dated May 27, 1966, a copy of the document was sent to Mr. Spruille Braden. On June 2, 1966, Mr. Braden replied, "I do not have a copy of No. 191, 7/9/38, p. 3 and therefore cannot definitely say that there is a connection between the document therein mentioned and the enclosure to your letter, but I would be 99% sure that they are one and the same."

The document's significance can hardly be overestimated, for it establishes the following:

(1) The Chaco settlement was accomplished by secret diplomacy.

(2) The Chaco settlement was not effected by arbitration, the proposed boundary having been established by agreement on July 8–9, 1938. In his letter of June 2, 1966, Braden established that the secret document signed July 8–9, was "just as valid as the award made on the tenth of October."

According to No. 191, p. 3, only three copies of this act were made. The original went to the Argentine president. Certified copies went to the Paraguayan and Bolivian foreign ministers.

[1] United States, National Archives, Washington, D.C., Department of State, RG 59, Decimal File 724.34119/1460, no. 191, Braden (Buenos Aires) to Sec'y State, July 9, 1938, p. 3.
[2] *Ibid.*

APPENDIX VIII

Treaty of Peace, Friendship, and Limits between the Republics of Bolivia and Paraguay[1]

The Republics of Bolivia and Paraguay (Paraguay and Bolivia) with the intention of definitively consolidating peace and of putting an end to the differences which gave rise to the armed conflict in the Chaco; inspired by the desire to prevent further disagreements; keeping in mind that between states forming the American community there exist historic, fraternal bonds which should not disappear because of divergencies or events which ought to be considered and solved in a spirit of reciprocal understanding and good-will; in execution of the undertaking to conclude a definitive peace which both Republics assumed in the peace protocol of June 12, 1935, and in the protocolized act of January 21, 1936, represented:

the Republic of Bolivia, by His Excellency Dr. Eduardo Diez de Medina, Minister of Foreign Affairs, and His Excellency Dr. Enrique Finot, Chairman of the Delegation of that country to the Peace Conference,

and the Republic of Paraguay, by His Excellency Dr. Cecilio Báez, Minister of Foreign Affairs, His Excellency General José Félix Estigarribia, Chairman of the Delegation of that country to the Peace Conference and Their Excellencies the Delegates Luis A. Riart and Efraím Cardozo,

present in Buenos Aires and duly authorized by their Governments have agreed to conclude under the auspices and moral guaranty of the six mediatory governments, the following definitive treaty of peace, friendship, and limits:

Article I. Peace is hereby reestablished between the Republics of Bolivia and Paraguay (Paraguay and Bolivia).

Article II. The dividing line between Bolivia and Paraguay (Paraguay and Bolivia) in the Chaco shall be that determined by the Presidents of the Republics of Argentina, Brazil, Chile, United States of America, Peru, and Uruguay in their capacity as arbitrators in equity, who, acting *ex aequo et bono*, will give their arbitral award in accordance with this and the following clauses:

(a) The arbitral award shall fix the northern dividing line in the Chaco,

[1] United States, Department of State, *The Chaco Peace Conference*, pp. 148–151.

in the zone comprised between the line of the Peace Conference, presented May 27, 1938, and the line of the Paraguayan counter-proposal, presented to the Peace Conference for consideration June 24, 1938, from the meridian of Fortín 27 de Noviembre, i.e., approximately meridian 61°55′ west of Greenwich, to the eastern limit of the zone, excluding the littoral on the Paraguay River south of the mouth of the River Otuquis or Negro;

(b) The arbitral award shall likewise fix the western dividing line in the Chaco, between the Pilcomayo River and the intersection of the meridian of Fortín 27 de Noviembre, i.e., approximately 61°55′ west of Greenwich, with the line of the award in the north referred to in the previous paragraph.

(c) The said line shall not go farther east on the Pilcomayo River than Pozo Hondo, nor farther west than point on the line which, starting from Fortín d'Orbigny, was fixed by the Neutral Military Commission as intermediary between the maximum positions reached by the belligerent armies when fire was suspended on June 14, 1935.

Article III. The arbitrators shall render the decision after having heard the parties and according to their true knowledge and understanding, taking into consideration the experience acquired by the Peace Conference and the suggestions of the military advisers to that organization.

The six Presidents of the Republics mentioned in article II are empowered to give the award directly or through plenipotentiary delegates.

Article IV. The arbitral award shall be given by the arbitrators within a maximum of two months after the ratification of the present treaty, obtained when and as stipulated in article II.

Article V. The award having been given and the parties notified, the latter shall immediately name a mixed commission composed of five members, two named by each party, and the fifth designated by common agreement of the six mediatory governments, in order to apply on the ground the dividing line drawn by the arbitral award and to set the boundary markers.

Article VI. Within thirty days after the award, the Governments of Bolivia and Paraguay (Paraguay and Bolivia) shall proceed to accredit their respective diplomatic representatives in Asunción and La Paz (La Paz and Asunción) and within ninety days shall fulfill the award in its principal aspects, under the supervision of the Peace Conference which the parties recognize to have authority to settle definitely any practical questions which may arise in this connection.

Article VII. The Republic of Paraguay guarantees the amplest free transit through its territory, and especially through the zone of Puerto Casado, of merchandise arriving from abroad destined to Bolivia and of the products proceeding from Bolivia for shipment abroad through the said zone of Puerto Casado, and the right of Bolivia to install customs agencies and construct depots and warehouses in the zone of the said port.

Regulations governing this article shall be the subject of a later commercial convention between both Republics.

Article VIII. The arbitral award having been executed through the application of the dividing line and the setting of boundary markers, the Governments of Bolivia and Paraguay (Paraguay and Bolivia) shall negotiate directly, government to government, the other economic and commercial conventions they deem proper to develop their reciprocal interest.

Article IX. The Republics of Bolivia and Paraguay (Paraguay and Bolivia) reciprocally renounce all actions and claims deriving from responsibilities for the war.

Article X. The Republics of Bolivia and Paraguay (Paraguay and Bolivia) renewing the non-aggression pledge stipulated in the protocol of June 12, 1935, solemnly bind themselves not to make war on each other or to use force, directly or indirectly, as a means of solution of any present or future difference.

If, on any occasion, such differences are not resolved by direct diplomatic negotiations, they undertake to have recourse to the conciliatory and arbitral procedures offered by international law and especially the American conventions and pacts.

Article XI. The present treaty shall be ratified by the National Constitutional Convention of Bolivia, and by a national plebiscite in Paraguay; in both cases ratification must take place within twenty days after the date of signature of this treaty. Ratification shall be exchanged within the briefest period possible, before the Peace Conference.

Article XII. The parties declare that in case the ratification referred to in the preceding article should not be obtained, the text and content of this treaty cannot be invoked as basis for allegations or proofs in future actions or procedures of international arbitration or justice.

In witness whereof the representatives of Bolivia and Paraguay (Paraguay and Bolivia), together with the plenipotentiary delegates representing the mediatory countries on the Peace Conference, sign and seal the present treaty in three copies at Buenos Aires, on the 21st day of the month of July, nineteen hundred and thirty-eight.

(Signed)

E. Diez de Medina
Enrique Finot
Cecilio Báez
José F. Estigarribia
Luis A. Riart
Efraím Cardozo
José María Cantilo
José de Paula Rodrigues Alves
Orlando Leite Ribeiro
Manuel Bianchi
Spruille Braden
Felipe Barreda Laos
Luis Fernán Cisneros
Eugenio Martínez Thédy
Isidoro Ruiz Moreno
Pablo Santos-Muñoz

BIBLIOGRAPHY

Unpublished Government Documents

Archival Collections

Argentina. Ministerio de Relaciones Exteriores y Culto. Archivo de Relaciones Exteriores. Buenos Aires.

Documents are numbered in no special order and listed under the heading, *La conferencia de paz del Chaco*. The official conference records are found in sixty-two boxes, thirty-one of which are classified as *confidencial, reservado*, or *secreto*.

Bolivia. Ministerio de Relaciones Exteriores y Culto. Archivo de Relaciones Exteriores. La Paz.

Conference files have no general classification number. The documents and papers are tied together loosely in five bundles, with the following titles: *Tratado de paz, amistad y límites; Acta de organización de la comisión mixta; Acta de canje de ratificaciones (del tratado de paz, amistad y límites); arbitraje; and reparación de prisioneros*. The documents were, after a fashion, in chronological order.

Paraguay. Ministerio de Relaciones Exteriores. Archivo de Relaciones Exteriores. Asunción.

Records are found under the title *La conferencia de paz de Buenos Aires*. There is no general classification number. The notes and communiqués of the Paraguayan delegation are found in forty files, each of which is marked under the title listed above. There are also seven folios, the first of which is marked 27-2-E. These contained signed documents, treaties, and agreements relating to the peace conference.

United States. National Archives. Washington, D.C. Department of State, Diplomatic, Legal, and Fiscal Branch. Record Group 59. Decimal File:

711.00: Inter-office Memoranda after 1936
724.3415: Chaco diplomatic materials 1913–July 9, 1935

724.34119: Chaco Peace Conference materials July 1935–August 1939

824.6363: Oil Activity in Bolivian Oriente 1924–1938

Uruguay. Ministerio de las Relaciones Exteriores y Culto. Archivo de Relaciones Exteriores. Montevideo.

File 1980/29: *Paraguay y Bolivia: La cuestión de límites* (1932–1945). Documents are found in six large folios. Arrangement is chaotic and each folio bears a variety of records from this period.

Private Collection (Properties of Señor Carlos Pastore, Montevideo, Uruguay)

Ayala, Eligio. *Política de la defensa militar del Chaco*, n.d.

Gobierno de la República de Bolivia. Carta Confidencial. Minister of Foreign Relations Don Juan Cancio Flecha to Don Antonio Quijarro, confidential agent, June 4, 1901.

Congreso Paraguayo. *Acta del Congreso—20 de mayo de 1904—Sesión secreta*, n.d.

―――. *Acta de una reunión realizada por el presidente de la república, Emilio Aceval, con los diputados y senadores, y el señor vice-presidente de la república, y los ministros secretarios de relaciones exteriores, interior, de hacienda, de justicia, culto, de instrucción pública y de guerra y marina*, July 5, 1901.

―――. *Acta de consejo de ministros de 17 de febrero de 1887*, n.d.

Consejo de Ministros Paraguayos. *Acuerdo en consejo de ministros del día 22 de octubre de 1879*, n.d.

PUBLISHED GOVERNMENT DOCUMENTS

Argentina. Ministerio de Relaciones Exteriores y Culto. *La conferencia de paz del Chaco 1935–1939*. Buenos Aires: E. L. Frigerio e Hijo, 1939.

―――. *La neutralidad argentina en el conflicto boliviano-paraguayo*. Buenos Aires: Jacobo Peuser, Ltda., 1933.

―――. *La política argentina en la guerra del Chaco*. 2 vols. Buenos Aires: Guillermo Kraft, 1937.

Bolivia. Ministerio de Relaciones Exteriores y Culto. *Bolivia-Paraguay: Exposición de los títulos que consagran el derecho territorial de Bolivia, sobre la zona comprendida entre los ríos Pilcomayo y Paraguay, presentada por el doctor Mujía, enviado extraordinario y ministro plenipotenciario de Bolivia en el Paraguay*. Prepared by Ricardo Mujía. 5 vols. La Paz: Empresa Editora de *El Tiempo*, 1914.

————. *La conferencia de Mendoza y el conflicto del Chaco.* La Paz: Imprenta Eléctrica, 1933.

Great Britain. *British and Foreign State Papers*, 1853–1854, XLII, 1256–1258. "Argentine Confederation and Paraguay—Treaty of Limits, Commerce and Navigation between Argentine Confederation and Paraguay, July 15, 1852."

League of Nations. *Dispute between Bolivia and Paraguay. Observations of the Paraguayan Government on the Chaco Commission's Report, August 6, 1934.* Series of Publications, Political, C.134.M.140. VII (1934).

————. *Dispute between Bolivia and Paraguay. Report of the Chaco Commission, May 11, 1934.* Series of Publications, Political, C.154.M.64. VII (1934).

————. *Dispute between Bolivia and Paraguay. Report as Provided for under Article 15, Paragraph 4 of the Covenant, November 24, 1934.* Series of Publications, Political, A.5 (extract). VII (1934).

————. *Dispute between Bolivia and Paraguay. Resolution Submitted by the Sixth Committee to the Assembly of the League of Nations, September 26, 1934.* Series of Publications, Political, A.58.VII (1934).

————. *Dispute between Bolivia and Paraguay. Statement of the Paraguayan Case Submitted to the Assembly by the Paraguayan Government, September 6, 1934.* Series of Publications, Political, A.19.VII (1934).

————. Information Section. *The League of Nations from Year to Year.* 5 vols., 1932–1936. Geneva: League of Nations Publications, 1933–1937.

————. Official Journal. *Dispute between Bolivia and Paraguay. Appeal of the Bolivian Government under Article 15 of the Covenant.* Special Supplement 124. Geneva: League of Nations Publications, 1934.

————. *Dispute between Bolivia and Paraguay. Appeal of the Bolivian Government under Article 15 of the Covenant.* Special Supplement 133. Geneva: League of Nations Publications, 1935.

————. *Dispute between Bolivia and Paraguay. Records of the Special Session of the Assembly.* Special Supplement 132. Geneva: League of Nations Publications, 1934.

Paraguay. Congreso Nacional. *La paz con Bolivia ante el poder legislativo.* Asunción: Imprenta Nacional, 1939.

————. Ejército. *La guerra del Chaco: Partes del conductor.* Ayudantía General, Sección Histórica e Imprenta. Asunción: Imprenta Nacional, 1950.

————. Ministerio de Hacienda. Dirección General de Estadística y Censos. *Boletín estadístico del Paraguay*, V, no. 13/15, 1961.

————. Ministerio de Relaciones Exteriores. *Cuestión de límites con Bolivia*. 2 vols. Asunción: Imprenta Nacional, 1919.

————. *Libro Blanco. Documentos relativos a los acuerdos de Mendoza y la declaración del estado de guerra con Bolivia*. Asunción: Imprenta Nacional, 1933.

————. *Memorándum de la delegación del Paraguay sobre canje y repatriación, Buenos Aires, 15 de octubre, 1935*. Asunción: Imprenta Nacional, 1935.

United Nations. Economic and Social Council. Economic Commission on Latin America. *El desarrollo económico de la Bolivia*. No. 4: Analysis y Proyecciones del Desarrollo Economico, 1958.

United States. Commission of Inquiry and Conciliation, Bolivia and Paraguay. *Proceedings of the Commission of Inquiry and Conciliation, Bolivia and Paraguay, March 18, 1929–September 13, 1929*. Baltimore: The Sun Book and Job Printing Company, 1929.

————. Congress. Senate. *American Petroleum Interests in Foreign Countries. Hearings* before a special committee investigating petroleum resources, Senate, on S.R. 36 (extending S.R. 253), 78th Cong., 1st sess., 1946.

————. *Munitions Industry: Chaco Arms Embargo*. Prepared by Manley O. Hudson. 74th Cong., 2d sess., Senate Committee, Print 9, 1936.

————. Department of Commerce. Maritime Division. *A Statistical Analysis of the World's Merchant Fleets: 1958*. Statistics and Special Studies Office. Washington, D.C.: Government Printing Office, 1959.

————. Department of the Interior. *Geology and Mineral Resources in Paraguay: A Reconnaissance*. Prepared by Edwin B. Eckel, Charles Milton, and Pedro Tirado Sulsona. Geological Survey Professional Paper 327. Washington, D.C.: Government Printing Office, 1959.

————. Bureau of Mines. *1963 Minerals Yearbook*, IV. Washington, D.C.: Government Printing Office, 1964.

————. Department of State. *The Chaco Peace Conference*. Publication 1466. Conference Series 46. Washington, D.C.: Government Printing Office, 1940.

————. *Papers Relating to the Foreign Relations of the United States, 1928–1939*. Washington, D.C.: Government Printing Office, 1929–1940.

————. *Report of the Delegates of the United States of America to the International Conference for the Maintenance of Peace at Buenos Aires —1933*. Washington, D.C.: Government Printing Office, 1934.

————. *Report of the Delegates of the United States of America to the International Conference for the Maintenance of Peace at Buenos Aires —1936*. Washington, D.C.: Government Printing Office, 1937.

————. *Report of the Delegates of the United States of America to the Sixth International Conference of American States at Habana, Cuba— 1928*. Washington, D.C.: Government Printing Office, 1929.

————. *Sixth International Conference of American States—Final Acts, Motions, Agreements, Resolutions and Conventions at Habana, Cuba— 1928*. Washington, D.C.: Government Printing Office, 1929.

BOOKS

Amarilla Fretes, Eduardo. *La liquidación de la guerra de la triple alianza contra el Paraguay*. Asunción: Imprenta Militar, 1941.

Arze Quiroga, Eduardo, ed. *Documentos para una historia de la guerra del Chaco: Seleccionados del archivo de Daniel Salamanca*. 2 vols. La Paz: Editorial Don Bosco, 1951.

Audibert, Alejandro. *Los límites de la antigua provincia del Paraguay*. Buenos Aires: Imprenta *La Economia* de Lustoni Hnos., 1892.

Avila, Fredrico. *Bolivia en el concierto de la Plata*. Mexico, D.F.: Editorial Cultura, 1951.

Ayala Moreira, Rogelio. *Por qué no ganamos la guerra del Chaco*. La Paz: Talleres Gráficos Bolivianos, 1959.

Báez, Cecilio. *Historia diplomática del Paraguay*. 2 vols. Asunción: Imprenta Nacional, 1931–1932.

————. *Paraguayan Chaco*. New York: n. p., 1904.

Bemis, Samuel Flagg. *The Latin-American Policy of the United States*. New York: Harcourt, Brace and World, 1943.

Benítez, Justo Pastor. *Estigarribia: El soldado del Chaco*. 2nd ed. Buenos Aires: Ediciones Nizza, 1958.

Braden, Spruille. *Algunos aspectos del panamericanismo*. Buenos Aires: Imprenta de la Universidad, 1936.

Bunge, Augusto. *La guerra del petróleo en la Argentina*. Buenos Aires: n. p., 1933.

Calvo, Roberto Querejazu. *Masamaclay*. La Paz: Empresa Industrial Gráfica E. Burillo, 1965.

Campos, Alfredo. *Misión de paz en el Chaco Boreal.* 2 vols. Montevideo: Centro Militar, 1954.

Cardozo, Efraím. *El Chaco en el régimen de las intendencias.* Buenos Aires: Imprenta Nacional, 1930.

———. *Breve historia del Paraguay.* Buenos Aires: Editorial Universitaria de Buenos Aires, 1965.

Carnegie Endowment for International Peace. *The Hague Conventions of 1899 (I) and 1907 (IV) Respecting the Laws and Customs of War on Land.* No. 5, Division of International Law. Washington, D.C.: Carnegie Endowment for International Peace, 1915.

Carrillo, Horacio. *El ferrocarril al oriente boliviano.* Buenos Aires: Casa Editora Coni, 1922.

Carvalho, Delgado de. *História diplomática do Brasil.* São Paulo: Companhía Editora Nacional, 1959.

Cole, Elío M. A. *El drama del Paraguay.* Buenos Aires: Editorial Claridad, 1935.

De Ronde, Phillip. *Paraguay: A Gallant Little Nation.* New York: Putnam, 1935.

Díaz Arguedas, Julio. *Cómo fué derrocado el hombre símbolo.* La Paz: Editora Universo, 1957.

Díaz Machicado, Porfirio. *Historia de Bolivia: Salamanca—La guerra del Chaco—Tejado Sorzano—1931–36.* Vol. III. La Paz: Editorial Gisbert, 1955.

Diez de Medina, Eduardo. *De un siglo al otro.* La Paz: Imprenta Alfonso Tejerina, 1955.

———. *Problemas internacionales.* La Paz: n.p., 1936.

Domínguez, Manuel. *El Chaco Boreal fué, es y será del Paraguay.* Asunción: Imprenta Nacional, 1927.

Duguid, Julian. *Green Hell.* London: The Century Company, 1931.

Eguino, Justo Rodas. *La guerra del Chaco: Interpretación de política internacional americana.* Buenos Aires: Editorial la Facultad, 1938.

Fernández, Carlos José. *La guerra del Chaco.* 4 vols. Buenos Aires: Impresora Oeste (Vols. I, II), 1956; Talleres Gráficos *Lumen*, 1962 (Vol. III); 1966 (Vol. IV).

Finot, Enrique. *The Chaco War and the United States.* New York: L. and S. Printing Co., 1934.

Gandía, Enrique de. *Historia del Gran Chaco.* Buenos Aires: J. Roldán y Compañía, 1929.

————. *Historia de Santa Cruz de la Sierra.* Buenos Aires: Talleres Gráficos Argentinos, 1935.

Gondra, César. *La diplomacia de los tratados: Paraguay y Bolivia.* Buenos Aires: Imprenta Didot, 1906.

González-Blanco, Pedro. *Los derechos inobjectables de Bolivia al Chaco Boreal.* Madrid: Imprenta Sáenz Hermanos, 1934.

Gubetich, Hugo Ferreira. *Geografía del Paraguay.* 4th ed. Asunción: n.p., 1960.

Gunther, John. *Inside Latin America.* New York: Harper and Bros., 1941.

Hudson, Manley O., ed. *International Legislation.* Vol. V. Washington, D.C.: Carnegie Endowment for International Peace, 1948.

Hull, Cordell. *The Memoirs of Cordell Hull.* Prepared with the assistance of Andrew Berding. 2 vols. New York: Macmillan Co., 1948.

Laconich, Marco Antonio. *La paz del Chaco.* Montevideo: Editorial Paraguay, 1939.

La Foy, Margaret. *The Chaco Dispute and the League of Nations.* Ann Arbor: Edwards Brothers Press, 1946.

Laguna, Adolfo. *La diplomacia paraguaya en la cuestión del Chaco Boreal.* Buenos Aires: Herrero Hnos., 1932.

Loureiro, Pizarro. *La conferencia de paz del Chaco.* Rio de Janeiro: Rousol e Cia., 1936.

Marof, Tristan. *La tragedia del Altiplano.* Buenos Aires: Editorial Claridad, 1934.

Mecham, J. Lloyd. *The United States and Inter-American Security, 1889–1960.* Austin: University of Texas Press, 1962.

Mello Franco, Afranio de. *Estudios de história internacional recente.* Rio de Janeiro: Impressa nas oficinas Pimenta de Mello e Cia., 1941.

Mercado Moreira, Miguel. *Historia diplomática de la guerra del Chaco.* La Paz: Talleres Gráficos Bolivianos, 1966.

Moore, John Basset, ed. *History and Digest of the International Arbitrations of which the United States Has Been a Party.* 6 vols. Washington, D.C.: U.S. Government Printing Office, 1898.

Osborne, Harold. *Bolivia.* London: Royal Institute of International Affairs, 1934.

Pan American Union. *Status of Inter-American Treaties and Conventions.* Series 5. Washington, D.C.: Pan American Union, 1964.

Pérez, Carlos E. *La agresión de Bolivia en el Chaco y el uti possidetis.* Santiago, Chile: Imprenta R. Neupert, 1932.

Raine, Philip. *Paraguay.* New Brunswick, N.J.: Scarecrow Press, 1956.

Ramírez, Juan Isidro. *La paz del Chaco: En defensa de la línea de hitos.* Buenos Aires: Imprenta Ferrari Hnos., 1942.

Ríos, Angel F. *La defensa del Chaco.* Buenos Aires: Imprenta Ayacucho, 1950.

Rivarola, Vicente. *Memorias diplomáticas.* 3 vols. Buenos Aires: Editorial Ayacucho, 1952–1957.

Saavedra, Bautista. *El Chaco y la conferencia de paz de Buenos Aires.* Santiago, Chile: Editorial Nacimiento, 1939.

Setaro, Ricardo M. *Secretos de estado mayor.* Buenos Aires: Editorial Claridad, 1936.

Standard Oil Company of Bolivia. *Confiscation: A History of the Oil Industry in Bolivia.* New York: Standard Oil Company of Bolivia, 1939.

Stefanich, Juan. *La diplomacia de la revolución.* Buenos Aires: Editorial el Mundo Nuevo, 1945.

———. *El 23 de octubre de 1931.* Buenos Aires: Editorial Febrero, 1948.

Steinberg, S. H., ed. *The Statesman's Yearbook, 1965–1966.* Vol. CII. New York: Macmillan Co., 1965.

Talbot-Booth, E. C., ed. *Merchant Ships.* London: Sampson, Low and Co., 1942.

Tiffin, Robert. *Monetary and Banking Reform in Paraguay.* Washington, D.C.: Board of Governors of the Federal Reserve System, 1946.

Toynbee, Arnold J., series ed. *The Republics of South America.* London: Royal Institute of International Affairs, 1937.

Ugarte, Manuel. *El destino de un continente.* 5th ed. Buenos Aires: Ediciones de la Patria Grande, 1962.

Vergara Vicuña, Aquiles. *La guerra del Chaco.* 7 vols. La Paz: Imprenta Unidas, 1940–1944.

Warren, Harris Gaylord. *Paraguay.* Norman: University of Oklahoma Press, 1949.

Wewege-Smith, Thomas. *Gran Chaco Adventure.* London: Hutchinson and Co., Ltd., 1937.

Welles, Sumner, ed. *The Intelligent American's Guide to the Peace.* New York: Dryden Press, 1945.

Ynsfran, Pablo Max. *The Epic of the Chaco: Marshal Estigarribia's Memoirs of the Chaco War, 1932–1935.* Institute of Latin-American Studies, vol. 8. Austin: University of Texas, 1950.

Zook, David H., Jr. *The Conduct of the Chaco War.* New Haven: Bookman Associates, 1960.

ARTICLES

Bolivia. *Bolivia*, 8, no. 3 (March–April 1941), 5–8; 8, no. 4 (May–June 1941), 6–7.

Braden, Spruille. "A Resumé of the Role Played by Arbitration in the Chaco Dispute." *Arbitration Journal*, 2, no. 4 (October 1938), 387–395.

―――. "Chaco Peace Conference." Department of State Press Releases, 20, no. 484, Publication 1278 (January 7, 1939), 1–9.

Carson, James S. "Can International Arbitration Work?" *Arbitration Journal*, 2, no. 1 (January 1939), 54–57.

Cooper, Russel, and Mattison, Mary. "The Chaco Dispute." *Geneva Special Studies*, 5, no. 2 (1934), 1–25.

González Tuñón, Raúl. "Argentine Realities." *Living Age*, 359 (November 1935), 240–243.

Green, Philip L. "Bolivia at the Crossroads." *Bolivia: A Survey of Bolivian Activities*, 8, no. 3 (March–April 1941), 14–15.

Gutiérrez Guerra, René. "Bolivia and the Standard Oil Company." *Bolivia: A Survey of Bolivian Activities*, 8, no. 3 (March–April 1939), 20–37.

Kain, Ronald S. "Behind the Chaco War." *Current History*, 42, no. 5 (August 1935), 468–474.

Kirkpatrick, Helen P. "The Chaco Dispute." *Geneva Special Studies*, 7, no. 4 (June 1936), 22–43.

Klein, Herbert S. "American Oil Companies in Latin America: The Bolivian Experience." *Inter-American Economic Affairs*, 18, no. 2 (Autumn 1964), 47–72.

Morris, Roberto M. "Bolivia." *Bulletin of the Pan American Union*, 70, no. 2 (February 1936), 169–171.

"The News in Brief." *Petroleum Press Service*, 35, no. 8 (August 1968), 315–316.

Pan American Union. *Bulletin of the Pan American Union*, 72–80 (1938–1945).

Schor, P. S. "Dust in the Chaco." *Living Age*, 359 (October 1935), 150–159.

Warren, Harris Gaylord. "Political Aspects of the Paraguayan Revolution 1936–1940." *Hispanic American Historical Review*, 30 (February 1950), 2–25.

NEWSPAPERS

Christian Science Monitor, December 13, 1933.
New York Times, February 16–21, 1928.

LETTERS AND INTERVIEWS

Bianchi, Manuel (through James Bradshaw). Letter, December 1, 1967.

Bozzano, José (Captain, Paraguayan Navy, ret.). Interview, Asunción, Paraguay, October 14, 1965.

Braden, Spruille. Interview, New York City, June 8, 1965; letters, November 2, 1965, and April 14, May 9, June 2, 1966.

Caldwell, Robert G. (through Robert Davies). Letter, July 15, 1966.

Cardozo, Efraím. Interview, Asunción, Paraguay, October 15, 1965; letter, May 22, 1966.

Mérida, Víctor. Interview, Buenos Aires, Argentina, September 21, 1965.

Pastore, Carlos. Interview, Montevideo, Uruguay, August 20, 1965.

Ramírez, Juan Isidro. Interview, Asunción, Paraguay, October 10 and 15, 1965; letter, November 25, 1965.

Santos-Muñoz, Pablo. Letter, November 15, 1965.

INDEX

ABCP powers: and Washington Committee of Neutrals, 36–37, 69, 70–71, 81–82; mediation attempts of, 73–74, 75–76, 76 n., 83–85, 86–87; compared to League of Nations, 95; members of, in new group, 97; invited to Chaco Peace Conference, 107
Aceval, Benjamin: 9
Acre, region of: 24
Advisory Military Commission: 205 and n., 230–231
Agua Rica: 35
Alcalá, José: 196
Altiplano (of Bolivia): 21, 22, 24
Altiplano Indians: social status of, 22; as soldiers, 41, 42, 44
Alvarado, Manuel Ramón: 189
Alves Bastos, Major: 118
Alvéstegui, David: 150, 150–151 n.
Amambay mountains: 4
Andrada e Silva, José Bonifácio de: 97, 111
Antofagasta, Chile: 55, 62
Apa River: 4, 9
Araguaya, Baron of: 6 n.
Arana, Miguel Suárez: 9
Araya, Raúl Rodrigues: 168 n.
Arbo, Higinio: 37 n., 127
Argaña, Luis: 197
Argentina: and Paraguay River ownership, 3–4; and Brazil against Paraguay, 4–5; and violation of Triple Alliance, 5–6; cession of Villa Occidental Zone to, 6–7; plot to cede Chaco Boreal to, 6 and n., 7–8; and Pinilla-Soler Protocol, 11–12; demilitarization proposals of, 14; refuses to attend Washington Conference, 29; objects to outside interference in negotiations, 32–33; offers to arbitrate dispute, 35; and Paraguay, 41 and n., 58–60 and nn., 63, 100, 132, 142, 163, 164, 166, 172 and n., 182–184, 193, 196–197, 213; and Standard Oil, 46–47 and nn., 47–48, 49, 51; and Royal Dutch Shell, 49; and United States, 52–54, 63, 66–67, 82, 142 and n., 149, 184, 185–186; seeks to become leader of Americas, 53–54; seeks to become arbitrator of Chaco dispute, 53, 54; and Bolivia, 54–58, 56 n., 147–155, 183 and n., 237–

238; Chile opposes status of, 63; and Brazil, 63, 143 and n., 213; and peace efforts, 67, 84–85, 85 n.; and proposed Brazil-Argentina mediation, 69 and n.; and joint statement by American republics, 70–71; joins Chile in negotiations, 94, 96–97; hosts mediation group, 98; on territorial committee, 190; and military commission, 193; opposes economic conference, 216. SEE ALSO ABCP powers; Justo, Agustín; Martínez Pita, Rodolfo; Ortiz, Roberto; Podestá Costa, Luis A.; Saavedra Lamas, Carlos
Argentine Foreign Office: 98 and n., 202
Argentine-Paraguayan Recognition Treaty: 3
Argentine Quebracho Company: 20 and n.
Arica, Chile: 62
arms shipments. SEE supplies, military
Asunción, Paraguay: 1869 fall of, 4–5; as port, 42, 50, 50–51 n.; League Committee of Inquiry at, 87
Audibert, Alejandro: 17
Audiencia of Charcas: 23, 26
Ayala, Elías: 207 n.
Ayala, Eusebio: as military leader, 43; and relations with Argentina, 59–60; empowered to declare war, 85; and war responsibility issue, 124 and n.; insists that mediators meet Paraguayan demands, 130, 131 and n.
Ayala-Mujía Protocol: 12, 14

Báez, Cecilio: 193, 194, 196 and n.
Bahía Negra: as boundary point, 4, 8, 178, 180, 181, 188, 190, 192, 194, 212 n.; Puerto Pacheco on site of, 9–10; as recommended port site, 30 and n., 38, 213; described, as port, 50 n.
Ballivián: capture of, 41, 44; as boundary point, 181, 188, 212 n.
Barreda Laos, Felipe: in mediation group, 97; in Buenos Aires negotiations, 100 and n.; heads Peruvian delegation, 111; and Saavedra Lamas, 113, 114 n.; on war responsibility issue, 121–122, 125; and international tribunal plan, 122–123, 123 n.; and December 1937 peace formula, 188; territorial-dispute strategy of, 189–

DATE DUE

MAY 1 1 1982		
Renewed		
NOV 0 7 1992		
NOV 2 2 1992		

PRINTED IN U S.A